ROB MUNDLE is a bestselling author, journalist and competitive yachtsman whose family heritage is with the sea, dating back to his great-great-grandfather who was the master of square riggers.

For over forty years Rob has combined his passions for sailing and writing. He has written thirteen books, reported on more than thirty Sydney to Hobarts (and competed in three), and covered seven America's Cups, four Olympics and numerous international events. He is the winner of many sailing championships, a regular competitor in local and international contests and has sailed everything from sailboards and 18-foot skiffs through to supermaxi yachts and offshore multihulls.

Rob has an intimate knowledge of the waters Bligh explored and traversed, having sailed the Solent, the English Channel, the Mediterranean, the northern waters of the Great Barrier Reef, Torres Strait, along the eastern archipelago of Indonesia, the West Indies, Fiji, New Caledonia, Hawaii, Cape Town, Tasmania, New Zealand, New Hebrides and Scandinavia – all in Bligh's wake.

ALSO BY ROB MUNDLE

BLIGH

Master Mariner

Rob Mundle

First published in Australia and New Zealand in 2010
by Hachette Australia
(an imprint of Hachette Australia Pty Limited)
Level 17, 207 Kent Street, Sydney NSW 2000
www.hachette.com.au

Trade paperback edition published in 2011
This edition published in 2016

10 9 8 7 6 5 4 3 2 1

National Library of Australia
Cataloguing-in-Publication data:

Mundle, Rob.
Bligh: master mariner / Rob Mundle.

ISBN 978 0 7336 3739 1 (pbk).

Includes bibliographical references and index.
Bligh, William, 1754–1817.
Explorers – Biography.

910.92

Cover design by Design by Committee adapted by Kinart Pty Ltd
Cover image The Gull's Way by Richard Willis/Bridgeman Art Library,
    London
Author photo by Prue Stirling
Maps by Ian Faulkner
Text design by Graeme Jones
Typeset in Bembo by Kirby Jones

*To those individuals who, like Bligh,
have stood proud through adversity,
slander and ridicule and gone on to
achieve great things*

HMS *Resolution*

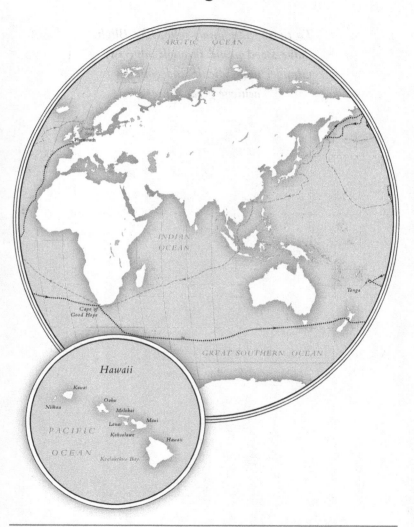

1776 - 1780

Captained by Cook

Navigated home by Bligh

HMS *Bounty*

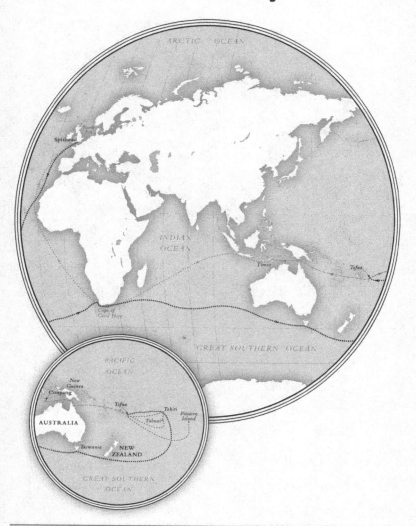

1787 - 1790*

Spithead

ATLANTIC
OCEAN

PACIFIC
OCEAN

Tofua   Tahiti   Pitcairn
Island

Cape
Horn

...... Route pre–mutiny
- - - Open–boat route
····· Bligh's route home*
- - - *Bounty* under Christian's
Command

Contents

PART III

CAPTAIN BLIGH

Author's Note

I first met Captain William Bligh when I was seven years old, the same age he was when he stepped aboard HMS *Monmouth* as a young cadet. My *Monmouth* was a small wooden packing case I'd rigged with a broomstick for a mast and an old roll-up window blind for a sail. My ocean was the backyard lawn at home, and I would sit out there aboard my ship on windy days with the sail straining and the horizon on my mind. I had learned about the captain at school in what I would later realise was a somewhat narrow and biased version of a much larger nautical life.

Now I have the chance to tell my story of a man too often misunderstood. First and foremost, my *Bligh* is the story of a bloody great sailor – one of the best: a master mariner, brilliant marine cartographer and navigator, and a fearless leader of men in battle.

I'm a sailor and a writer, but not an historian, and my research of the era and the man stands on the shoulders of the work of the many erudite authors, historians and even novelists who have gone before me. For a sense of Bligh's motivations and preoccupations, I have relied on the many expressive letters he wrote and received during his lifetime. I have also dramatised many moments in

Bligh's story, blending my own experience of sailing the waters he traversed into the action and narrative.

My *Bligh* is by no means the definitive account of his life. Instead, it is a tribute to an extraordinary life spent at sea on magnificent ships, and in particular the incredible 3600-nautical-mile open-boat voyage in the Pacific during which Bligh saved the lives of seventeen men. Accordingly, I have not dwelt on the politics of the *Bounty* mutiny or the tough time he had as the fourth governor of New South Wales, both very big stories in themselves and the subject of many dedicated and excellent works.

This is the biography of a sailor.

I dips m'lid to Captain Bligh.
— *Rob Mundle*

BLIGH

BLIGH

Tofua, 1789

The Stones

'**M**attee!' the barely clad, russet-skinned chief bellowed at near point-blank range into the face of Lieutenant William Bligh, RN. The simultaneous stare from the chief's brutal brown eyes confirmed his intentions. He retreated a short distance up the rock-strewn beach and, with a few incisive words to the 200 equally menacing-looking tribesmen encircling Bligh and his eighteen scruffy seafarers, urged them to attack.

The warriors began clacking together the stones they held firmly in their hands – diamond-hard black volcanic rocks washed smooth by the sea for eons. Then the rhythmic, haunting, monotonous sound began rising to a crescendo. It was a signal: the foreign trespassers were to be massacred. If it occurred, it would be a pivotal point for British maritime history in the eighteenth century.

There was little chance the Englishmen would be able to defend themselves. They had no firearms, only four cutlasses, two of which were aboard the small open launch riding the gentle surge of the sea at the water's edge, just yards away. The launch was their only hope for escape – and survival – and reaching it required an immediate, effective plan, timed to perfection.

Bligh, then aged 34, could have been forgiven for thinking he was experiencing some level of déjà vu. A decade earlier, in 1779, he had seen his mentor and commander aboard HMS *Resolution*, the legendary navigator and explorer Captain James Cook, RN, clubbed and stabbed to death by 'islanders' on a beach in the Hawaiian Islands.

Ten years on, Bligh found himself with the remnants of his own crew, totally isolated on a rocky beach in the South Pacific – on the remote Tongan island of Tofua (or Tofoa, as Bligh spelled it), a rugged, five-mile-wide circular speck on the ocean, the tip of a volcanic seamount. Now he faced a similar fate to Cook. At this point Bligh must also have been wondering why Cook, when he landed in 1777 on a tiny coral atoll nearby, the long and narrow Lifuka (during his second exploration of the South Pacific), named the region the Friendly Archipelago. At the time Cook noted the reason: 'as a lasting friendship seems to subsist among the inhabitants and their courtesy to strangers entitles them to that name'.

However, there would be a major difference between the two incidents, should Bligh and his men die at the hands of this far from courteous mob. Full details of Cook's death reached England via a letter carried by another ship preceding *Resolution* home, but if Bligh and his motley mariners – the first Europeans to set foot on Tofua – were killed, then the world would never know of their fate. Worse still, it would never know that just four days earlier, on 28 April 1789, they had been the victims of a mutiny aboard HMS *Bounty*, of which Bligh was captain. That had occurred little more than 30 nautical miles away to the south-south-west, just over the horizon from where they stood at that very moment.

Bligh and those who joined him had already been taunted by death twice in the previous four days, but had managed to escape its clutches. Now, though, it almost certainly wasn't going to be third time lucky.

The man who had led the mutiny, Fletcher Christian, and his 24 rebels were acting so irrationally they could easily have killed their captain and his followers by running them through with a bayonet, or throwing them overboard. Incredibly, as if there was a tinge of remorse in his rebellious bones, Christian chose to spare them, at least for the short term. His decision was to cast them adrift in mid-ocean, but in tormenting circumstances. Initially they were to be put aboard the ship's small, worm-eaten and rotting cutter, but eventually they were granted the slightly larger launch, which was in better condition. As magnanimous as this gesture towards salvation might have appeared, Bligh and his loyalists were actually closer to death than survival, simply by being aboard a small boat on the open sea.

Of robust construction, *Bounty*'s heavy carvel-planked timber launch was a mere 23 feet long, 6 feet wide and less than 3 feet deep. It was used as the ship's anchor-handling longboat and as the tender for transporting up to eight individuals to another vessel or to shore. Christian and his snarling supporters insisted eighteen of their former crewmates should join Bligh. This meant that with everyone aboard, along with some meagre provisions and personal effects that the mutineers grudgingly released to them, the ocean was all but lapping at the gunwales. Even in the benign sea conditions they were experiencing at the time, the freeboard was considerably less than the length of a forearm. The vessel was barely seaworthy: even the slightest of waves could have swamped it, or it might easily have been capsized by a sudden gust of wind pressing too forcefully into the two lugsails it carried. This act by the mutineers was nothing short of premeditated murder; as far as they were concerned there was next to no chance the grossly overloaded boat could reach shore.

With *Bounty* now under the command of Fletcher Christian and the launch cast adrift, the mutineers were enjoying raucous celebrations. Occasionally, as the ship sailed away ever so slowly in the light breeze, when their mirth mellowed, those on the quarterdeck looked aft over the heavy timber taffrail just to confirm the castaways were becoming an ever-decreasing dot in the ship's wake. This hedonistic group of sailors had commandeered the ship because they had no desire to swap an idyllic, carefree South Pacific way of life for a bleak and cheerless existence back home in England. They were also rebelling against what they saw as their captain's hard hand of authority. Now though, following their successful mutiny, they were on a course that would take them back to their decadent lifestyle of the previous five months with the alluring women they had come to know in the South Pacific paradise of Tahiti. Most importantly, they were determined never to be found. Christian and his men were certain the overloaded launch would soon be overwhelmed in rough weather and disappear, taking those aboard and the story of the mutiny to the depths. With the passing of time, when *Bounty* failed to arrive in her home port the ship would be registered as lost at sea without trace, with all hands. The mutineers would then have achieved their goal: establishing a new life in paradise with the 'flesh-pots of Tahiti'. They would also have provided the world with the ingredients for one of its greatest ever maritime mysteries.

Bligh's official directive when he sailed from England on this mission had been to travel halfway around the world to Tahiti and load the ship with juvenile breadfruit plants. Then, on the passage back to England, *Bounty* would stop in the West Indies, where the plants would be offloaded. They were to be cultivated there to provide food for the slaves labouring under the control of English masters.

But that wasn't to be. *Bounty* was now heading back to Tahiti, albeit on a circuitous route to the west–north–west because the mutineers wanted to disguise their intentions. Bligh already knew their destination, however, because during the mutiny many of the rebels were heard to shout with great gusto, 'Huzza for Otaheite!' (Hurray for Tahiti!).

With nineteen men crowded aboard the launch, space was at a premium. Bligh, who was at the tiller in the stern sheets, was steering a course to the north–east while those manning the oars rowed hard. Little was said. They could only wonder what hand fate might deal them as they watched their ship sail away. Bligh's initial intention was to try to get the launch to Tofua, which he knew from his experience in this region with Captain Cook was some 30 nautical miles away. By the middle of the day everyone was heartened: they could see the outline of the towering volcano that stood as the centrepiece of the island they hoped to reach before nightfall.

All day Bligh's mind had been running wild. Why the mutiny? Why had he not sensed it was brewing? And, how were they going to survive? Where should they head? Tofua was the obvious answer to start with. He hoped it would be a source of food, particularly breadfruit, and water, because he wanted to minimise their reliance on the paltry provisions the mutineers had allowed them. His plan then extended to stage two: to sail to Tongataboo, another Tongan island, about 100 nautical miles south of Tofua. He hoped that once there, King Paulehow, whom Bligh had met with Cook, would support them while they prepared their boat for the next stage of their voyage, to a destination yet to be decided.

Bligh's overpowering realisation was that there was little to no chance of them ever being rescued by a passing ship and repatriated to England, so it was up to him and his men to save themselves.

His mind then moved to the west, across the Pacific and to the East Indies, where the Dutch were known to have a colony, but he didn't know exactly where. That was the nearest site of European civilisation and their only real hope for salvation, but it was more than 3600 nautical miles away across an often treacherous open ocean. Worse still, their only means of getting there was the launch, and there was a high probability it would be overcome by wind and wave on such a long and arduous passage.

But first things first: they had to reach Tofua, an island that became known to Europeans in 1643 when Dutchman Abel Tasman sailed through the region. Until then Tasman had only seen low-lying atolls in this archipelago, so he took time to sketch Tofua, which he named Amatofua. Fortunately for the *Bounty* discards, the seas remained relatively calm through to the afternoon when a light and favourable easterly wind sprang up and propelled them towards their goal. The breeze held, so after more than twelve hours of rowing and sailing the launch was guided into the lee off the north-western corner of Tofua. Night had fallen, so Bligh decided they would remain at sea and make landfall the next morning under the safety of daylight. The call was for two oars to be manned throughout the night in a rotating watch system so the launch could be held in the calm waters of the lee. Those men not on watch had to endure a fitful sleep in cramped and extremely uncomfortable conditions.

After sunrise they cruised along the shore until, around mid-morning, they found a small cove. They anchored in shallow water there, just beyond the surf-line, about three boat-lengths off the rocky beach. Bligh felt a great sense of relief and his men could have been forgiven for thinking they had achieved safe sanctuary, and the first step to survival.

Once ashore, their initial search for food and water was disappointing. The scouting party returned with only a few quarts of water and not even a coconut or breadfruit. As a result their supper that night was a mouthful of bread and a glass of wine, which the mutineers had included in their provisions. Bligh then decided that since they were not certain the island was uninhabited, for their own safety they should all stay aboard the launch that night.

The following day a strong wind and rough seas prevented them from departing the cove in which they were anchored, so Bligh opted to take the launch along the lee shore to broaden their search for food. Eventually they spotted coconut palms atop a high cliff and some crew went ashore to retrieve coconuts. They collected twenty: enough for each man to enjoy one that evening after they returned to their original anchorage. Once again they slept aboard.

Bligh was becoming frustrated and anxious to depart Tofua, but strong winds and rough seas made it unsafe to set sail, so they stayed hemmed in in the bay. To make good out of the delay he further widened the quest for food and water, and even took part in the search himself. He and some of his men used vines to haul themselves up a steep cliff, then moved inland further than any previous expedition by other crew members, but the extra effort brought little benefit: only a few gallons of water and some plantains.

When the group reached the top of the cliff on their way back to the cove, Bligh bent down to pick up one of the vines so he could safely descend the escarpment, and as he did he suffered a severe attack of what appeared to be vertigo, but it could also have been a dizzy spell brought on by acute hunger. Fortunately, some of his men were able to grab him before he toppled over the edge, and then, after he regained his balance, they supported him during the difficult descent.

Soon after, when Bligh was joined by the rest of his men back in the cove, they took stock of the day's effort and it was nothing short of extremely disappointing: they had secured no fish or food of any significance. This prompted the leader to write in his log, 'We considered ourselves on as miserable a spot as could well be conceived.' However, there was possibly a positive side to the day: there had been a sign of people living on the island – some deserted huts – and they had also found a cave in the cove large enough for Bligh and some of his crew to sleep in that night. Those remaining aboard the launch would be more comfortable.

On the following day, during what was by then a desperate search for water and food, some of the crew made contact with apparently friendly islanders, two men, a woman and a child, who presented them with two coconut shells full of water. A little later the situation appeared to be improving for Bligh and his men when the two men they had met returned to the beach with a further 30 members of their tribe, most of whom brought plantains and coconuts which they exchanged for buttons and beads. However, these provisions were few and Bligh quickly realised it was unlikely they would find sufficient supplies on this island for the next stage of the voyage to Tongataboo.

The following morning, to the surprise of Bligh and his crew, the mood had changed; the tide of welcome was swiftly turning against them. There was obvious tension in the air. Many more tribesmen gathered on the beach and two canoes arrived, one carrying an elderly local chief, Macca-ackavow. Soon after, when the men Bligh had sent into the gullies in search of water returned, they had a young chief, Eefow, with them. By this time Bligh was alarmed. Trouble might be brewing, so he made every effort to establish a favourable rapport with the chiefs by presenting them with an old shirt and a knife, but before long there was no doubt the Englishmen were facing a perilous predicament. Suddenly they were unwelcome visitors. The number of men on the beach was increasing and the threat of hostility heightened, so Bligh surreptitiously formulated a plan of escape.

The first confrontation came when a group of the islanders tried to drag the launch onto the beach by the stern line. This was attached to the grapnel that had been set among the rocks. Bligh immediately went on the offensive: when he showed his commanding demeanour and brandished his cutlass, 'everything became quiet again'. Even so, with his concerns for the safety of his crew escalating, he decided his only option was to wait for nightfall and make good an escape. He wrote in the notebook that he was using as a log:

> The beach was lined with natives and we heard nothing but
> the knocking of stones together which they had in each hand.
> I knew very well this was the sign of an attack. At noon,
> I served a coconut and a breadfruit to each person for dinner,
> and gave some to the chiefs, with whom I continued to appear
> intimate and friendly. They frequently importuned me to sit
> down, but I, as constantly, refused; but it occurred both to
> Nelson [*Bounty*'s botanist] and myself, that they intended to
> seize hold of me if I gave them such an opportunity. Keeping,
> therefore, constantly on our guard, we were suffered to eat our
> uncomfortable meal in some quietness.

Recognising that if he or any of his men showed signs of fear it would probably bring immediate and fatal consequences, Bligh had those on shore begin casually and confidently transferring food, water and equipment to the launch. At the same time the master on board the launch was informed that Bligh wanted the vessel to be kept as close to the beach as possible so, in the event of an attack, they could quickly board it.

Bligh's log continued:

Every person who was on shore with me now boldly took their proportions of things and carried them to the boat, when the chiefs asked me if I would not stay with them all night, I said 'No, I never sleep out of my boat, but in the morning we will again trade with you, and I shall remain until the weather is moderate, that we may go as we have agreed, to see Paulehow at Tongataboo'. Macca-ackavow now got up and said 'You will not sleep on shore; then Mattee,' (which directly implies 'We will kill you') and I saw no more of him.

With the noise from the knocking together of the stones ever louder, and Eefow urging his men to attack, Bligh decided to move to the next stage of his survival plan: he took a hostage, a prominent tribesman, Nagatee, whom Bligh remembered meeting when he was at Tongataboo with Captain Cook. He firmly grabbed Nagatee's arm and restrained him. The intention was, if an attack occurred, to be ruthless: he would have no hesitation in killing his hostage.

This small advantage was quickly lost when, with a sudden and sharp jolt, Nagatee broke free of Bligh's grip. It was time to make an audacious move and board the launch. Mustering every ounce of their English pride, Bligh and his men strode purposefully past the warriors, through the small surf, then clambered over the side and into the launch. However, as Quartermaster John Norton made his way towards the launch he noticed the stern grapnel was still secured on the beach, so without hesitation he turned back to release it. 'I heard the master and others calling him to return while they were hauling me out of the water,' wrote Bligh. 'I was no sooner into the boat than the attack by about 200 of them began – this unfortunate poor man was first knocked down and the stones flew like a shower of shot. Many men got hold of the stern fast [anchor line] and were near hauling us on shore and would certainly have done it if I had not had a knife in my pocket to cut it.'

With the stern line severed, some of Bligh's men then frantically hauled on the anchor line at the bow so they could get away from the beach as fast as possible. Bligh looked back and saw two of the islanders with Norton, continually beating his head with large stones while five others were fighting over who would get his trousers as a trophy. Nearby, other men were filling their canoes with stones, to pursue the Englishmen and renew the action.

The now desperate sailors pulled hard on the line, but the forward grapnel was fouled under a rock and refused to budge from the bottom – until one of its flukes broke. The men holding the six long and heavy hardwood oars slid them into the slots in the gunwale, then began rowing as hard as they could, straining every muscle in their bodies in a frantic bid to get the heavy and cumbersome launch away from the beach and to safety on the open sea. While Norton's ghoulish murder drove their high stroke rate, it soon became apparent that with so many men aboard, they could not outpace the islanders pursuing them in their faster canoes. In no time they were circling the launch, attacking the Englishmen with an unrelenting bombardment of rocks, 'which they did so effectually as nearly to disable all of us,' Bligh later wrote in his notebook.

Bligh's men tried in vain to return the fire by hurling back the rocks that had landed in the launch, to little avail. It seemed inevitable they would succumb to their attackers and be killed, until Bligh seized upon one last tactical chance – the element of surprise. Having witnessed the islanders on the beach fighting over Norton's trousers, he instantly grabbed some clothes from the bilge and tossed them high into the air and into the sea, making sure their attackers could see what he was doing. It was a stroke of genius: the clothes were seen as a far greater prize than the lives of the Englishmen, so the islanders, distracted from the chase, immediately stopped paddling and picked up the sodden garments. Bligh and his men now had the slight advantage they needed, which, coupled with the fact that night was beginning to close in, led to the tribesmen quitting the pursuit and returning to their island.

With the threat now over, the men on the oars eased their stroke rate while the bow of the launch continued to press into the surge of a rising sea. After the horrific slaughter of shipmate Norton, the remaining crewmembers realised how close they had come to death. In fact it had been an entire day of narrow escapes. Bligh, for one, appreciated that had the warriors cornered them in the cave where they had slept the previous night, it would have been impossible to get away.

A profound sense of relief settled on the scene aboard the launch, as it continued to move away from the island and deeper into the night. Bligh now pondered his next move. Going to Tongataboo was out of the question: it would be far too dangerous to go there without firearms or any genuine form of defence to counter another attack, especially considering Nagatee, having observed their escape, might return to his home in Tongataboo and alert the local islanders as to what had happened. It was highly likely that even if their lives were spared when they landed there, the launch plus the compass and quadrant, which the mutineers had allowed Bligh to take for navigation purposes, would be seized and not returned. He held no doubt it was too much of a risk.

Bligh's mind was now seized by an unshakeable determination: he must somehow return to England and present an account of the mutiny. Reflecting upon the events, he wrote:

> I felt an inward satisfaction which prevented any depression of
> my spirits. Conscious of my integrity, and with anxious solicitude

for the good of the service in which I had been engaged, I found my mind wonderfully supported, and I began to conceive hopes, notwithstanding so heavy a calamity, that I should one day be able to account to my King and country for the misfortune.

Even so, there was no apparent way to achieve this. They were on a course to no place in particular, even though, as Bligh recorded: 'I was earnestly solicited by all hands to take them towards home.'

As they distanced themselves from the shore, the launch sailed into the clutches of a menacing gale that was producing seas with the potential to overwhelm it. There was no option but to run with this weather, as Bligh described:

> It was about eight o'clock at night when we bore away under a reefed lug fore-sail and, having divided the people into watches and got the boat in a little order, we returned God thanks for our miraculous preservation and, fully confident of his gracious support, I found my mind more at ease than it had been for some time past.
>
> At daybreak the gale increased; the sun rose very fiery and red, a sure indication of a severe gale of wind. At eight it blew a violent storm and the sea ran very high, so that between the seas the sail was becalmed, and when on the top of the sea it was too much to have set: but we could not venture to take in the sail for we were in very imminent danger and distress, the sea curling over the stern of the boat, which obliged us to bale with all our might. A situation more distressing has perhaps seldom been experienced.

He had an obligation to keep his men safe and secure, so Bligh declared that after the experience they had just survived on

Tofua, it would probably be unsafe to land on any other island in the region. Their only hope was to sail a direct course to the Dutch East Indies, a passage they had already considered as almost impossible under the circumstances confronting them. He stressed to his men, who were listening intently to their leader, that the only place along the way where they might be able to safely stop to replenish their food supplies would be on the north-east coast of New Holland (Australia), which had been discovered by Captain Cook almost two decades earlier.

On considering the alternatives, every man decided they would prefer to back their ability as seafarers over certain death at the hands of islanders. Bringing added influence to this decision was the rudimentary knowledge Bligh held of the north-east coast of New Holland and Torres Strait, gleaned from Cook when Bligh sailed with him between 1776 and 1779. So, the East Indies it was, and with that decision made, the crew then agreed with a crucial demand from Bligh: they must be prepared to live on an absolute minimum amount of food and water each day if they were to have any chance of reaching their destination.

The men then prepared the boat for what would be an undertaking of gargantuan proportions. When everything was ready they set a course to the west-north-west towards the northern coast of New Holland, which would possibly be their first stop en route to the Dutch East Indies. Bligh logged the moment:

> ... after examining what our real stock of provisions was,
> and recommending this as a sacred promise forever to their
> memory, I bore away across the sea, where the navigation is
> dangerous and but little known and in a small boat 23 feet
> long from stem to stern, deep loaded with 18 souls, without a
> single map and nothing but my own recollection and general

knowledge of the situation of places, assisted by an old book of latitude and longitude to guide me ...

What followed was one of the greatest ever feats of navigation, seamanship and human endurance – a perilous 47-day passage of more than 3600 nautical miles that spanned a merciless and storm-ravaged open ocean: eighteen men in a tiny boat, with little food and little hope, defied hideous odds and lived to tell the story.

In maritime history only Sir Ernest Shackleton's death-defying seventeen-day voyage in 1916, and convict Mary Bryant's escape in a stolen boat from Sydney to Timor two years before Bligh's ordeal come close. Shackleton's epic passage over 750 nautical miles from Elephant Island to South Georgia Island came after his ship, *Endurance*, was crushed by ice and sunk in the remote and frigid waters of the Antarctic Ocean, south-east of Cape Horn. With five men Shackleton sailed a dilapidated lifeboat through a hurricane and surf-like seas until they reached their destination and orchestrated the rescue of the 22 shipmates they left behind.

As the centuries have passed, history and Hollywood have conspired to malign Bligh – a man who could justifiably lay claim to being one of the great master mariners. All too often today's attitudes have been applied to judge eighteenth-century actions.

These attitudes supposedly make for a better story – but not this time!

ADVENTURE BAY,

VAN DIEMAN'S LAND

PENGUIN ISLAND

BAY OF FREDERICK HENRY.

SCALE of MILES

PART I

Master Bligh

PART 1

Master Bligh

CHAPTER ONE

Plymouth, 1754

The boy becomes a seafarer

Voyages into the South Pacific by the great mariners of the eighteenth century – such as Cook, Bligh and Furneaux – revealed a paradise that could not have been more starkly different from everyday life in England at the time. Little wonder then that the *Bounty* mutineers, especially those with few family ties, opted not to return home. They weren't the first to do so: there had already been deserters from many of the ships that had sailed to those shores. Even Captain Cook had trouble with deserters in Tahiti after he anchored HMS *Endeavour* at Raiatea, 140 nautical miles north-west of Papeete, during his first voyage of discovery. And Samuel Wallace, captain of HMS *Dolphin*, who discovered Tahiti in 1767, saw how the charms of the Tahitian women brought trouble among his crew. He wrote: 'the commerce which our men had found means to establish with the women of the island, rendered them much less obedient to the orders that had been given for the regulation of their conduct on shore, than they were at first ...'

It was 22 years after Captain Wallace made those observations that Bligh also became a victim of the hypnotic effect of this tropical paradise. But his situation was far worse: more than half his crew had mutinied and as a consequence he found himself, along with some loyalists, marooned on a small Pacific island 13000 nautical miles from home. It was the last thing this accomplished seafarer could have imagined when, after joining the Royal Navy as a seven-year-old cadet in his hometown of Plymouth, he put to sea for the first time as a crewmember of HMS *Hunter*, aged fifteen.

The name Bligh is more Cornish than pasties. It can be traced back to the Domesday Book in the eleventh century. Three centuries later, during the reign of Edward III, official records reveal that the family of Bligh held estates in Cornwall. So it is not surprising that a number of villages in Cornwall have laid claim to being the birthplace of William Bligh, none more so than St Tudy, in the countryside 200 miles south-west of London. After residing in nearby Bodim during the sixteenth century, some of Francis Bligh's forebears had moved to St Tudy in 1680. But according to noted Bligh historian and academic George Mackaness, it is more likely that William Bligh was born in Plymouth, 30 miles to the south-east of St Tudy. The St Andrew's Church register in Plymouth declares: 'William the Son of Francis and Jane Bligh was born on the ninth day of September 1754, about one o'clock in the morning'. He was baptised in the same church less than a month later.

William's mother, Jane Pearce, had been a widow with one daughter, Catherine, when she married Francis. She was over 40 years old when William was born; it is highly likely he was the only child of this union. There are no records to the contrary.

The England of Bligh's childhood saw the birth of the Industrial Revolution, an event that over the next century transformed the world forever, and nothing was more pivotal to England's burgeoning wealth and power at this time than the Royal Navy.

In the year Bligh was born, the navy comprised nearly 500 ships and some 75000 men, and seaports dotted the entire English coastline for defence, maintenance and trade purposes. The Royal Navy had six dockyards in England, the largest being at Portsmouth, however Plymouth became the main naval base when the French replaced the Dutch as the greatest threat to the country's security. Originally known as Plymouth Yard when it was founded in 1690, Plymouth Dock was the home port for the Western Squadron during the eighteenth century. Even during peacetime the dockyard was busy as ships were laid-up: they remained afloat but their guns, masts, sails and rigging were removed and placed in storage. Peace also presented the opportunity for these ships to be repaired and to have new ships built.

In the early eighteenth century, English novelist Daniel Defoe described Plymouth as: 'a town of consideration and of great importance to the public. It is situated between two very large inlets of the sea and in the bottom of a large bay, which is very remarkable.'

In fact, Plymouth was remarkable in many ways. In addition to its prominence as a naval port, it was a vital centre of trade for England, both coastal and to distant destinations, including the West Indies, the American colonies and the Mediterranean. This amalgam of naval activity and commerce created a vibrant and diverse community for its few thousand residents. By 1758, Plymouth had achieved such significance on a national scale that a turnpike – a toll road – was built between the town and London, a distance of more than 200 miles.

Due to its proximity to the western entrance of the English Channel, Plymouth remained of high strategic and commercial importance to England for centuries: it gave ships-of-sail unimpeded access to the North Atlantic and beyond. For this same reason,

Plymouth was the port of origin for so many famous voyages, and departures for battle.

In December 1577 Francis Drake set sail from this port on what would be the first circumnavigation of the world by an Englishman. When he returned three years later he had news of many discoveries, but what brought him most fame, plus deep gratitude from his queen – Elizabeth I – was that he presented her with one of the richest prizes ever to be taken in battle: coins, jewels and precious metals valued then at £450 000. He secured this immense treasure after his defeat of the Spanish ship *Nuestra Señora de la Concepción* during a confrontation off the coast of Peru. The queen's half-share of the booty exceeded the rest of the crown's revenue for the entire year, so it wasn't surprising she dubbed him Sir Francis Drake in a ceremony on the deck of his ship, *Golden Hind*, near London the following year.

Drake's name became synonymous with Plymouth in 1588 when, legend has it, he chose to complete a game of bowls at Plymouth Hoe, overlooking the harbour, instead of immediately responding to news that the 150-strong Spanish Armada was on approach, intent on invading England and overthrowing the queen. Drake had apparently placed more importance on completing the game of bowls than putting to sea. The true reason he didn't set sail immediately was adverse tide and wind. When he did lead the English ships into battle they put down the foreign threat over a period of months in a most resounding fashion.

Plymouth also farewelled the Pilgrims on *Mayflower* on 16 September 1620 as they set sail for the New World, and two months later established the Plymouth Colony in what is now Plymouth, Massachusetts. It was also the point of departure for all three voyages into the Pacific undertaken by Captain James Cook, the first of which came almost 150 years after the Pilgrims set sail.

A defeated Napoleon, too, left Plymouth on the *Bellepheron* in 1815 on his way to exile in St. Helena.

With so much maritime activity centring on Plymouth, William Bligh seemed destined for a life as a seafarer. It was a destiny inevitably influenced by his father, a lifetime employee of HM Customs in this naval town. During William's formative years he spent time with his father aboard the revenue boats, used to ferry customs officials to ships that had entered the port and were at anchor, to collect duty from the master. However, being a customs official also had a grave element of danger to it: smuggling was rife across this part of England, and customs men, who were supposed to help control it, stood the chance of being murdered. Even so, the smugglers were seen by many to be an acceptable part of the local community. At Mousehole, one of the westernmost villages on the coast, charges were laid against village officials for accepting bribes and cooperating with smugglers, while the Penzance collector of customs described one villager, Richard 'Doga' Pentreath, as 'an honest man in all his dealings though a notorious smuggler'. But it was Plymouth, one of the busiest ports in England, that was the largest market for contraband, primarily because of its vastness and the volume of shipping arriving there from foreign ports.

Young Bligh grew up against a backdrop of trade, travel and war. When he was just two years old, the Seven Years War, in many ways the world's first global war, began. It involved all major European powers and saw Great Britain, Prussia and a coalition of German states confronting an enemy comprising France, Russia, Sweden, Austria and Saxony and, eventually, Spain. The Dutch Republic and Portugal were also involved. The bloody encounters, which resulted in as many as 1.4 million deaths, came to an end with the signing of the treaties of Hubertusburg and Paris in

February 1763. With Spain and its allies defeated, Britain emerged as the greatest colonial power, its control extending as far as India and North America.

It was during the latter years of the war that seven-year-old William Bligh was entered on Admiralty records as a ship's boy, or servant to the captain, on the battle-hardened HMS *Monmouth*. In command of this veteran ship was a 23-year-old Scot, Keith Stewart, who is believed to have been a friend of Bligh's mother, Jane. More interestingly, young William Bligh's brother-in-law, John Bond – who was married to Bligh's half-sister, Catherine – was a naval surgeon aboard the same ship.

It was the custom in Georgian England for a Royal Navy captain to have favoured youths or youngsters from the lower classes join him on a man-of-war as servants so each boy could achieve, at the earliest possible age, the six years' sea time required for a career in the navy. Naval regulations stipulated that each captain was allowed four servant boys for each 100 crew, and with *Monmouth* having a complement of between 500 and 600 men, Captain Stewart could have had more than twenty cadets in service. In addition to receiving an education from the schoolmaster employed aboard each of the larger navy ships, these youngsters acted as cabin boys for their superiors and also 'learnt the ropes', learning about the many features of a ship-of-sail, seafaring, the tying of knots, the handling of sails and steering. They were taught to draw, read and write, something most ordinary seamen aboard the ship could not do. In battle many of these youngsters were required to work as 'powder monkeys', their task being to run gunpowder from the ship's magazine to the cannons. Discipline was always strong for cadets while on board a ship, but there was no class distinction: lower-class lads lived and learned alongside the sons of gentlemen and officers.

Aged seven, Bligh's career path was already set: he was destined to be a naval officer, and while he was on the bottom rung of the ladder of naval service he could not have wished for a better opportunity. *Monmouth*, named after a town in south-eastern Wales that has a history dating back to the Roman occupation of England, was a ship with an extremely proud heritage. She was a 70-gunner that had been in service for almost twenty years, and it would be another five years before she was decommissioned and broken up. Her illustrious career saw her collect many battle honours, however, there was no greater achievement than her close-quarters encounter with the new 80-gun French flagship *Foudroyant*, on 28 February 1758, just four years before Bligh went aboard.

By this time in British naval history its sailors had learned how to fight a battle successfully at night, something the French had not mastered. *Foudroyant* was sailing off Cartagena, on Spain's Mediterranean coast, when she was intercepted by three British ships, including *Monmouth*. Despite *Foudroyant* boasting significantly superior firepower, *Monmouth*'s then captain, Arthur Gardiner, had no hesitation in engaging the enemy. He broke his ship away from the British squadron and at eight o'clock at night the action began. In a blazing and unrelenting battle where the sky was vividly illuminated as if by lightning, lethal cannonballs were blasted towards the enemy, bringing carnage to both sides. At ten o'clock *Monmouth*'s mizzenmast was blown to pieces and soon after *Foudroyant*'s main mast went crashing over the side in a tangle of rigging, sails and timber. At midnight *Foudroyant* had virtually no cannons left operational, and it took only one destructive broadside from HMS *Swiftsure* when she arrived on the scene for the French to strike their colours.

Bligh did not see such action as a cadet, nor even go to sea on *Monmouth*. Just eight months after joining the ship he was paid off and returned to shore. It is highly probable this was due to the signing of the Treaty of Paris, which ended the Seven Years War, just ten days prior to him leaving the ship. The treaty, which recognised a British victory, brought peace, and this led to the Royal Navy decommissioning a large proportion of its fleet and standing down the majority of its men. No doubt it meant that Captain Stewart, of *Monmouth*, was no longer entitled to his quota of cadets and Bligh, along with many others, would have most likely then returned home where he would continue his education and possibly share work experience on the water with his father.

With peace prevailing across Europe, the British began to turn their seafaring skills towards exploration, and soon became obsessed by it. As a result there were few opportunities for employment within the navy, and this might explain why there are no records relating to William Bligh for seven years following his departure from *Monmouth*. However, there is no doubt he continued his education and was an avid student because by the time he reappeared, he had developed impressive skills and acquired considerable knowledge in mathematics, science, writing and illustrating – exceptional talents so apparent in the meticulous logs and charts he created later in life.

It was in 1770, the same year that Captain Cook confirmed the existence of the Great South Land, New Holland, on the opposite side of the world, that the name William Bligh reappeared in naval records and set him on a course which a few years later would see him linked to the great explorer. It might have been the recent death of his beloved mother, and his father's remarriage, that led fifteen-year-old William to re-enter the navy on the pay sheets of HMS *Hunter*. It was 27 July and he was registered as an able-bodied seaman (AB), or able seaman.

Aboard *Hunter*, a small ten-gun sloop, Bligh had his first taste of being at sea and under sail. He made his first trans-Atlantic passage to the Caribbean and later crossed the Irish Sea to Dublin. As an AB he learned about a ship's rig and sails, how to relay messages between decks, how to command the ship's small boats, how to run a watch system and how to supervise the gun batteries.

For Bligh this posting was, in essence, an apprenticeship, a period during which he would mark time and accumulate the experience and contacts needed to further his career. It was not uncommon for a young man with his sights set on moving up to the next rank, a midshipman, to be appointed an able seaman while waiting for a vacancy to occur. Bligh, at this time, was a midshipman in every sense but name: he was carrying out the same duties as midshipmen on the quarterdeck and also messed with them.

He was already impressing his superiors because by February 1771, a mere seven months after he joined *Hunter*, he was promoted to midshipman, a position he retained when he was transferred to a considerably larger 32-gun ship, HMS *Crescent*, a few days after his seventeenth birthday. He remained with *Crescent* (formerly the French privateer *Rostan*, which had been captured by the British in 1758) for three years when the ship spent much of its time on the West Indies station, where it was actively involved in helping quell slave uprisings. His service aboard this ship saw him hone his skills further.

As the name suggests, a midshipman was a sailor who was accommodated amidships, in the middle section of the ship between the men who lived forward and the officers who were aft. Royal Navy regulations stated that no one could 'be rated as a master's mate or midshipman who shall not have been three years at sea'. All midshipmen were expected to work the ship as well as learn navigation and seamanship. Royal Navy slang saw a midshipman often referred to as a 'snotty'. There were two popular theories relating to this seemingly derogatory term. One related to a general absence of handkerchiefs among midshipmen, so they had no option but to deal with a runny nose by wiping it on their sleeves. The other story claims that the three buttons sewn onto the cuffs of a midshipman's jacket were put there to stop this practice.

During his posting aboard *Hunter*, or later with HMS *Ranger*, Bligh may have visited Douglas, the largest town on the Isle of Man, and if so, might have met Elizabeth Betham, a strikingly attractive young woman who would eventually steal his heart. She was one year older than Bligh, and her father, like Bligh's, was a collector of customs, and he was also the water bailiff in Douglas.

In September 1774 Bligh joined *Ranger* – a small eight-gun sloop that had been in service since 1752 – as it presented a greater chance for advancement through the ranks. Unlike many of his fellow midshipmen, he did not have the family background to further his career through connections or money. His only assets were his talent and his determination. So, to ensure that he could take full advantage of any opportunities *Ranger* offered, he chose to step back to the position of AB just so he could be on board.

It was a wise move as Admiralty records would soon reveal that Bligh displayed the talents of a sailor who was 'intended for the quarterdeck'. This was confirmed when, just one year later, he was promoted to the rank of midshipman, and with it came the title of master's mate: he was now a direct assistant to the sailing master and took a more responsible role in the operation of the ship. The posting brought an increase in pay from 2 pounds, 5 shillings to 3 pounds, 16 shillings per month.

Had he stayed with *Ranger* he would almost certainly have seen action in the American colonial rebellion in 1776, but eighteen months after signing on, his brilliance was further recognised by his superiors: he was rewarded with what would have been at the time a much sought after transfer. He was appointed to the notable position of sailing master aboard the 111-foot, 462-ton sloop HMS *Resolution*, under the command of Captain James Cook. This ship was being prepared for Cook's third voyage of discovery into the Pacific. Cook had returned from his second voyage in June 1775 and was due to set sail again with the same ship just one year later. The primary aim for the new expedition was to discover a passage around the northern coast of North America, from the Pacific to the Atlantic, and thus eliminate the need to traverse the treacherous waters of the Southern Ocean where Cape Horn and the Cape of Good Hope stood as notorious obstacles. There were additional instructions, such as 'collecting samples of plants, fruit, metals and stones; establishing a friendship with the natives of the region, and claiming uninhabited locations along the way in the name of His Majesty'.

Bligh's appointment as sailing master, which he took up on 20 March 1776, was a remarkable achievement for the 21-year-old, who was then still in the junior ranks. On 1 May that year he was presented with his lieutenant's 'Passing Certificate'. The transfer to *Resolution* and promotion to a senior rank confirmed he had continued to display exceptional talent to his superiors, even though he had been seen by some to be an 'awkward fellow' because of his supposed hair-trigger temper and a propensity for impatience.

Prior to being awarded his certificate, Bligh went before a board of three captains for an examination relating to seamanship, navigation and discipline. Various propositions would likely have been put to him, such as: 'An enemy is observed; give orders for clearing your ship and make all the necessary preparations for engaging.' Bligh was also required to present proof of his length of service, journals he kept while a midshipman, and certificates from his superiors confirming his sobriety and diligence. He had to convince the board he had the ability to work a ship under sail, reef a sail, splice ropes, work the tides and demonstrate his aptitude as a navigator. While he had then qualified as a lieutenant, it did not automatically entitle him to the new commission. Instead, he would have to wait until a position became available within the ranks.

As sailing master on *Resolution*, Bligh was primarily in charge of navigation and the sailing of the ship. In consultation with the captain he decided and plotted the course, and nominated the sails to be set. He also maintained the maps and instruments needed for navigation, a responsibility that demanded meticulous attention to detail, particularly on voyages of exploration where charts were more often than not inaccurate, or worse still, nonexistent.

Cook had been encouraged to include Bligh in his crew with the strongest recommendation from the Admiralty's highest office. Lord John Montagu, the 4th Earl of Sandwich, was in his third period as First Lord of the Admiralty, and was patron of Cook's Pacific ambitions. Lord Montagu was also funding the purchase and fit-out of *Resolution*.

Montagu was obviously well aware of the growing reputation the promising young midshipman, Bligh, held as a navigator, surveyor and seaman. Accordingly, Cook had no hesitation in signing him on for his third Pacific voyage, one that would embrace exploration and discovery. Cook realised that, even with only six years at sea to his credit, Bligh was displaying every attribute needed to complement Cook's own abilities and serve the voyage well. His view of Bligh was that the young man 'under my direction could be easily employed in constructing charts, in taking views of the coasts and headlands near which we would pass, and in drawing plans of the bays and harbours in which we should anchor', adding that attention to detail in these duties was 'wholly requisite if we should render our discoveries profitable for future navigators'.

The two seafarers also shared a common bond: Cook, then aged 47, and Bligh both came from modest origins, and while Bligh spent all of his younger years on the waterfront in Plymouth, Cook's passion for the sea emerged at the age of sixteen when he moved to the scenic coastal village of Staithes, in North Yorkshire, and became entranced by its sheltered harbour and the ocean that lay beyond. Both men had entered the Royal Navy through the junior ranks on the lower deck, and had enjoyed an impressive rise based on their talent and skill. By comparison, had either man been enlisted as a boy into the British Army, and not the Royal Navy, there is a high probability neither would have achieved such levels of distinction during their careers. The reason was simple: to have the best chance of climbing the ranks in the army in the eighteenth century you had to be from the aristocracy or at least be extremely well connected. But in the navy a sailor's ability as a mariner was generally considered more valuable than his social status, even though there was a considerable element of bias towards the nobility within the fleet.

It is likely that before *Resolution* set sail, Bligh met for the first time the acclaimed botanist Sir Joseph Banks, a man who was destined to become a mentor and great supporter of Bligh's naval career. Banks had been with Cook on his first Pacific voyage of discovery between 1768 and 1771 – the historic passage to Tahiti that led to the discovery of New Zealand and Australia's east coast, but one which also saw the ship run aground on a coral reef and go close to foundering. Ironically, it was when Cook was saving his ship on the tropical north-east coast of Australia that Bligh returned to the navy as a fifteen-year-old.

For Cook's third voyage, part of the *Resolution*'s refit for her planned three-year expedition involved the relatively new procedure of sheathing and filling the hull for protection from teredo worms – 'the termites of the sea'. This was being carried out at the naval facility at Deptford, on the Thames, just downstream from the centre of London. Unfortunately, however, the results of the apathy and shoddy workmanship of the dockyard workers would not become truly evident until the ship was being pressed on the high seas, or when the heavens delivered a torrential downpour. The ingress of water under those circumstances made for a miserable existence for all on board. It can also be safely said that the responsibility for much of the inferior workmanship and delays during the refit period rested with Cook. Before his previous voyages he had played an extremely active role in overseeing every aspect of the preparation of his ships, ensuring the work was done to appropriate standards, but this time he was otherwise occupied: completing the writing of his journal from the preceding voyage, sitting for a portrait, and forever studying charts relating to the proposed course for this third mission.

The importance the government placed on Cook's passage to the South Pacific became apparent on 8 June when *Resolution* was anchored in the lower reaches of the Thames so that armaments, water and stores could be put aboard. On this day the entire crew was ordered to assemble on deck in their best dress, or slops – a name originating from the old English word *sloppe*, meaning breeches (the Royal Navy still refers to its clothing stores as 'Slop Stores'). With most sailors being relatively poor they made their own clothes, so their garb varied considerably in style and colour, blue being the preference. On this occasion the fundamentals for the sailors would have been baggy breeches, often made from old canvas sails, cotton or linen tunic tops with long sleeves, weskits (vests made from fabric or leather), possibly knitted stockings and simple leather shoes. Like the clothing, their headwear varied greatly in colour, design and material: there was the basic tricorn, knitted caps, monmouth caps, apple pastie hats with their turned-up brims, and canvas hats that were tarred black to make them waterproof. Their hair was generally tied back in a ponytail and often coated with tar so that it remained in place – hence the term 'jack tar'. The commissioned officers on the day were in all their finery: blue frockcoats with white lapels, white breeches, stockings and black bespoke shoes with buckles. Bligh and other lower-ranked warrant officers were identified by their blue breeches. It was mid-afternoon when the cause for this call for full regalia became apparent. With all pomp and ceremony, including cannon fire and the shrill of pipes, the First Lord of the Admiralty, the 4th Earl of Sandwich, was welcomed aboard along with other dignitaries. They spent considerable time inspecting the ship under Cook's guidance, and then, with formalities complete, they joined him for a special dinner in the great cabin.

Before departing English shores, *Resolution* would make two additional stops. Early on 26 June she anchored at the Downs, off the south-east corner of England, where two small open boats, specially built for the expedition in nearby Deal, were taken on board. Then it was on to Plymouth, where Cook would wait for the right weather conditions – a favourable wind and tide – so they could safely weigh anchor, clear the coast and sail south into the Atlantic. While in Plymouth *Resolution* was joined by the 229-ton full-rigged ship *Discovery*, which was to be the consort vessel for this voyage. Given Cook had come close to losing *Endeavour* while exploring Australia's north-eastern coast, he insisted on having a support vessel for future expeditions. It meant there was always a vessel that could either come to the aid of a grounded ship or transport the crew back to England should one of the vessels be wrecked.

For this latest mission, *Resolution* had a crew of 112 and *Discovery*, 70. The total complement included 35 marines. On

12 July 1776, just eight days after the Declaration of Independence in the American colonies on the other side of the Atlantic, dawn gave way to a gloomy and wet English summer day. The wind and tide were suitable for sailing, however, so on Cook's call, and with sailing master William Bligh coordinating many of the procedures, the sails and rig were readied while some of the crew turned to the windlass handspikes and waited for the order to weigh anchor. When that came they began their labour, hauling aboard the anchor warp until the anchor itself was raised high enough above the water for it to be hoisted to the cathead and lashed into place. Simultaneously, they eased the clew and buntlines, and the sails unfurled from their heavy timber yards. Then, with blocks and pulleys screeching under the load, the crew hauled away on the braces, sheets and tacks before belaying them. Soon all sails, including the spanker and foresails, were set to suit the wind angle and *Resolution* was making way. Cook's third passage into the Pacific had begun, two months behind schedule.

Resolution's initial course would take her to the south from Plymouth into the English Channel. As she gained momentum and increased bearing on the coastline many crewmembers spent time absorbing the expansive but grey-tinged view of the English countryside with some level of despondency. Bligh would not see home for more than four years, but tragically for his famous captain, this would be the last time that Cook would cast his eyes on the coast of England.

CHAPTER TWO

South Pacific, 1776

Captain Cook's final voyage

R*esolution* made slow progress down the English Channel on her way to the wide open waters of the North Atlantic, achieving an average of around 4 knots until she passed the first of many milestones, Ile d'Ouessant (Isle of Ushant), the westernmost point of France and a graveyard for the many ships that had failed to clear its treacherous rocks in rough weather.

At this stage Cook was comfortable with *Resolution*, the vessel he had referred to as 'the ship of my choice ... the fittest for service of any I have seen'. However, he would soon be rethinking that statement, simply because of the poor way the ship had been prepared in Deptford for this expedition. If only he had spent more time there, supervising the often slipshod and sometimes corrupt workers.

While *Resolution*'s displacement was 100 tons greater than the famous HMS *Endeavour*, there were distinct similarities between the two ships – including both being designed as colliers. The similarities pleased the captain: both featured long, straight buttock lines; the underbody sections of the hull were wide and flat for much of the overall length; and each had buoyant and bulbous apple-cheeked bow sections. It was likely that Cook's all-too-vivid memories of the near disaster he faced on his first voyage with *Endeavour*, becoming stranded on the Great Barrier Reef, influenced his enthusiasm for *Resolution*. The exceptional buoyancy of the *Endeavour*, provided by her underwater shape, certainly contributed to her being floated free and saved.

Originally launched in 1770 as the *Marquis of Granby*, *Resolution* was renamed when she was purchased for £4115 by the Navy Board fourteen months later. Her one distinct difference from *Endeavour* was that she was a more modern, three-masted, ship-rigged sloop-of-war, while *Endeavour* was a simple bark.

Prior to her departing England in 1772 for Cook's second Pacific odyssey, *Resolution* underwent a major rebuild, including the addition of an upper deck and raised poop, primarily to accommodate the requirements of botanist Sir Joseph Banks, who was to be aboard. However, it quickly became apparent in sea trials that the ship was then disturbingly top-heavy and would prove very difficult to handle in strong winds and high seas: she would certainly be more prone to capsize if caught in a Southern Ocean storm with too much sail set. As a consequence of these doubts, it was decided that the new structures should be removed. Banks was so disgusted by this decision that he subsequently refused to join the expedition.

This time around, as good a ship as she was, *Resolution* retained the inherent poor manoeuvrability of any similar square-rigged ship of the era, something that became all too evident for sailing master Bligh, his captain and the entire crew at an early stage of the voyage when she nearly foundered. After stopping at Tenerife, off the north-west coast of Africa, on 1 August for three days to repair leaks, Bligh, as Cook's navigating officer, set a course to the south towards the Cape Verde Islands. It was around nine o'clock in the evening and on the captain's watch when the surgeon,

William Anderson, who happened to be on deck, peered through the darkness and was shocked by what he saw. Bonavista Island was lying dead ahead, and he could see white water breaking on rocks at an alarmingly close distance. Obviously it had gone unnoticed by everyone else on deck. He was about to shout a warning to Cook, when the captain also spotted the danger, which he too realised was perilously close. He immediately ordered the helmsman to change course and the crew on deck to rush to their stations and man the heavy hemp braces, sheets and tacks to change the angle of the yards, so the sails would be set most effectively for the new course to safety. It was a crisis moment. *Resolution* slowly responded to the helm then began to heel in response to the pressure that came with the new wind angle, a pressure that saw the ship gradually claw her way forward and escape the impending danger by the narrowest of margins. Anderson's account of the incident, in part, read:

> ... just as I was going to mention my suspicions he [Cook] observed something of the same sort and ordered them to starboard the helm. In less than a minute the cry of hard-a-starboard became general and we could now see a range of breakers at a very small distance: upon which we were steering a direct course. Orders were given to brace the yards sharp up; but I who could only be an idle spectator in this scene of confusion went abaft and had a clear prospect of our impending danger. For the space of ten minutes I thought it utterly impossible we should avoid striking on the rocks: but the manoeuvre with the sails being pretty quick I had the pleasure to see the ship lie parallel to them.

Cook's grave concern for the safety of his ship was still evident in his more modest account of the incident:

... at 9 o'clock in the evening we saw the island of Bonavista
bearing south distant little more than a league, though at this
time we thought ourselves much further off, but this proved
a mistake; for after hauling to the eastward until 12 o'clock
to clear the sunken rocks that lie about a league from the SE
point of the island, we found ourselves at that time close upon
them, and did but just weather the breakers. Our situation for a
few minutes was very alarming ...

While Bligh held the important role of sailing master there are
surprisingly few references to him in Cook's lengthy record of this
voyage, right up until the time of the captain's murder. Intriguingly,
no logbook or journal – which the always meticulous Bligh would
have inevitably kept for the duration of the voyage – has ever been
found. This might be explained by the fact that at the conclusion
of any voyage it was the responsibility of commissioned officers to
lodge their accounts of the voyage with the Admiralty, but Bligh,
being still only a warrant officer, was not required to hand over any
of his documents.

The first significant mention of Lieutenant William Bligh
came when his captain decided a feature of the Kerguelen Islands
should take Bligh's name. *Resolution* had sailed from Cape Town
in company with *Discovery* on the first of its numerous missions: to
locate and confirm the position of this rugged and barren archipelago
of 300 islands, which had been discovered four years earlier, in
1772, by French navigator Yves-Joseph de Kerguelen de Trémarec
when he was searching for 'the Great Southern Continent'.

The two ships were pressed hard and deep into the Southern
Ocean before a frosty and fog-laden westerly wind until they reached
what Cook believed was the likely latitude of the Kerguelen Islands
– 49 degrees south. They continued east on that latitude until they

were close to the longitude where they expected to actually locate the islands, and once at that point Cook initiated his plan to sail a zigzag course to the east to maximise the chance of finding their goal. The lookouts aloft, who were scanning the horizon 10 nautical miles away, were rewarded on Christmas Eve. Cook's journal read:

> ... at six o'clock in the morning, as we were steering to the eastward, the fog clearing away a little, we saw land, bearing south-south-east, which upon nearer approach we found to be an island of considerable height ... Soon after, we saw another of the same magnitude, one league to the eastward; and between these two, in the direction of south-east, some smaller ones ... A third high island was seen ... a high round rock, which was named Bligh's Cap. Perhaps this is the same that Monsieur de Kerguelen called the Isle of Rendezvous; but I know nothing that can rendezvous at it, but fowls of the air; for it is certainly inaccessible to every other animal.

The young sailing master was impressing his captain with his abilities and dedication; it was a huge honour for Bligh, a man ever willing to learn, to have his name immortalised on a chart he would have created with his legendary captain. This chart and the many others that would come from this voyage would prove invaluable for the growing number of explorers and seafarers who would sail in the wake of *Resolution*.

On Christmas Day 1776, both *Resolution* and *Discovery* anchored in an inlet on the eastern side of the northern tip of the main island, and fittingly Cook named it Christmas Harbour. Over the next 48 hours Bligh carried out directions from his captain to survey the shoreline and sound the depths of this harbour and another to the south. To do this, Bligh boarded a pinnace and left the ship, which remained at anchor, and directed the crew with him to row or sail to various points within the bay. As they progressed, Bligh made pencil sketches of the outline of the bay and the general topography. At the same time, using a lead-line, the depth of water at various points was noted so that a relatively accurate idea of the sea floor could also be established. On returning to the ship he transferred all the information from his notebook onto a large-scale chart – which was so accurate it could be used safely today by anyone travelling to this isolated domain.

While conducting his surveys, Cook also requested Bligh to 'look for wood; for not a shrub was to be seen from the ship'. He reported back to his captain that he had landed on both shores of the harbour and found them to be barren and rocky with no sign whatsoever of a tree or shrub. 'I could have very properly called the island Desolation Island to signalise its sterility, but in order not to deprive M. de Kerguelen of the glory of having discovered it, I have called it Kerguelen Land,' Cook mused.

The one thing that was in ample supply was pure, clear water, so both ships fully replenished their supplies. With that done, it was very much time to set sail for two reasons: a schedule that was becoming tighter by the day because of the late departure from England; and because a number of the animals that had been put aboard *Resolution* by King George – with a view to them being used to establish herds on South Pacific islands – were dying as a result of the sub-Antarctic conditions.

If the animals were feeling the cold one can only imagine how brutal the conditions at these high latitudes must have been for the crew. While their clothing was comfortable in a practical sense, it did little to protect them from the elements. Most wore long trousers and short-waisted vests for the majority of the time, but when it was cold they donned heavy woollen pullovers. Few, if any, of those working on deck or aloft wore leather shoes of any type as they found bare feet gave them far better grip on the wet timber or when climbing the ratlines.

With the clewlines and buntlines eased and the sails then falling away from their yards, everything that was set was trimmed to harness the prevailing westerly wind. Before long *Resolution*'s figurehead, a proud white horse, was showing the way eastwards to the next stop, New Zealand. *Discovery* was in close company.

However, a few days later, in the middle of the inhospitable Southern Ocean, fate intervened and the intended course had to be changed. A cold and savage squall hammered the ship, catching the crew unawares. Suddenly *Resolution* was being pressed far too hard – the sound of tortured timber, rig and sails left no doubt everything was grossly overloaded. Before the crew could react and reduce sail the fore topmast carried away, snapping like a dry stick. The backstays and shrouds supporting it had failed due to the enormous stress the squall had brought to the highest sail on the foremast, the fore top-gallant. For the next 24 hours, while the ship rolled awkwardly on the large Southern Ocean swells, crew scrambled up and down the ratlines, first going aloft to clear the broken mast, sail and rigging, and then to install replacements.

While the ship was being repaired mid-ocean, Cook took stock of his situation, especially the amount of provisioning that remained. He quickly realised a new problem had emerged: the need for firewood and water for the ship, plus fodder and water for the animals, was becoming urgent. There was not enough to get them to New Zealand. Something needed to be done, so the moment repairs were completed and the ship was back on course under full sail he declared there would be a change of plan: *Resolution* and *Discovery*, both of which had remained in visual contact throughout this time, would alter their course to the north once they reached the southern tip of Van Diemen's Land and then anchor in Adventure Bay.

Cook was well aware of this destination: Captain Tobias Furneaux, commander of *Adventure*, the support ship to *Resolution* during Cook's previous Pacific expedition, had anchored there in 1773. On that voyage, the two ships had become separated and lost contact in a dense fog. On realising he was on his own, Furneaux decided to sail towards what he knew to be Van Diemen's Land, now Tasmania, the southern point of which had been discovered by Abel Tasman 131 years earlier, and consequently positioned on charts. On 11 March *Adventure* dropped anchor in a superbly sheltered, east-facing bay that lies 30 miles south of where the state capital, Hobart, is located today. It was a true haven – a long ribbon-like strip of golden sand with a dense forest as the backdrop and high hills beyond: a place where his men soon gathered an abundant supply of wood and water for the ship. After a brief stay, *Adventure* headed east once more and a few weeks later Furneaux rendezvoused with Cook in New Zealand. He reported most favourably on the attributes of the bay, which he had named after his ship.

Cook's change of plan this time around would prove to be a fortunate, and inevitably historic, twist of fate in Bligh's favour because, once arriving there on 27 January 1777, the young sailing master was again able to apply his exceptional surveying abilities and chart in fine detail Adventure Bay and much of the adjacent Storm Bay. It was the first time this part of the world had been explored and surveyed to any extent, yet it is only in more recent times that Bligh has been properly recognised for the important contribution he made to the early exploration of this region. It was also during this exercise that he made his first observations of indigenous people on a foreign shore, although there is no record of him coming into direct contact with them himself. What initial contact there was came to an abrupt end when, after the Aboriginals demonstrated their skills with spears, a *Resolution* crewman decided to demonstrate to them his firearm, so raised his musket and fired. This was enough to send the Aboriginals into a panic: they put their hands over their ears and took fright, quickly disappearing into the bushland.

Having discovered the east coast of New Holland only seven years earlier, and there being no further exploration of the region since then, Cook voiced a theory while in Adventure Bay that he believed Van Diemen's Land was part of New Holland, in fact the southern point of the continent. This belief stood unchallenged until the discovery by Matthew Flinders and George Bass in 1798 of what would become known as Bass Strait – the stretch of water separating mainland Australia from the island state of Tasmania.

Once water, wood and fodder was collected and put aboard both ships, and Cook presented the Aboriginals with a pair of pigs for breeding purposes, *Resolution* and *Discovery* weighed anchor three days after their arrival. A course was set towards Cape Farewell on the north-western corner of New Zealand's south island. After averaging 4 knots over the next eleven days the Cape was sighted, and once it was abeam the two ships moved further east to Queen Charlotte Sound before anchoring in Ship Cove, which Cook had named when he stopped there on his first expedition with *Endeavour* in 1770. Cook presented some of the livestock that was aboard *Resolution* to the local Maoris, and then, quite innocently, he initiated what would become a future environmental problem for the region: he released two pairs of rabbits into the wild.

The ships remained in this anchorage for almost two weeks, and in that time both vessels were refurbished with some new rigging and spars which it was hoped would see out the remainder of the planned circumnavigation. The next scheduled destination was Tahiti, but when New Zealand faded over the western horizon and the ships entered the South Pacific, the weather turned against them: the strong east-south-east trade wind they were expecting had a mood change – it became very light in strength and variable in direction, making for what *Discovery*'s captain, Charles Clerke, described as 'an exceedingly tedious passage'.

During this leg, Bligh and other officers observed with concern a change in the behaviour of their captain, a man they always saw as being very considerate of his crew, especially when it came to their health. Cook was informed that food had been stolen from the ship's stores, and when the perpetrators were not found he became so incensed that he halved the meat ration for each man, only to have the majority of his crew baulk at this punishment and refuse to take any. This act ignited the captain's temper to the degree where he declared their actions to be mutinous.

With the gentle winds continuing unabated the progress towards Tahiti remained slow, compounding a problem that began with the late departure from England: it was no longer possible to complete this voyage in the time frame originally designated. Cook and every one of his men had to accept they would now lose an entire season, and as a result they would fall behind schedule by almost a year. That realised, and with water supplies aboard both ships dangerously low, Cook decided that the course would be changed away from the Society Islands and Tahiti, and set towards the Friendly (or Tongan) Islands to the north-east, where supplies could be obtained. This led to the two ships cruising through the island-laced tropical waters in the north of the group for many weeks, and Bligh charted and sketched for his captain many of the islands they had sailed past or visited. The information he gathered, which included the latitude and longitude of islands, and the depth of water around them, led to Bligh creating charts which, providentially, would greatly benefit him after the *Bounty* mutiny twelve years later.

Resolution and *Discovery* eventually sailed south to Tongataboo, and once there Cook decided they should stay for a month so he could observe an eclipse of the sun on 5 July 1777. Soon after arriving, the captain's temperament again showed disturbing signs of being unexpectedly volatile. The most disconcerting time came after Cook had become obsessed by the fact that a considerable number of islanders were pilfering whatever they could from his men and the ship. The captain decided the only way to bring this to a rapid end was by meting out a brutal punishment to the guilty. It was a level of retribution that shocked everyone. Midshipman George Gilbert noted in his log:

> This [thieving], which is very prevalent here, Captain Cook
> punished in a manner rather unbecoming of a European, viz by
> cutting off their ears, firing at them with small shot, or ball, as
> they were swimming or paddling to the shore; and suffering the
> people as he rowed after them to beat them with the oars, and
> stick the boat hook into them ...

Bligh described his captain's actions as 'a most ludicrous performance'.

Additionally, there was confusion among the two crews: they could not understand why they were spending so much time in Tongataboo when their actual destination was Tahiti. Questions were also asked as to why, during this time, Cook – a man who lived to explore – did not dispatch Bligh and others to search for a group of nearby islands known to the islanders, yet undiscovered by the Europeans. These islands were only three days' sailing time to the north of Tongataboo. The islanders referred to this place as 'Fidgee' – today, Fiji – a place which, ironically, Bligh was to discover after the *Bounty* mutiny.

When *Resolution* and *Discovery* finally departed Tongataboo they took a long, looping course to the south then east, so they could sail the safest and fastest possible route to Tahiti and make their final approach riding the trade winds towards the north. They arrived there on 12 August, and almost immediately Bligh had his first taste of breadfruit, a local food that would have a major impact on his life.

During the six weeks they were in Tahiti, Cook grew even more irrational: his outbursts were so extreme that some of his crew were beginning to think he was in the early stages of a mental illness. This view was reinforced when two of the ship's goats tethered on shore were stolen. Contemporary opinion on what ailed Cook varies, one diagnosis of his symptoms of fatigue, loss of health, loss of interest and depression may indicate that he was suffering from a parasitic infection of the lower intestine. Nevertheless, Cook's totally unwarranted reprisal was to burn down the islanders' huts and destroy canoes.

On departing Tahiti, *Resolution* and *Discovery* embarked on the most important stage of the exploration. It was a long passage to the north into a region unknown to them: the North Pacific, where their quest was to find an ice-free route around the top of North America and into the Atlantic. The voyage was uneventful until Christmas Eve 1777 when they were about 1200 nautical miles to the north-west of Tahiti and almost on the equator – which was when a low-lying and undiscovered coral atoll loomed over the horizon. After both ships anchored off the atoll, Cook once again showed his faith in Bligh's ability as a navigator and seaman when, only hours after having named it Christmas Island, he sent him on a mission to find a safe passage through the outer reef and into the island's lagoon, something other members of the crew sent before him had failed to achieve. Bligh did this, but the only passage he could find was too narrow for the ships to navigate.

In mid-January 1778, some two weeks after leaving Christmas Island, when the two ships were sailing deeper into the northern hemisphere, Cook made yet another discovery. The call 'Land ho!' came from the lookout aloft, then soon after there was another shout: an additional island was in sight. With that Cook had become the first European to discover what he named the Sandwich Islands in honour of his close ally and patron, the 4th Earl of Sandwich, John Montagu. It was Hawaii.

Cook went ashore at the first opportunity with the express desire to befriend the local inhabitants and with this achieved, he set about exploring the surrounding expansive chain of rugged and spectacular islands. As part of his exploration he commissioned Bligh to conduct surveys as they went and chart the region to the best of his ability.

Five weeks later, *Resolution* and *Discovery* were back on the high seas, heading for the north-western tip of North America. Three weeks of extreme, punishing weather challenged their endeavours, with conditions so bad that by the time they reached Nootka Sound, on what is today Vancouver Island, *Resolution*'s rig was in such poor condition that she was in danger of being dismasted. Cook had to call for major repair work to be carried out, including making replacement masts. By 26 April they were again under sail and heading towards Bering Strait, a passage that would later see them recognised as the first British ships to sail the north-west coast of North America. From this point the mission became nothing short of a daring and highly dangerous exercise in which ice would become the chief adversary. But before they even reached the strait, *Resolution* went extremely close to being wrecked on rocks off Unalaska Island. Cook had his ship sailing fast in strong winds and a thick fog when, fortunately, an extremely alert lookout high up the mast shouted to the deck that he could hear breakers ahead. The immediate reaction was to change course and slow the ship: something that was achieved with less than 200 yards to spare.

On 12 August, *Resolution* passed through Bering Strait and six days later crossed into the Arctic Circle. Soon after, when they were north of Icy Cape, their passage was blocked when they were confronted by a wall of ice which Cook described as being 12 feet high and stretching from horizon to horizon. For the next three days the expedition leader did everything possible to complete his mission, but on 21 August he had no alternative but to surrender to nature and abandon his plans.

By the end of October, five months after they began their quest and with the threat of winter looming, Cook decided it was time to retreat and head south so they could winter in safety, the plan being to continue the expedition beyond Bering Strait the following year. However, with this call came a surprise: instead of staying in an ice-free zone relatively close to this region, Cook elected to return all the way back to the Sandwich Islands. This wasn't to be an easy passage. They departed Unalaska on 26 October, and the following day – Cook's birthday – the two ships were battered by a severe gale and huge seas; three crewmen were badly injured by the violent motion of their ships, but worse still, John Mackintosh, Captain Clerke's servant aboard *Discovery*, died when he fell down the main hatchway.

After 30 days of sailing they arrived in the waters of the Sandwich Islands, and much to Cook's delight, the first island to come into sight was a new find, Maui, followed soon after by 'the big island', Hawaii. Cook initiated an extensive exploration of these islands and regularly called on Bligh to survey the coastline, and it was following one of these missions, after the ships had rounded the southern tip of Hawaii, that Bligh recommended to his captain that Kealakekua Bay, which he had visited in the ship's launch, was a sheltered anchorage with a suitable landing spot on shore. As part of his survey of this bay Bligh had checked the depth of the water, then went ashore to search for fresh water. In doing so he became the first European to set foot on the island of Hawaii.

Early on 16 January 1779, Cook took his quill, dipped it in ink and penned in the ship's journal what would be his final note:

> Seeing the appearance of a bay I sent Mr Bligh with a boat from each ship to examine it, being at this time three leagues off. Canoes now began to arrive from all parts, so that before 10 o'clock there were not fewer than a thousand about the two ships, most of them crowded with people and well laden with hogs and other productions of the island. One of our visitors took out of the ship a boat's rudder. He was discovered, but too late to recover it. I thought this a good opportunity to show these people the use of firearms, and two or three muskets and as many four-pounders were fired over the canoe which carried off the rudder. As it was not intended that any of the shot should take effect the surrounding multitude of natives seemed rather more surprised than frightened. In the evening Mr Bligh returned, and reported that he had found a bay in which was good anchorage and fresh water. Here I resolved to carry the ships to refit and supply ourselves with every refreshment the place could afford.

In the first days of February, Cook had both ships weigh anchor and began a slow passage north along the coast of the island. On 8 February, when they were near its northernmost tip, a severe storm blasted in and caused damage to *Resolution*'s foremast, so serious that both ships were forced to return to Kealakekua Bay for repairs to be made. Once *Resolution* was anchored securely, the crew noted with some level of concern that the previously friendly attitude of the islanders had all but evaporated, and they didn't know why. One theory is that the islanders believed Cook was their god, *Lono*, and that they had lost faith in him when he sailed from the bay.

Regardless of this change of attitude, Cook sent his men ashore to set up camp so they could begin work on a replacement foremast and repair torn sails. The disquiet among the islanders remained evident, but it wasn't enough to deter Cook from going ashore to inspect his carpenters' progress. While there he and some of the men with him became embroiled in an incident involving an islander who had stolen items from *Discovery*. The situation escalated and soon the islanders were pelting rocks at the Englishmen, who defended themselves by firing rounds of shot high into the air in the hope of frightening their assailants. By nightfall tempers had calmed, but the next morning, 14 February, a major confrontation was inevitable: *Discovery*'s largest cutter had been stolen. In response, Cook decided that if he was to recover this boat and find the culprits, he should blockade the bay.

Bligh, firm in the belief that a heavy hand must be shown to defuse the situation, was directed by Cook to take command of *Resolution*'s cutters and some small boats from *Discovery*, lead them on to the bay and confront the islanders. Bligh, as sailing master, opted to take no chances and insisted that his men load their muskets with ball instead of shot so they could be most effective in the event of a mass attack. It was already clear to the Englishmen that such an attack was highly likely, simply because of the number of warriors appearing around the bay and on the hills behind. As he headed to the shore, Bligh took the initiative by intercepting, then firing upon, a number of canoes that had been launched into the bay, killing some of the occupants. After observing this, Cook decided he too should go ashore so he could confront the local king, Kalaniopu'u, and his warriors over the theft of the cutter. On reaching the beach, the captain went straight to the king's hut, intending that the king might return with him to *Resolution* so the two of them could, hopefully, resolve the warlike atmosphere on shore. Also, by having Kalaniopu'u aboard *Resolution*, Cook would hold a valuable hostage. The king agreed to go with him, but as Cook and his guard of marines led the men towards the beach there was high confusion on both sides, partly because some islanders thought their king was being kidnapped.

In a flash, fierce fighting erupted and spread rapidly. The islanders began stabbing, stoning and spearing the Englishmen, who retaliated with shot as quickly as their muskets could be reloaded. When Cook found himself abandoned by his guard of marines, who had taken up the fight to protect him, he came under attack. David Samwell, a surgeon aboard *Discovery*, described the blood-curdling scenario as it unfolded:

> An Indian [sic] came running behind him, stopping once or
> twice as he advanced, as if he was afraid that he [Cook] should
> turn round. Then, taking him unaware, he sprung to him,
> knocked him on the back of his head with a large club taken
> out of a fence, and instantly fled with the greatest precipitation.
> The blow made Captain Cook stagger two or three paces.
> He then fell on his hand and one knee and dropped his musket.

As he was rising another Indian came running at him, and before he could recover himself from the fall, drew out an iron dagger he concealed under his feathered cloak and stuck it with all his force into the back of his neck. This made Captain Cook tumble into the water where it is about knee deep.

Here he was followed by a crowd of people who endeavoured to keep him under the water, but struggling very strongly with them he got his head up, and, looking towards the pinnacle which was not above a boat's hook length from him, waved his hands to them for assistance, which it seems was not in their power to give.

Finally, it took just one massive blow to Cook's head from a club wielded by a warrior to end his life. His body was dragged onto the rocks, where a frenzied attack continued on the corpse.

Bligh watched in horror from the cutter as his captain was struck down, along with four marines. Outraged, he determined to do whatever he could to reinstate English authority over the scene. The second highest ranking officer, Charles Clerke, immediately and rightfully assumed leadership of the expedition and command of *Resolution*, even though he was so seriously ill that he could barely stand. He declared they should depart the bay as soon as possible, so ordered Bligh, among others, to go ashore with the strongest possible group of armed men, primarily marines, to support those left there, expedite the evacuation of the camp and bring back, among other equipment, the partially repaired foremast and sails.

Once on the beach, Bligh and his men came under attack from islanders throwing spears and rocks. Retaliating with shots from their muskets, Bligh and his men bravely carried out Clerke's orders and coordinated the recovery of the foremast and sails.

Despite the best efforts to prepare the ships for sea, they were in no position to weigh anchor so remained in the bay overnight. By morning the tension between the two warring sides had receded, but later, during the afternoon, the situation took a macabre turn when a parcel was delivered to Clerke aboard *Resolution* by one of the king's priests. Clerke took the parcel to his cabin, opened it and discovered the grisly contents – burnt portions of Cook's dismembered corpse.

Simmering hatred for the islanders among the crews of the two ships exploded with the news of this ghoulish presentation and they took an opportunity for revenge when a watering party that went ashore to collect supplies was attacked. In the melee that followed many islanders were killed and the village razed.

At this stage Clerke was convinced the bodies of the four marines who had died on the beach alongside Cook – John Allen, Thomas Fatchett, Theophilus Hinks and James Thomas – would not be found, but he was determined to recover all he could of Cook's remains. Five days after their captain's death, Clerke was summoned ashore to receive, as the *Resolution*'s Lieutenant King recalled in his journal, 'a bundle wrapped very decently'. It contained more body parts, mainly bones and two hands still with the flesh attached which were identified as Cook's. During the evening of 22 February the contents of both parcels were then consigned to the deep in a ceremony in accordance with Royal Navy tradition. As a final salute, ten rounds from the four-pounder cannons boomed across the bay at 30-second intervals.

With that solemn ceremony completed, Clerke called for the ships to be readied for sea. This order was accelerated by the fear that word of the battle at Kealakekua Bay, and Cook's death, might precede them to other destinations among the islands where they might want to make landfall.

Clerke, a popular captain, decided to stand by Cook's decision to return to the frozen waters of the north-west region of North America and try to find a safe route into the Atlantic, but not before a more extensive exploration of the Sandwich Islands. Over the ensuing weeks, as the two ships sailed in company from magnificent island to magnificent island, life was ebbing from the new commander – the victim of consumption (tuberculosis). Before long he accepted that he could no longer carry out his duties effectively, so he implemented a new chain of command among his senior officers. John Gore, a much-admired American-born seafarer, who joined *Resolution* as a third lieutenant having already logged two circumnavigations, was appointed as the new leader and captain of *Resolution*, and Lieutenant King took up the captaincy of *Discovery*. Then, when it came time for Clerke to delegate the vital role of navigator for the expedition, without hesitation he chose 24-year-old Lieutenant Bligh, who subsequently noted in his journal: 'Captain Clerke being very ill in a decline he could not attend the deck, and thus he publicly gave me the power solely for conducting the ships & moving as I thought proper.'

By August, as the two ships retraced their course towards the Bering Sea, Clerke was on the verge of surrendering to his illness. On 10 August he managed to write one last letter, this one to his great friend, Sir Joseph Banks:

My ever honoured Friend,

The disorder I was attacked with in the King's bench prison has proved consumptive, with which I have battled with varying success, although without one single day's health since I took leave of you in Burlington Street. It has now so far got the better of me, that I am not able to turn myself in my bed, so that my stay in this world must be of very short duration ...

Now my dear and honoured friend, I must bid you a final adieu. May you enjoy many happy years in this world and in the end attain that fame your indefatigable industry so richly deserves. These are the most sincerely and warmest wishes of your devoted, affectionate and departing servant,

Chas. Clerke

Clerke, who died ten days later aged 38, was for everyone who knew him, a good man. He had been aboard for all three of Captain Cook's voyages of discovery, and prior to those completed a circumnavigation aboard HMS *Dolphin*. Before Cook's third voyage he had committed himself to serving time in the fleet debtor's prison for a debt a brother, Sir John Clerke, had incurred, and it was there that he developed the tuberculosis that would eventually kill him.

Bligh held dear the directive from Clerke when he was appointed navigator for the expedition: 'to explore the Sandwich Isles as much as you can & from thence carry the ships to Kamchatka & thence to do your utmost endeavours to discover the NW passage'. Making his task even more satisfying was the fine rapport he established with *Resolution*'s new captain, one that lasted for the remaining fourteen months of the voyage.

The charter for the two ships to search for the Northwest Passage proceeded without great incident, but also without success. The ice confronting them once again formed an insurmountable barrier through to the Atlantic.

It is easy to understand why discovery of a north-western route from the Atlantic to the North Pacific was so important to the British because, at the point where the ice became impassable, the two ships were little more than 4000 nautical miles in a direct line from England – less than two months' sailing time. But, with no other option, they were forced to turn back and take the long route home – a course that saw the ships sail along the coast of Siberia (some of which Bligh sketched and mapped) then via Japan, Macau, the Cape of Good Hope and finally north into the Atlantic to England, a distance of more than 18 000 nautical miles.

Four years and three months after their departure, on 4 October 1780, *Resolution* and *Discovery* dropped anchor at the Nore, a sandbank on the River Thames. When 26-year-old Lieutenant William Bligh stepped onto the dock from one of *Resolution*'s launches and was welcomed home, he was a changed man in so many ways: his skills as a navigator, seafarer, cartographer and sailor had been honed under the guidance of one of the great navigators and explorers. He had sailed around the world, witnessing all at once the beauty and brutality of the South Pacific. He had excelled in the fourteen months after Cook's death when it was his duty as navigator to guide the two ships through uncharted territory beyond Bering Strait, back home safely to England.

As he walked confidently along the cobblestone street leading away from the dock, Bligh could afford to stand proud: few navy lieutenants his age, if any, had achieved as much. Surprisingly, though, there were no direct rewards, especially in the form of an immediate promotion, but what was most relevant for this ambitious young naval officer was the fact that he was now very much in the gaze of his superiors, and most importantly, Sir Joseph Banks.

Inevitably he would have been wondering what would come next, and within two months that course was set. In December 1780 England declared war on the Dutch – the Fourth Anglo–Dutch War. Destiny would now take Bligh into battle.

CHAPTER THREE

Dogger Bank, 1781

Into battle

With both *Resolution* and *Discovery* back in England, the crew of each ship was stood down. It had been an extraordinary coming of age for Bligh – he had witnessed the death of Cook and Clerke, and in December 1780, he was to lose his father. Francis Bligh, the man who had guided his son into a life with the Royal Navy, died and was buried at St Andrew's Church in Plymouth.

As a youngster Bligh had been very close to his father, and now he felt the full impact of the loss of his remaining parent, as he was his father's only son. A generation had passed. He found comfort in immersing himself in his charts from the recently completed voyage with Captain Cook, refining details so they could be included in the official account of what was a successful, yet tragic, expedition. But before long he realised he needed to escape: it was time for him to take a well-deserved and extensive holiday in the lush countryside of the west of England before visiting Douglas, on the Isle of Man in the Irish Sea. It was during the sojourn there that Bligh either reacquainted himself with or met for the first time Elizabeth Betham, an intelligent, well-educated woman. With much in common, the two developed an

MUNDLE

overwhelming romantic rapport, so much so that one month later, on 4 February 1781, they were married in the parish church in the nearby village of Onchan.

It was a marriage between a strong woman and a determined man who were, for much of their lives, separated by the sea. However, their devotion and love for each other were always evident in the tender and caring letters they exchanged over the long years apart. For Bligh, it would prove to be a fortuitous liaison for his already promising career: his new wife's uncle was Duncan Campbell, one of England's most prominent and successful commercial shipowners, a plantation owner and merchant in the West Indies, and the contractor in charge of convict hulks in the Thames. Campbell, who was also very well connected with the government of the day, was quickly impressed by the 26-year-old Bligh, taking him under his wing and becoming a life-long mentor and confidant. Bligh's wife, affectionately known as Betsy, was also a close friend of 55-year-old Campbell's second wife, Mary, a woman 30 years his junior.

Just ten days after the start of the post-nuptial celebrations, Betsy gained a rapid induction into the reality of being a naval wife, when her husband received some anxiously awaited news: he had been appointed master of HMS *Belle Poule*, under Captain Philip Patton, and he was expected aboard post-haste.

A ship in the French Navy, *Belle Poule* was captured by the English in 1780 off Ile-d'Yeu in the Bay of Biscay. Bligh's appointment coincided with her being commissioned into the Royal Navy. When he boarded the refitted, Bordeaux-built 30-gun frigate, she was already a veteran of hydrographic surveys to the Indian Ocean, campaigns in the West Indies and famous battles. Most notably, when sailing under the French flag in June 1778, she engaged HMS *Arethusa* in a fierce encounter which led to France's

42

involvement in the American War of Independence in support of the colony. And just eight years earlier, Jean-François de Galaup, Comte de La Pérouse, who greatly admired the achievements of Captain Cook, walked the decks of *Belle Poule*. Like Bligh, he was destined to achieve fame in the Pacific, but tragically disappeared there, probably in 1788.

By the time Bligh took up his posting as the master of *Belle Poule*, England was again at war with many of its neighbours, including the French, the Spanish and the Dutch. Across the Atlantic, battles were raging with the American colonists. For Bligh, to be engaged in a successful conflict meant a far greater chance of promotion, so he was eager to put to sea.

That was to be the case. In mid-April the tidy little *Belle Poule* and the 74-gun HMS *Berwick*, under the command of Bligh's first captain, Keith Stewart, engaged the heavily armed 400-ton French privateer *Calonne*, or *La Calogne*. This took place near the Firth of Forth on Scotland's east coast, after *La Calogne* had captured the small and unarmed merchant brig *Nancy*, which had been en route to Newcastle from Aberdeen. Initially the crew of the French ship believed the then unidentified *Belle Poule* and *Berwick* were whaling ships from Greenland, but by the time they realised their mistake it was too late. *Berwick* then *Belle Poule* loomed up alongside the French ship and caught the crew unawares. They began pounding *La Calogne* with cannon fire for an hour, until the French struck their colours, surrendered and the British took their ship as a prize.

Bligh was now 'blooded' in battle but most importantly, as sailing master of *Belle Poule*, he had played a significant role in ensuring his ship remained as safe as possible by not exposing her unnecessarily to enemy fire, or by being outmanoeuvred.

In August *Belle Poule* was one of seven smaller naval vessels backing the same number of ships-of-the-line in a squadron escorting a large fleet of merchant vessels from the Baltic Sea to England. The squadron was under the command of Vice-Admiral Sir Hyde Parker, 5th Baronet, whose flagship, the 74-gun HMS *Fortitude*, was the lead vessel. The vice-admiral's second son, also Hyde Parker, was the captain of the 38-gun, fifth-rate HMS *Latona*, which was part of the squadron.

Parker Senior had been warned that a superior force of Dutch warships was in the area escorting a convoy, but he was unfazed. The ships' lookouts were on high alert, and just after dawn on 5 August 1781, as the English fleet was crossing Dogger Bank in the middle of the North Sea, they were rewarded. Referred to as having come from 'rotten row' because of their age, the British ships were better armed than the eight Dutch ships-of-the-line, which were under the command of Rear-Admiral Johan Zoutman.

After the British sighted the Dutch merchant convoy, on the horizon to the south-east, an engagement ensued. Vice-Admiral Sir Hyde Parker explained how the battle unfolded:

> I was happy to find I had the wind of them, as the great
> numbers of their large frigates might otherwise have endangered
> my convoy. Having separated the men of war from the
> merchant ships, and made a signal for the latter to keep their
> wind [and continue sailing towards England], I bore away with
> a general signal to chase.
>
> The enemy formed their line, consisting of eight two-
> decked ships, on the starboard tack. Ours, including the
> *Dolphin* of 44 guns, consisted of seven. Not a gun was fired
> on either side until within the distance of half musket shot.
> The *Fortitude* being then abreast of the Dutch Admiral, the
> action began ...

Suddenly the air reverberated with the booming sound of non-stop cannon fire as the adversaries tried to blast each other off the surface of the ocean. As each ship unleashed a fusillade of iron cannonballs, ranging from 18-pounders to 68-pounders, a massive shaft of flame shot from the muzzles of the cannons and the air thickened with pungent, gunpowder-laced smoke. Every cannonball that found its target during the broadsides delivered horrendous carnage: killing sailors, smashing the thick timber hulls and decks into splinters, shredding sails and bringing down rigs. Inevitably, some of the ships would have been using the recently introduced short-barrelled carronades, which could fire cannonballs capable of penetrating 3 feet into solid oak, causing the timber to explode.

Vice-Admiral Sir Hyde Parker described the rest of the battle:

> [The action] continued with an unceasing fire for three hours
> and 40 minutes: by this time our ships were unmanageable.
> I made an effort to form the line to renew the action and found
> it impracticable.
>
> The *Bienfaisant* had lost her main top-mast, and the *Buffalo*
> her fore yard; the rest of the [English] ships were not less
> shattered in their masts, rigging and sails; the enemy appeared to
> be in as bad a condition. Both squadrons lay to a considerable
> time near each other, when the Dutch, with their convoy,
> bore away for the Texel. We were not in a condition to follow
> them.

While the Dutch hightailed it towards the Texel – an island off Holland's north-west – the English set about dealing with their dead and wounded, and repairing their ships so they could set sail for home. The English toll was estimated to be 108 dead and 399 wounded, and for the Dutch, 140 dead and 400 wounded. It was a strategic victory for the English but a tactically indecisive result that went against the odds: the Dutch had the better ships yet Vice-Admiral Parker took up the less favourable windward position for the encounter. More remarkable was the fact that, for some unexplained reason, Rear-Admiral Zoutman did not take advantage of this when the broadsides began. It was later claimed that had Vice-Admiral Parker not been in the windward position, he would have exposed the merchant convoy he was protecting to the Dutch cannons.

The ships-of-the-line, which were the only vessels from both sides to engage in this battle, were the true warships of the era, each one being rated according to the number of carriage-mounted cannons it carried. They were the largest ships in the force and designed specifically to take part in front-line battles during a major fleet action. For this reason the small frigate *Belle Poule* was ordered to take up a position on the flank of the fleet, but there is no doubt the encounter was keenly observed and assessed by all aboard, including the master, Bligh.

Belle Poule's next task was to sail in the wake of the Dutch and confirm they really were on the run. It was soon after sun-up the following day when the ship's lookout reported an incredible sight: three masts of a Dutch ship-of-the-line protruding above the surface of the ocean, and the ship's pennant fluttering forlornly in the morning breeze from the main topgallant mast. It was the 74-gun *Hollandia*, the second most important ship-of-the-line in the Dutch fleet, which was so badly damaged in the battle that it could not reach shore, instead sinking in 22 fathoms off the Dutch coast and settling on the bottom in an upright position. *Belle Poule* drew alongside the submerged ship and hove to. Captain Patton then had one of his ship's launches take him to *Hollandia* so he could strike the pennant in the name of the Royal Navy and subsequently present it to Hyde Parker.

It was not until early September that *Belle Poule* completed its mission and reached port – this time Sheerness Docks on the Isle of Sheppey, near the entrance to the Thames, which, along with its protective fort, was established in 1672. It was here on 5 October 1781 that Bligh received the news of an appointment he had worked so assiduously to achieve: finally, he was a commissioned officer. He had been appointed fifth lieutenant of *Berwick*, a ship launched at Portsmouth Dockyard in 1775 then commissioned into the service three years later when France entered the American War of Independence. *Berwick* joined the Channel Fleet under the command of the Hon. Keith Stewart.

Bligh expected *Berwick*, then under the captaincy of John Fergusson, to be the ideal ship for his first posting as a lieutenant but it proved to be a frustrating experience. As part of the Channel Fleet, life aboard *Berwick* was boring and monotonous as she lay at anchor in the Downs, waiting for the call to intercept the Dutch fleet should it break from its cover in the Texel, but that didn't happen. Following their losses at Dogger Bank the Dutch no longer wanted to engage the English.

At this time the two sides were engaged in the Fourth Anglo– Dutch War, a conflict that came about as a result of the Dutch failing to support England, a supposed ally, during its war with the American colonies. Fortunately for the newly appointed lieutenant, the posting aboard *Berwick* would last only a few months. During the posting *Berwick*'s captain granted him compassionate leave so he could join his beloved Betsy, then domiciled in Leith, Scotland, for the birth of their first child. On 15 November, Harriet Maria Bligh, the first of their six daughters, arrived.

After spending the following six weeks as a family man, Bligh's next posting commenced on 1 January 1782, when he took up the same position, fifth lieutenant, aboard the 80-gun third-rate ship-of-the-line *Princess Amelia*, another veteran of the Battle of Dogger Bank, in which it saw the loss of nineteen men including its captain, John Macartney, and had 56 wounded.

Yet again it was a brief tenure: after just eleven weeks with this ship, on 20 March he made an important advance in his career – to a first-class ship-of-the-line, the 80-gun HMS *Cambridge*, as a sixth lieutenant. Much of the complement of *Princess Amelia* was transferred with him. *Cambridge*, which was 166 feet in overall length on the gun deck and displaced more than 1600 tons, was then acting as a guard ship at Portsmouth. One of near twenty lieutenants among a crew that numbered more than 800, Bligh worked under the guidance of the first lieutenant, who was the ship's second-in-command. Bligh's primary responsibility was to ensure the crew completed their duties as expected.

With his momentum through the ranks now accelerating, Bligh decided to try to use the influence of his wife's uncle, Duncan Campbell, to secure an even higher appointment as soon as possible. This came about because he had learned that Vice-Admiral John Campbell, a relative of Betsy's uncle, was to be based in Newfoundland, where he would become governor and commander-in-chief of a wide stretch of ocean known as the Newfoundland Station. This region on the western side of the Atlantic was of great strategic importance to England due to its proximity to the extremely valuable fishing grounds of the Grand Banks, and its location relative to the navigation route between Europe and the New World.

For the aspiring young Lieutenant Bligh, this was the place to be: being elevated to the post of commander of a ship at this station would be of immense worth to his career.

At the suggestion of Duncan Campbell, Bligh wrote to Vice-Admiral Campbell seeking a commission with his fleet:

Sir,

It was the only satisfaction I had after a long and laborious voyage to be introduced to you through the means of my best friend Mr Campbell ... and I am induced again to make myself known to you.

From Mr Keith Stewart's partiality to me from my services I have since gained promotion as a Lieutenant, and now ... have allowed myself to hope I may come under your cognizance.

Allow me, Sir, to wish to go in any manner under your command – I have experienced hard service; but shall never complain whilst sailing under your notice.

I am, Sir, with great respect,

Your most obedient humble Servant

Wm Bligh

Unfortunately for Bligh, the time was not right, so he remained as part of the crew aboard *Cambridge*. Royal Navy records state that on at least two occasions in May and July 1782 *Cambridge* moved from Spithead to the Downs, where she was stationed as part of a fleet under the command of Lord Viscount Howe, a notable naval officer recognised for exceptional service during the American War of Independence and the French Revolutionary Wars and who would soon become a Vice-Admiral of the Blue. Howe's ship was the now legendary 100-gunner HMS *Victory*. (Lord Howe Island, off Australia's east coast, was named after him, as was Cape Howe on the New South Wales–Victorian border.)

Also around this time *Cambridge* underwent a refit, something that proved to be a costly exercise for the crew. Much to their frustration, the refit fell well behind schedule and as a result *Cambridge* was not part of Vice-Admiral Samuel Barrington's coastal patrol fleet – to which it was then attached – when the fleet captured thirteen well-laden merchant ships in an enemy convoy crossing the Bay of Biscay. The prize for the victors was a large cash bounty, which was divided among the officers and crew of the participating ships. Bligh wrote of this with great displeasure: 'It has been no small mortification for me not being out with Admiral Barrington as it was intended we should join him ... I imagine officers will get 200 pounds.' It was an amount that would have brought much-wanted financial security to Bligh and his family.

When the refit was finally completed, *Cambridge* joined a flotilla of 183 vessels, including 34 ships-of-the-line and twelve smaller naval vessels under the command of Howe. The flotilla had been assembled to relieve the English fortress at Gibraltar, which had been under siege since 1779.

Cambridge's crew comprised 850 seamen and officers, and an eighteen-year-old ship's boy named Fletcher Christian – the same Fletcher Christian who would later lead the mutiny against Lieutenant Bligh aboard *Bounty*. While aboard *Cambridge*, Christian became well aware of Bligh, who is said to have taught the youngster how to use a sextant. The two are also said to have dined together at times, and Christian would later acknowledge in his diary that Bligh had treated him 'like a brother'.

On 11 September 1782 the relief fleet set sail from Spithead. It would prove to be fortuitous timing because a few days later the fortress, which was under the authority of Governor Lieutenant-General George Eliott, came under a relentless all-out attack by the Spanish and French, an assault so intense that for the first time the English were on the verge of capitulating. The odds were grossly in favour of the enemy: they had 90 warships, including 44 ships-of-the-line, 300 transports and ten heavily armed purpose-built floating batteries. The French also had 12 000 infantry aboard the ships, while a further 40 000 soldiers surrounded the outpost on land. The English garrison numbered a mere 5300 men.

Incredibly, though, even with this massive imbalance in numbers, adverse weather and a tactical blunder by the French and Spanish played into the hands of the English who had arrived off Cape St Vincent on 9 October. The British fleet was able to wedge its way into the port at St Vincent free from attack and take the dominant position because a storm suddenly broke over the scene, causing the enemy ships to run for shelter. At the same time the British managed to retain some semblance of formation while on approach to the fortress, and through superb seamanship and great determination they achieved their goal before the French and Spanish vessels could return to the desired position and engage in battle. Howe's convoy was able to reach shore and deliver additional supplies to the garrison that would last more than a year, plus a fresh complement of infantrymen to ensure its security. With his mission fulfilled, Howe then directed his ships to return home to Spithead while the French and Spanish could only look on while trailing them. Days later, Howe decided it was time to confront the enemy still lurking in his fleet's wake and dispose of them once and for all. This turned into an inconclusive long-range cannon fight with minimal loss of life and no loss of vessel on either side. When the hostilities ended, *Cambridge* reported the loss of just three men during the battle, and the ship was essentially undamaged. The success of this mission was such that 'prize money' was distributed among the officers. Lieutenant Bligh took home £22.

While the siege of Gibraltar produced an overwhelming victory for the British, the Royal Navy's fleet on the opposite side of the Atlantic had fought a losing battle in the American War of Independence, one which came to an ignominious conclusion for them at the end of 1782. With that war lost and Gibraltar secure, the Royal Navy returned to a peacetime footing. Almost the entire fleet arrived back in home waters, and with no battles to be fought, the culling of officers, seamen and marines began immediately. Within weeks the number of full-time men in the force had been reduced from 100000 to just 30000. Lieutenant Bligh was one of those stood down on half-pay: two shillings a day.

This made for tough times for the Blighs, now resident in Douglas on the Isle of Man, but fortunately the period of virtual unemployment was short-lived. Aged 28 and having been at sea for nearly thirteen years, Bligh was now a highly accomplished seafarer, well versed in all aspects of a ship's operation as well as engagement in battle. Obviously the sea was his passion, but it represented his career path, and knowing little else he could only hope an opportunity would arise that would see him setting sail again soon.

Fortunately, Duncan Campbell, who employed many ship's captains in his merchant marine operations, was all too aware of his nephew's experience and exceptional seafaring talents, so was quick to offer him a job. Bligh was eager to accept the offer so immediately sought and received permission from the Admiralty to do so. He then wrote to Campbell:

Douglas, Isle of Man, July 18, 1783 – I am glad to hear you
think it likely I may soon be wanted in Town [London] as
I am anxious to show you that whatever my services may be,
my endeavours in every respect will not be wanting either
in exercise or care ... I shall be ready at an hour's notice and
nothing can stop me now but a contrary wind, which at this
season of the year is not likely to happen ... Your very obliged
and affectionate and humble Servant, Wm Bligh.

For Bligh, this exciting venture into merchant shipping would prove to be financially rewarding and advantageous for his career as, for the first time since going to sea, he had his own command – as captain of *Lynx*, the finest and fastest ship in Campbell's fleet, which operated mainly on the trans-Atlantic route to the West Indies. The region was the world's largest source of sugar so this product made up a considerable proportion of the cargo *Lynx* carried on return passages to England.

Bligh was not to walk the quarterdeck of a Royal Navy ship for more than four years. Instead he would stay in the employ of Duncan Campbell out of London, and as a result he moved his wife and two daughters – Mary had been born that year – to 'Town', where they settled in Lambeth. It would be home for the family for a quarter of a century.

Peace continued to prevail for England throughout 1784. In June of that year the first edition of the official, three-volume account of Cook's voyage was published in London. With Cook's death, Lieutenant James King – who had kept a detailed journal relating to the expedition – was entrusted with the responsibility to complete Cook's work, *A Voyage to the Pacific Ocean*, and commissioned to write the third volume. Bligh, who had penned his own equally detailed journal during the voyage, was infuriated by King's account.

As Cook's second lieutenant on *Resolution*, King had shared the responsibility for astronomical observations with him. Bligh, his junior, had worked alongside him in the preparation of charts and sketching views of coastlines but they shared little tolerance for each other and clashed frequently. Bligh was adamant that King, and other officers, had taken credit for more of the published information than was fair, in particular *his* charts and maps. Having received a copy of the third volume, Bligh set about making a myriad of margin notes, recording in no uncertain fashion his displeasure and disdain over King's work. On the title page of the volume crediting the maps and charts 'from the original drawings made by Lieut. Henry Roberts, under the direction of Captain Cook', an indignant Bligh, wrote his own credit:

> ... none of the Maps and Charts in this publication are from the original drawings of Lieut. Henry Roberts; he did no more than copy the original ones from Captain Cook, who besides myself was the only person that surveyed and laid the Coast down, in the *Resolution*. Every plan & Chart from [the time of] C. Cook's death are exact Copies of my Works.

Bligh's barbs did not miss King when it came to the death of Captain Cook. King was quoted as describing Cook as a beloved and honoured friend. To this, Bligh countered: 'A most hypocritical expression, for his death was no more attended to in the course of a few days than if he never existed.'

But tragically, less than six months after the publication of Cook's official journal in June 1784, King himself died from consumption. He was only 34. Bligh's journal of his voyage with Cook has never been found. Ironically, his relationship with his young midshipman on *Providence*, Matthew Flinders, would be strained over a similar point of recognition on credit for the charts and maps that resulted from that voyage.

This same year, 1784, Bligh stepped down as captain of *Lynx*, having made numerous Atlantic crossings, and took up senior positions aboard two other vessels in the Campbell fleet, *Cambrian* and *Britannia*. Campbell also had him work for a period as the company's agent in Port of Lucea in Jamaica.

While Bligh continued to ply the Atlantic in the shadow of the slave trade, fate was charting a new course for his life, one that would merge the West Indies, the breadfruit plant (which he first tasted in Tahiti when there with Captain Cook) and his well-established career as a naval officer of considerable repute. The catalyst in all this would be the two men who were unquestionably his guiding lights, Sir Joseph Banks and Duncan Campbell.

Two centuries earlier the existence of the breadfruit tree became known across Europe as a consequence of voyages into the South Pacific. However, it wasn't until William Dampier returned to England in 1691 from his voyage to the region that the English took a genuine interest in the plant. Dampier praised its virtues as a food that could be prepared in many forms. Then, in 1769, when Cook and Banks arrived in Tahiti, they too were impressed by its value, even though Cook disliked its flavour, describing it as being 'as disagreeable as that of a pickled olive generally is the first time it is eaten'. He also went on record as saying, 'Its taste is insipid with the slight sweetness somewhat resembling that of a crumb of wheaten bread mixed with the Jerusalem artichoke.'

Dr Daniel Solander, a botanist with Captain Cook's first voyage to the Pacific disagreed:

> ... the bread-fruit of the South Sea Islands within the tropics, which was by us during several months daily eaten as a substitute for bread and was universally esteemed as palatable and nourishing as bread itself. No one of the whole ship's Company complained when served with bread-fruit in lieu of biscuit; and from the health and strength of whole nations, whose principal food it is, I do not scruple to call it one of the most useful vegetables in the world.

Before long, crews of all ships visiting the South Pacific during this era would prefer the starchy and dense breadfruit over their ships' bland, hard tack bread, known then as biscuits, which had to be soaked in liquid to be edible.

Inevitably, word of the potential of breadfruit spread to the West Indies. In April 1772, the then captain-general of the British West Indies, Valentine Morris, wrote to his good friend Sir Joseph Banks suggesting that the introduction of breadfruit to those islands would be a great benefit to all the inhabitants, especially the slaves, and lessen 'the dependence of the sugar islands on North America for food and necessaries'. However, no real consideration was given to this suggestion because England was in a protracted period of war; Britannia had to exert its authority on the high seas.

Twelve years later, in 1784, when Bligh was sailing the Atlantic for Duncan Campbell, Hinton East, another well-known plantation owner with holdings in Jamaica, took up the cause when he wrote to Sir Joseph and suggested breadfruit would be:

> ... of infinite importance to the West Indian Islands, in
> affording a wholesome and pleasant food to our negroes, which
> would have the great advantage of being raised with infinitely
> less labour than the plantain, and not be subject to danger from
> excessively strong winds. The time is not very distant when
> measures will be taken by proper authority for bringing about
> this desirable event.

Then, during a visit to England two years later, Hinton East met with Sir Joseph and reiterated the importance of an expedition to the South Pacific to obtain juvenile breadfruit plants for the West Indies. With other plantation owners reinforcing East's suggestion, Sir Joseph took the proposal to King George III – to whom he was an adviser – who then gave orders for a breadfruit expedition to be formed and prepared to sail on what would be a major undertaking, spanning at least six months. Not surprisingly, it was decided that a navy ship would take up the challenge, and that it would be under the command of a naval officer. Accordingly, Sir Joseph then assumed the role of organiser for the project, which would depart around August 1787.

The Society for Promoting Arts and Commerce, of which Sir Joseph Banks was president, was already involved indirectly in the quest for breadfruit, having offered a 'premium' – a gold medal – to the first person who transported 'from the islands of the South Sea to the islands of the West Indies, six plants of one or both species of the bread-fruit tree, in a growing state'.

Bligh was aboard *Britannia* on his final two passages as a merchant captain when it was confirmed by the king and the government that the proposed breadfruit voyage to Tahiti would go ahead. Here, once again, Fletcher Christian appears in Bligh's life: he was second mate aboard *Britannia* for their final voyage back to London, a position Bligh awarded to him after he had impressed the captain as an all-round seafarer. Bligh now considered him a friend.

As *Britannia* closed in on the coast of England, another element in the next chapter in Bligh's life was unfolding: a ship was purchased by the Admiralty for the breadfruit expedition into the Pacific. Only one more question remained: who would be captain? It was soon decided it would be one of the Royal Navy's most promising young officers, Lieutenant William Bligh – but he wouldn't know this for some weeks.

CHAPTER FOUR

Spithead, 1787

Preparation for the South Pacific

Lieutenant Bligh came ashore after *Britannia* reached the Downs on 31 July 1787, and exactly one week later he received 'flattering news'. It came from the office of Sir Joseph Banks, a man of considerable political and social influence, who, like Duncan Campbell, became a friend and mentor. The letter advised Bligh he had been named as commander and purser for the breadfruit expedition to the South Seas.

Profoundly honoured, Bligh wrote of his gratitude in a letter to Banks:

No. 4 Broad-Street, St George's, East
August 6, 1787.
Sir,
I arrived yesterday from Jamaica and should have instantly paid
my respects to you had not Mr Campbell told me you were
not to return from the country until Thursday. I have heard
the flattering news of your great goodness to me, intending to
honour me with the command of the vessel which you propose
to go to the South Seas, for which, after offering you my

most grateful thanks, I can only assure you I shall endeavour, and I hope succeed, in deserving such a trust. I await your commands, and am, with the sincerest respect,

Yours, etc.

Wm Bligh.

Campbell and Banks jointly created this exceptional opportunity for the talented 32-year-old Bligh. When it came to nominating the commander, Banks had no hesitation in recommending Bligh given the impressive role he played in the successful completion of Cook's third Pacific voyage, especially after the captain was murdered. Campbell, too, held his niece's husband in high regard following the four years of service Bligh completed with him in his merchant service.

Sir Joseph had proposed the expedition and received King George III's endorsement, but when he and the then-titled Commissioners for Exercising the Office of Lord High Admiral of the United Kingdom of Great Britain and Northern Ireland – later known more simply as the Admiralty – set about looking for a ship, there was none within the Royal Navy's fleet of around 300 vessels that could be suitably converted for the mission. So they turned to the merchant service, or more specifically, Duncan Campbell, for assistance.

Bethia, a small trading ship that had been built in Hull in 1784, was chosen then purchased by the Navy Board for approximately £1950. After being renamed His Majesty's Armed Vessel *Bounty* in recognition of the king's generosity, she was dispatched to Deptford and put into dock for a refit, which was to be supervised by both Bligh and Sir Joseph. The modifications were to be extensive and unique because this was to be a voyage like no other: a botanical undertaking in which *Bounty* would become a floating greenhouse.

Campbell detailed the sale of *Bethia* in a letter to his son, Dugald, who was residing in Jamaica:

> Bligh is now fitting out a small ship in the King's Service which
> I helped procure him the command of, he is going to Otaheetee
> to bring the breadfruit plant to your Island and St. Vincent. This
> command is what I alluded to in a former letter. Though he
> goes out only as a Lieutenant yet if his conduct is approved it is
> the sure road to being made a Captain. On his return, this Lord
> Howe [the First Lord of the Admiralty] has absolutely promised.

The latter point rankled Lieutenant Bligh after his appointment was announced. He was obdurate in his own mind that as master of the vessel it was only fitting that he be promoted to the rank of captain, a theory reinforced by the recent precedent of another lieutenant, Robert Moorsom, who had been elevated to that position for a surveying voyage to the East Indies. Bligh subsequently wrote to Duncan Campbell saying the difficulties Moorsom would confront 'are not likely to be any way equal to those I am to encounter'. But there was nothing he could do about it – except make a success of the mission and hope for the appropriate recognition.

Bounty was by the standards of the day a small ship – a 90-foot, three-masted and full-rigged vessel with a beam of just 24 feet, a draft of 11 feet, 4 inches and a displacement of 220 tons, as compared to Cook's *Endeavour* at 368 tons, and *Resolution* at 462 tons. The design featured no superstructures, which meant all accommodation and facilities were below deck. The tallest of the three masts stood at 87 feet; the fore and main masts each carried 3 yards while there were 2 on the mizzenmast. In keeping with superstition at the time, *Bounty*'s 'pretty' figurehead under the bowsprit was a woman dressed in a riding outfit. It was created around the theory of the day that a female figurehead, often bare-breasted, would shame the seas into being calm.

If Bligh had been consulted on the selection of a ship for the expedition then *Bounty* would certainly not have been his choice. After his experiences with Captain Cook in the Southern Ocean and across the Pacific, he would have preferred a larger ship, but *Bounty* it was and he had to do the best he could with her. One thing in *Bounty*'s favour was that like Cook's *Endeavour*, she had been designed as a collier, so while she was a small vessel she featured high internal volume and excellent carrying capacity.

The safe transportation of the plants was the ultimate challenge, and everything to do with the refit centred around that. Crew comfort was secondary: even the great cabin, as Bligh explained, was modified: 'the great cabin was appropriated for the preservation of the plants ... it had two large skylights and on each side three scuttles for air, and was fitted with a false floor cut full of holes to contain the garden pots in which the plants were to be brought home ...' Water would be at a premium when caring for the breadfruit plants, so an ingenious system of capturing any overflow was created. The deck was covered with lead and pipes were fitted at the forward corners of the cabin to carry any excess water that drained from the plants into tubs below deck for future use.

Not even the commander was spared when it came to the plants having priority over everything else. He had a small cabin near the side of the ship as his sleeping quarters, and an equally small area amidships for dining. The ship was so short of space that the arms chest containing weapons had to be located in the quarters of the mates and midshipmen, a circumstance that would, months later, greatly assist the mutineers. On deck, *Bounty*'s armament was also kept to a minimum: four short-carriage 4-pounder cannons and ten half-pounder swivel guns.

During the refit Bligh revealed his talent and skills as a far-sighted and highly experienced master mariner when he called for two major modifications to *Bounty*, both designed to make her a safer and more manageable ship, particularly when locked in the teeth of a savage Southern Ocean gale and enormous seas. Both decisions were influenced by his experiences as master for Captain Cook aboard *Resolution*. The first call was for the masts to be reduced in height: this involved the removal of the masts from the ship so the lower of the three sections could be shortened. The lower and topsail yards were also reduced in length. 'I thought them too much for her,' Bligh commented, 'considering the nature of the voyage.'

Then, when *Bounty* came out of the dock at Deptford on 3 September, Bligh effected another major alteration – a reduction in the amount of ballast, which was primarily iron. With the meticulous foresight of a seasoned mariner he 'gave directions that only nineteen tons of iron should be taken on board instead of the customary proportion which was forty-five tons'. He reasoned: 'The stores and provisions I judged would be fully sufficient to answer the purpose of the remainder, for I am of opinion that many of the misfortunes which attend ships in heavy storms of wind are occasioned by too much dead weight in their bottoms.'

When it came to the selection of the crew, it was inevitable Bligh would have a significant input, particularly with the appointment of officers. This was seen as a captain's right, and more often than not those chosen were friends and acquaintances with whom the captain had previously shared favourable experiences at sea. Alternatively the chosen men had come with strong references from family or respected friends and associates. Such was the case with Fletcher Christian. Christian having impressed Bligh himself when sailing with him aboard *Britannia*, was also strongly recommended for the *Bounty* voyage by Captain Taubman, a relation of Christian's who made a special trip from the Isle of Man to London to present his case to the captain.

Signing onto any ship meant you put your life in your captain's hands; trusting their judgement and skills as a seafarer. Many of Bligh's other *Bounty* crew had already sailed with him, or were recommendations from Banks, other captains, friends and family connections. Lawrence Lebogue, who had been his sailmaker aboard *Britannia*, took up the same position on *Bounty*. Quartermaster John Norton and the young seventeen-year-old Thomas Ellison also came across from *Britannia*, as did Robert Lamb who became *Bounty*'s butcher. From Bligh's extended family and friends came *Bounty*'s midshipmen Thomas Hayward, John Hallett (aged fifteen), Peter Heywood (also fifteen) and George Stewart. The gunner, William Peckover, had also sailed with Captain Cook on all three voyages. There were two other significant appointments, both of which would bring Bligh grief. The master, John Fryer, was unknown to Bligh prior to the *Bounty* mission but was chosen for the position because of the impressive way he worked when the ship was being prepared for the voyage. The most frustrating appointment was that of Thomas Huggan, the surgeon. Bligh disliked him from the moment he first saw him and considered him a lazy and incompetent drunkard, so much so that he immediately tried to find a replacement. He was unable to achieve this, so as a precaution he appointed a surgeon's mate, Thomas Ledward, a man who held medical qualifications.

How the remainder of the crew came to be aboard is not clear, however. As was the case with the majority of Royal Navy vessels, most were drawn from the lower levels of society: men whose backgrounds, be they fine or fearsome, would remain unknown.

There is ample evidence to suggest Bligh was highly aware of the need to have his crew as comfortable as possible and in good health for the duration of the voyage. For example, his exceptional experience under the tutelage of Captain Cook saw him insist before leaving London that the crew manning *Bounty* included a fiddler, the latter's role being to bring entertainment during their long evenings at sea, promoting the crew's physical wellbeing by involving them in dancing for exercise.

Bligh's only serious problem prior to departure had nothing to do with *Bounty*'s crew, her seaworthiness or appropriateness: it was all to do with her overall length. At just 90-feet, *Bounty* was deemed too small to include a complement of marines on board – a militia to protect the captain and defend the ship. If she had been a larger ship-of-war the captain would have been entitled to have more crew and marines on board, but as it was, he did not even have another commissioned officer to support him. Instead, he would have to place his faith in the lieutenants he had chosen, men he was certain would be trustworthy. In time, these expectations would prove to be very wrong.

Bligh had obviously registered his concerns about the ship – her shortcomings and the absence of a militia – with his family, because on 21 September 1787 his father-in-law, Richard Betham, replied to an earlier letter from Bligh, saying in part:

> ... I have a different idea of it [the voyage] from what I had conceived before I was acquainted with the circumstances of the vessel, and the manner in which it is fitted out.
>
> Government I think have gone too frugally to work; both the ship and the complement of men are too small in my opinion for such a voyage. Lord Howe may understand Navy matters very well, but I suppose mercantile projects are treated

by him with contempt. Yet, in my opinion, the bringing of the
breadfruit tree in the West India Islands must be as beneficial to
them, as the bringing of the potato plant from Virginia by Sir
Walter Raleigh to be cultivated in Great Britain hath been of
benefit to us and to all Europe. However, I'm most solicitous
about the success of the voyage on your account, that it may
not only be the means of your promotion but attended with
such emoluments as may enable you to live comfortably after
the toils of the sea are passed ...

I always imagined you would have been made Master and
Commander on your going out, and some navy officers here
persuaded me that you will have a commission for that purpose
to be opened with your instructions in a certain latitude at sea –
as no promotions in time of peace are made at land.

Unfortunately, Richard Betham's wish for a promotion for his son-
in-law during the early stages of the voyage did not eventuate. He
remained Lieutenant William Bligh.

Many others supported the belief that *Bounty* was not an
appropriate or suitably manned vessel for the voyage. One was
Lord Selkirk, who had hoped his son, Dunbar Douglas, would be
able to join *Bounty* on the voyage, but whom Bligh was unable
to accommodate because there wasn't an appropriate position
available. On 14 September, Lord Selkirk wrote to Sir Joseph
Banks regarding *Bounty*, saying in part:

I got some of these particulars from an officer of the Navy
who happened to be here just now on a visit; who tells me
that this establishment of Bligh's vessel is that of a cutter,
and says it is highly improper for so long a voyage; only 24
able seamen, and 21 of all others, without a lieutenant or any

marines, with only a surgeon, without a surgeon's mate which [misses] from its being considered as a cutter, whereas in a sloop of war, they have besides Lieutenant and a surgeon and his mate ...

While *Bounty* was being modified for the voyage to the South Seas, Governor Arthur Phillip, under instructions from King George III, had departed from England with the First Fleet to establish a convict colony at Botany Bay. Coincidentally, this and Bligh's expedition had a common link: Sir Joseph Banks was also the greatest advocate for the establishment of the penal colony. Then, as the eleven ships in the First Fleet headed south in the Atlantic, the possibility arose for the two voyages to become further intertwined.

Aware of the *Bounty* voyage, Phillip wrote from Rio de Janeiro to the under-secretary of state for the Home Department, Sir Evan Nepean, on 2 September 1787 with a suggestion: 'I likewise mentioned [in previous communiqués] the slops for the women not being sent down before we sailed, and the want of musket-balls and paper cartridges for the use of the garrison, as likewise tools to keep the small arms in repair; those articles will, I hope, be sent out in the ship that goes for the breadfruit.' However, *Bounty* was not required to carry a cargo for the new settlement.

It would have been a remarkable coincidence for Bligh to have visited the outpost during the earlier stage of its establishment, given his later appointment as governor of the colony. Even so, he is reported to have suggested a desire to visit Botany Bay during the leg of his voyage from Adventure Bay to Tahiti. Possibly, because the initial order for *Bounty* was to sail the shortest route to Tahiti – west-about around Cape Horn – consideration was not given to her carrying supplies for Governor Phillip. Bligh's orders were to take the alternative route, via the Cape of Good Hope and beneath what is now Australia, only if the prevailing weather conditions at the world's most fearsome cape, 'the Horn', prevented the ship from making a safe passage and entering the South Pacific.

It was this same order that was burdening Bligh: it imposed a rapidly escalating level of pressure onto the preparations because the later *Bounty* departed, the more likely she would be confronted by unfavourable and impenetrable headwinds at the Cape.

Prior to leaving, Bligh's calculations saw the ship provisioned for an eighteen-month voyage, with more supplies being secured along the way:

> In addition to the customary allowance of provisions, we were provided with sauerkraut, portable soup, essence of malt, dried malt and a proportion of barley and wheat in lieu of oatmeal.
> I was likewise furnished with a quantity of ironwork and trinkets to serve in our intercourse with the natives in the South Seas: and from the board of longitude I received a timekeeper [K2], made by Mr Kendal [sic].

Bligh was already well acquainted with English watchmaker Larcum Kendall's chronometers, based on John Harrison's ingenious marine timekeepers that allowed for navigation at sea with greater accuracy. Captain Cook had taken K1 and K3 with him on his second and third voyages into the South Pacific.

Bounty headed downriver from Deptford under the guidance of a pilot in early October and stopped at Long Reach, where the cannons and swivel guns were put aboard. The ship arrived at her final point of departure, Spithead, at the eastern end of the Solent, on 4 November.

The following day, in anticipation of the voyage ahead, Bligh wrote, in part, to Sir Joseph Banks:

Sir, I have been very anxious to acquaint you of my arrival here, which I have now accomplished with some risk. I anchored here last night, after being drove on the coast of France in a very heavy gale. However, by persevering, I am now in readiness, or will be in three days, to receive my final orders.

I once before made an attempt to get here, but was glad to go into the Downs again, although of all other places it is one of the most disagreeable to be in. I think I cannot have much worse weather in going round Cape Horn, and it is with pleasure I tell you I think the ship very capable. This also is another consolation to me, for my ideas of making a ship fit for sea and of those above were very different, and my conduct in troubling the Navy Board for alterations cannot be reprehensible, for had I not got the masts, yards, and tops all altered I should now be getting ready to go into the harbour ...

I shall take 18 months' provisions, which, with other supplies, will do very well, and my present intention is that, as I shall be late round Cape Horn, not to depend on touching there, but complete my water, if convenient, at Falkland Islands, for if I get the least slant round the Cape I must make the most of it ... The wind and weather is now very bad, and I fear will continue so for some days; but I assure you, sir, I will lose no time in proceeding on my voyage ... I shall take a pleasure of informing you of my progress as I go on, and I hope by the time my business is over here the wind will turn favourable. At present I could not move with it. I am particularly happy at receiving your letter of the 25th, and I trust nothing can prevent me from completing my voyage much to your satisfaction.

It would be three weeks before Bligh's 'orders' would arrive from the Admiralty, and while that was extremely frustrating for the captain it gave him the opportunity to go ashore and join his wife, Betsy. She had travelled to Portsmouth in the hope she could enjoy one final farewell with her husband as she was unlikely to see him again for at least two years. Most importantly, Mrs Bligh had been able to make the trip and take up lodgings because their third daughter, young Betsy, had recovered from a bout of smallpox.

During the time of farewell, Bligh remained adamant that his ship was not ideal for the task ahead, but revealed he was actually happy with her seafaring capabilities following a rough passage to the anchorage at Spithead. In a note to a friend he advised: 'My little ship I hope will do very well and have had a good trial of her having made my passage here when superior ships put back.'

Four days after arriving at Spithead, Bligh received his final orders from Lord Hood, the First Naval Lord of the Admiralty, and at the same time the entire crew received two months' pay in advance. With that done, the captain declared with a high degree of satisfaction that it was time to depart. While some crew manned the capstan and waited in readiness to weigh anchor, others scampered monkey-like through the rigging, unfurling the sails and ensuring everything was ready for sea. Soon after, with the anchor up and secured and the sails trimmed to suit the course, *Bounty* was finally on the move – some seven weeks behind schedule. It was 28 November 1787 and it must have been only because Bligh was exceedingly anxious to get underway that he did so in an opposing southerly wind. However, there was a favourable afternoon tide which he hoped would assist the ship in clearing the Isle of Wight and entering the English Channel. But that wasn't to be the case. After trying for some time and failing to clear St Helens, at the eastern end of the island, which was only 5 nautical miles out, Bligh had no option but to anchor and wait until the next morning, when he would reassess the situation: 'I got under sail again, for although the wind was not favourable being at south, the weather being moderate tempted me to try what could be done.'

On 1 December, with the wind still coming from the south, he decided to try once more, hoping that he could get *Bounty* to a point where she could sail down the English Channel towards the Atlantic, but again the attempt was foiled by the weather. He continued to try to beat the weather over the ensuing days: 'We made different unsuccessful attempts to get down Channel, but contrary winds and bad weather constantly forced us back to St Helens, or Spithead ...'

The frustration of these delays took his emotions from simmering to near boiling point, which was all too evident in his letter to Duncan Campbell on 10 December:

If there is any punishment that ought to be inflicted on a set of men for neglect, I am sure it ought on the Admiralty for my three weeks' detention at this place during a fine fair wind which carried all outward bound ships clear of the Channel but me, who wanted it most. This has made my task a very arduous one indeed for to get round Cape Horn at the time I shall be there. I know not how to promise myself any success and yet I must do it if the ship will stand it at all or I suppose my character will be at stake. Had Lord Howe sweetened this difficult task by giving me promotion I should have been satisfied ...

After a further two weeks of waiting for favourable weather, Bligh took the chance to see his 'dear little family' once more and then waited and reflected on his frustrations and ambitions in a letter to Duncan Campbell at the end of December:

> I had written to Sir Joseph Banks and told him that as my orders were not sufficiently discretional but enjoined me to make my passage round Cape Horn, I thought it hard at this late period of the year, and by return of post I received directions to do as I thought best. It is impossible to say what may be the result – I shall endeavour to get round, but with heavy gales, should it be accompanied with sleet and snow my people will not be able to stand it, and I shall not then hesitate to go to the Cape of Good Hope. Indeed I feel my voyage a very arduous one and have only to hope in return that whatever the event may be my poor little family may be provided for ... my little ship is in the best of order and my men and officers all good and feel happy under my directions. ... If I accomplish my passage round C. Horn, I have no doubt of being home in the two years, but on the contrary it may take six months longer.

There was no sign of the conflict that lay ahead. Bligh's perception that his crew were content was confirmed by many crewmembers, including the surgeon's mate, Thomas Ledward, who in a private note deemed his captain to be a passionate and kind-hearted man who showed respect towards him.

When the crew awoke to the sound of an easterly gale howling through the rigging on the morning of 23 December, they were elated: this was the first day in a month in which they had a wind coming from the ideal direction, and despite its bleak ferocity it could not be wasted. It was the perfect time to depart, and *Bounty* was straining hard on her anchor warps as if encouraging everyone to get going.

The magnitude of the moment, when there was no longer any question of his ship being forced back to anchor, was not lost on Bligh. 'The object of all former voyages to the South Seas undertaken by the command of his present Majesty, has been the advancement of science and the increase of knowledge,' he proudly wrote. 'This voyage may be reckoned to be the first where the intention has been to derive benefit from those distant discoveries.'

In no time *Bounty* was prepared for sea. By late morning she was sailing west through the Solent then past the Needles, a famous landmark at the western end of the Isle of Wight. Bligh then called for a west-by-south course 'down Channel with a fresh gale of wind at east ... At night the wind increased to a strong gale with a heavy sea.'

On reviewing his final orders from the Admiralty, Bligh recognised them as being direct and brief. They instructed him to sail as quickly as possible around Cape Horn to the Society Islands from where, after having potted and loaded as many breadfruit plants as deemed necessary, *Bounty* was to sail via Java and the Cape of Good Hope, calling at ports whenever necessary. Half of the plants were to be delivered to the Botanical Gardens in St Vincent and the remainder to Hinton East or his agent in Jamaica. With that task fulfilled, the ship was to then complete the circumnavigation by sailing directly to Spithead.

The captain's projections already confirmed that due to the delays with the refit and weather, plus the procrastination on the part of the Admiralty, his alternative option, to sail east-about via the Cape of Good Hope, would almost certainly be adopted. *Bounty* would arrive at the Horn so late in the season it would be near impossible to make headway against the howling westerly wind and raging seas that were predominant at that time of the year.

Because of this, Bligh had written to the Admiralty requesting he be allowed to change course and sail east-about to Tahiti via the Cape of Good Hope should *Bounty* be unable to clear Cape Horn. The Admiralty's response was in Bligh's favour. The addendum to his orders read:

The season of the year being now so far advanced as to render
it probable that your arrival with the vessel you command on
the southern coast of America will be too late for your passing
round Cape Horn without much difficulty and hazard, you
are in that case at liberty (notwithstanding former orders) to
proceed in her to Otaheiti, rounding the Cape of Good Hope.

Eye Sketch of Part of New Holland in the Bounty's
Launch by Lieut. Wm Bligh

PART II

Commander Bligh

CHAPTER FIVE

Cape Horn, 1788

Capitulation and the long way to Tahiti

The easterly gale showed no sign of abating when *Bounty* surged boldly out of the English Channel and into the North Atlantic with a real bone in her teeth. The white waves churning away from her bluff bow resembled large banks of snow being pushed aside. Understandably, she was under greatly reduced sail, but she was still being pressed hard. There was good reason for this. Bligh's experience told him that with the dangerous seas brought on by the gale it was essential that the ship maintained a reasonable and manageable speed to minimise the chance of being pooped and engulfed by one of the massive breaking rollers that regularly loomed up from astern, or being driven uncontrollably into a broach. He knew it would be far more dangerous to lower all sail, lie-a-hull and be at the mercy of the elements. If there was a positive in this situation, it was that *Bounty* was maintaining a course that would see her sail parallel to the coast of Portugal then head towards Tenerife for the first planned stop.

It was miserable and dangerous sailing on the high seas in what was the depths of winter. At one stage a crewman furling the main topgallant high above the deck lost his grip and almost fell.

Somehow he managed to grab hold of a stay and save himself from certain death.

The following day was Christmas Day 1787, and much to the pleasure of all on board both the wind and sea moderated slightly – but the rain, hail and sleet persisted. Still, this meant that the crew could enjoy modest yuletide celebrations in a slightly more amenable manner, even though they couldn't light a fire for cooking. As part of the celebration, Bligh ordered that each man receive an allowance of rum plus beef, and plum pudding, for dinner.

This respite was to be short-lived. By early morning on 26 December the wind rampaged once more and the seas were rising fast. A few hours later the wind was at storm force, and the waves had grown to such height and power that *Bounty* was beginning to labour under their onslaught, rolling violently and semi-submerging each time a wave broke over her, delivering a colossal cascade of white water. Two spare yardarms and a sweep oar on deck were ripped from their chain restraints and sent careering across the ship like rolling logs. Not much later another monster wave smashed into the larboard quarter, causing timbers and windows to implode. The safety of the ship was now under threat. A powerful surge of water bursting across the cabin claimed everything in its path, including a compass and some of the ship's valuable bread supply. Bligh described the dramas they faced right then as being 'of a very serious nature'. One more wave like that and only heaven knew what might happen. 'Fortunately no sea struck us while we were repairing the damage,' he added in the ship's log.

A few hours later the waves had become so savage that the helmsman could no longer sail a proper course; it was a case of having to guide the ship as best he could down the face of the waves rolling in from astern like giant mountain ranges breaking into avalanches of white water. The chaos continued: one wave carried away the larboard bumpkin and its iron braces, while another was so powerful that it stove in planks on the ship's cutter and launch, which were stacked one above the other on deck with the jollyboat stored atop them. It was only quick action by the crew in this threatening situation that prevented the small boats from being more badly damaged or possibly lost overboard. However, while they saved the boats, the crew had to face the devastating sight of seven hogsheads of beer – all full – being washed over the side. To add to their misery, two casks of rum carried below deck burst open during the pounding, spilling the contents into the bilge. Some crewmembers, though, just didn't care: they were still struggling to find their sea legs and overcome severe bouts of *mal de mer*.

It was difficult for many of the crew to comprehend that less than one week into what might be a two-year voyage they were already confronting survival conditions. Just one rogue wave, or one incident, could remove *Bounty* from the face of the earth without anyone ever knowing what happened. It was a chance Bligh and true seafarers recognised all too well, and at that moment Bligh could have reflected on Vice-Admiral Hyde Parker, who had led the fleet at the Battle of Dogger Bank in 1781. Little more than a year later, in December 1782, he set sail aboard HMS *Cato* – a ship considerably larger than *Bounty* – bound for his new posting in Bombay. The ship and its entire crew disappeared without trace during the passage.

The maelstrom raged until around noon on 27 December, when the conditions had eased to the point where Bligh believed he could safely lower sails and lie-to. His men were exhausted, so allowing the ship to drift downwind for a period gave everyone time to recover. It also meant the main and lower decks could be tidied and a fire lit to dry saturated clothing. When it looked as though the gale was abating later that day, the crew set the sails again and *Bounty* returned to a course of south-by-west. Much to everyone's relief, ideal sailing conditions – favourable and moderate northerly winds – prevailed until they reached Tenerife in the Canary Islands.

The anchorage at Tenerife was in an open bay influenced greatly by wind and sea, so to ensure the safety of the ship Bligh went to the extreme of mooring *Bounty* using four anchors. It was a five-day stop and during that time they took aboard additional supplies of water and wine.

Prior to departing the Canary Islands, Bligh announced he would be dividing the crew into three watches of four hours each, instead of two watches of four hours each. The master of the third watch would be Fletcher Christian. He explained his reasons for the new watch arrangement thus:

> I have ever considered this among seamen as conducive to
> health, and not being jaded by keeping on deck every other
> four hours, it adds much to their content and cheerfulness.
> Some time for relaxation and mirth is absolutely necessary,
> and I have considered it so much so that after four o'clock the
> evening is laid aside for their amusement and dancing.

Bligh's decision to do this was obviously influenced by his desire to proceed non-stop to Tahiti via Cape Horn after all. It would be a demanding passage that was very much weather-dependent and therefore of uncertain duration, so as a precaution he called for the crew's bread ration to be reduced by one-third, ensuring there would be enough to go the distance. This caused little concern as the majority didn't eat their full ration anyway.

When describing in detail the intention of the voyage to the crew, Bligh assured them there would be certain promotion for anyone whose endeavours earned it. He also distributed fishing equipment as conditions approaching the equator were ideal for such an activity. In a very short time, 'some dolphins were caught'.

Before long *Bounty* was exiting the region of the north-east trade winds and entering the Doldrums, near the equator, and as she did her speed dropped from a maximum of around 7 knots to just 3 or 4 knots. This equatorial region brought widely varying and rapidly changing sailing conditions around the clock. On some occasions the ship could be near motionless, trapped by an oily calm. In this windless environment the canvas set aloft hung forlornly like heavy drapes, their presence confirmed sporadically when they slatted with a thud against masts and spars as the ship lumbered through a swell-induced roll. At other times the wind would box the compass, blowing the sails aback with a sudden gust from an unexpected direction. Worse still, a cloud could bear down on *Bounty* with an accompanying rain squall so savage that she was immediately struggling under the pressure, heeling heavily and in danger of being dismasted, or at least having sails blown apart. The crew was forever on the lookout for these squalls and each time one of them struck, they had to man the sheets and furl the sails as quickly as possible so the loads on the ship were lessened. If there was a plus side, it was that the cloudbursts accompanying these squalls often brought torrents of rain with them. In one squall the *Bounty* crew was able to capture 700 gallons of precious drinking water in the run-off from canvas canopies.

This part of the passage was punishing both physically and mentally for those on board. The humid environment was stifling, especially below decks, and each time it rained things grew worse. Mildew thrived in the sultry conditions and the only way to freshen the air below was to light fires and sprinkle vinegar throughout. When the weather cleared, the crew could open the hatches and deadlights to bring some relief for those below, but the moment it rained, which was often, they had to be battened down. When the weather permitted, Bligh insisted that all wet clothing was brought on deck to be washed and dried. This order brought better comfort for the crew and lessened the chance of disease.

For much of the time, progress through the Doldrums was negligible: at one stage *Bounty* took twelve days to cover just 150 nautical miles – little more than 12 nautical miles a day. Then, on 6 February 1788, they reached the point where the south-east trade winds began to waft over them. Two days later, when *Bounty* crossed the equator, the due ceremony for those who had not previously 'crossed the line' took place. Twenty-seven of the crew were tarred then shaved with a piece of iron hoop. Later in the day Bligh granted every man half a pint of wine, a gesture that certainly helped enliven the dancing that followed.

As *Bounty* continued to ease her way deeper into the southern hemisphere the trade winds strengthened and she gained speed. By the end of the first week of March she was at full clip, around 7 knots. There was a noticeable fall in the air temperature as the southern hemisphere autumn began to take hold: the thermometer dropped 8 degrees Celsius in just one day. Bligh's ongoing determination to minimise the risk of ill-health among his men led to him calling for everyone to then dress in clothes more suited to a colder climate.

Bounty's speed was such that a few days later she caught up to an English whale-fishery ship, *British Queen*, which had departed England eighteen days before *Bounty*. When they drew alongside, Bligh learned that the ship was bound for Cape Town so he took the opportunity to transfer a letter he had written to Duncan Campbell so that it could be delivered back to England. The letter read:

We are all in good spirits and my little ship fit to go round a half score of worlds. My men all active good fellows, and what has given me much pleasure is that I have not yet been obliged to punish any one. My officers and young gentlemen are all tractable and well disposed, and we now understand each other so well that we shall remain so the whole voyage, unless I fall out with the doctor, who I have trouble to prevent from being in bed fifteen hours out of the twenty-four. I am at present determined to push round the Cape Horn without touching anywhere as I have plenty of water, but that must depend on the winds ... My men are not badly off either as they share in all but the poultry, and with much content and cheerfulness, dancing always from four until eight at night. I am happy to hope I shall bring them all home well.

Bligh's pleasure in not having to punish any of his crew was short-lived. In his log dated 11 March he recorded: 'Until this afternoon I had hopes I could have performed the voyage without punishment to anyone, but I found it necessary to punish Matthew Quintal with two dozen lashes for insolence and contempt to the master.' Quintal would later be one of the most active of the *Bounty* mutineers.

As always, the trade winds provided perfect sailing conditions and *Bounty* was reeling off the miles, but each mile gained meant the challenge of Cape Horn was that little bit closer. It became increasingly important for the ship to be as seaworthy as possible for the inevitable battering it would face in the almost always hostile southern latitudes. As part of the preparation, Bligh ordered for some new sails to be bent onto the yards, that all deck equipment be lashed down, and all rigging checked to minimise the chance of any problems developing that might impede a safe passage.

At two o'clock in the morning of 23 March, lookouts on *Bounty* peering through the darkness spotted the coast of Tierra del Fuego at the southern tip of South America. From that point Bligh had hoped to sail through the Straits le Maire between Isla de los Estados and the mainland, but a contrary southerly wind forced him to navigate down the craggy shoreline on the island's eastern side, a position from where his goal, Cape Horn, on Horn Island, was 140 nautical miles to the south-west. The following day would be the last time the crew would sight land until more than two months later, when Bligh finally abandoned his courageous effort to round the notorious landmark. Until then all onboard had to endure punishing conditions while they persisted with their bid to beat the odds and enter the Pacific from east to west at what was the wrong time of the year.

As *Bounty* pushed to the south to avoid any adverse currents and sail to a position where she could change course and achieve a safe rounding of Cape Horn, Bligh noted the magnitude of the situation they faced: 'Having now entered on our most difficult and grand part of our passage, I took every precaution to render the ship proof against the general attacks of the weather. I stood away close hauled to the southward and at noon I considered myself totally out of the way of the current round Cape Horn.'

The gales sweeping in from the west were relentless and even when they eased, the conditions remained miserable due to sleet, snow and rain. It was absolute torture for those on deck: *Bounty* was essentially a flush-deck ship, so there was virtually nowhere to seek protection from wind or wave. On 29 March, and over the following days, Bligh's log revealed the nature of the near-intolerable environment: 'We are obliged to be battened down fore and aft, the sea frequently breaking over us, however we keep tolerably dry below.' Then only a few hours later: 'I do not wonder at Lord Anson's "Account of the High Sea" for it exceeds any I have seen, and to be here in a laboursome ship must be an unhappy situation.' (Bligh is referring to an account of a rounding of Cape Horn in a violent storm by a fleet of ships led by Anson in March 1741, in which lives were lost.)

A glimmer of hope that they might be able to round the Cape came on 31 March when the wind changed direction to the north-by-west, then north-north-east, which allowed them to steer the ship on the much-desired course to the west for the first time. Even so, conditions remained atrocious, as Bligh noted: 'Fresh gale and sleet and rain with a very high confused sea.'

On 1 April, the wind blew from the south, allowing the ship to sail closer to the desired course. Misery still reigned, as Bligh's log revealed: 'As the wind came round we began to have very hard snow squalls, and at this time it was as much as we could do to bring the ship under the fore and main staysail. It blew a storm of wind and the snow fell so heavy that it was scarce possible to haul the sails up and furl them for the weight and stiffness.'

At all times Bligh maintained a caring watch over his men, appreciating the exceptional effort that was being asked of them during this desperate bid to enter the Pacific. He noted that he wanted to 'see after my people who had undergone some fatigue, and to take care that a proper fire was kept in and that no one kept on wet clothes. This being done and seeing them all comfortably dry, I ordered a large quantity of portable soup to be boiled ... which made a valuable and good dinner for them.' Additionally, in an effort to vary their diet, some crew took to catching some of the seabirds that were prevalent every day. This also provided the opportunity for some interesting research, as the captain reported: 'As we caught a good many birds but which were all lean and tasted fishy we tried an experiment upon them which succeeded admirably. By keeping them cooped up and cramming them with ground corn they improved wonderfully in a short time; so that the pintada birds became as fine as ducks, and the albatrosses were as fat, and not inferior in taste to, fine geese.'

Soon, though, the determination to forge a course that would see them safely around the 'corner' was outweighed by frustration. It was as if the Southern Ocean was as dogged about stopping their progress as they were about making headway, for Bligh's navigation indicated that after ten days of sailing as close to the direction of the wind as possible, his ship was still barely west of the longitude of Cape Horn. His exasperation surfaced in his log notes on 3 April:

> The gales we begin to experience are very heavy and
> distressing. At midnight I had hopes of a fair wind but an hour
> had scarce elapsed before I found, what would have done very
> well in moderate weather and little sea to have enabled me to
> clear the whole coast of Patagonia, I could do no more with
> than make a course directly for the land, however to make the
> most of it I carried a main topsail with four reefs in and a reefed
> foresail; but this was but little other than lying to as before ...
> it was not a little distressing after the exertions we have made
> thus far to see ourselves losing what we had got with some
> difficulty ... All I have to do now is to nurse my people with
> care and attention, and ... look forward to a new moon for a
> change of wind and weather.

Then came the captain's explanation of the weather they were dealing with: 'The snow does not lie on the decks but comes in large flakes and covers us for a while, and the hail is very sharp and severe. The sea from the frequent shifting of the wind is very irregular and breaking.'

The new moon failed to deliver. Instead, Bligh logged on 11 April that his ship could scarcely make headway against the wind and giant waves, which were almost as high as *Bounty* was long. With each one she would start rising, rising, rising up a near-vertical wall of dark water before exploding through the ugly crest in a huge cloud of white spray, only to then plunge into the abyss that followed. On descent the flogging sails sent a heavy and frightening shudder through the rig and the entire ship, and when she landed in the trough, the fo'c's'le (the forecastle at the bow where the crew quarters were located) was immediately buried under water. *Bounty* would labour, trying to free herself from the tons of water washing across her decks, and then, the moment she resurfaced, there was another of the ocean's ogres looming up ahead. It was a horrifying perpetual motion, a scene that persisted day and night, and all the crew could only wonder when their punishment would end. The Cape's reputation for desolation and death was justified: they could easily understand how so many ships and crews attempting to traverse those infamous waters before *Bounty* had disappeared without trace.

Making matters worse for the crew on deck was the wind and spray. It was as if the air was laced with shards of ice fresh from the yet-to-be-discovered frozen land – Antarctica – which was only a few hundred miles to the south. It cut through their wet and inadequate clothing like a hail of bullets.

All the time *Bounty* was being robbed of the ground she had gained to the west under the most trying of circumstances, fuelling Bligh's determination to make headway, to the degree where he had the ship carry more sail than would otherwise have been set in such conditions. Fortunately the crew shared his determination: 'my men and officers bear the fatigue with cheerfulness and health'. However, while the captain and his crew tried to cope with the incessant battering, the ship was starting to protest. Damage was evident: the constant pounding and wrenching was opening the seams between both hull and deck planks. This rendered the caulking ineffective in some areas, and without this the water could pour in. Soon there was so much water below that the bilge was awash, and the two large pumps mounted on the waist area of *Bounty*'s deck had to be manned every hour to keep the ship afloat. For the majority of the crew, especially those sleeping forward, being below was like enduring water torture. Bligh was so concerned that he had no hesitation in offering his own cabin to the men, setting it up as a dormitory for all those with wet berths to hang their hammocks.

On 13 April he noted:

> It is now three weeks since we came round Staten Land [Isla de los Estados], a time we have spent with much fatigue and almost constant bad weather, I now begin to see that this is a most improper time to venture into these seas ... upon the whole I may be bold to say that few ships could have gone through it as we have done, but I cannot expect my men and officers to bear it much longer, or will the object of my voyage allow me to persist in it.

Reinforcing the captain's concerns was the incidence of injury and ill-health for the first time since departing England. This was despite his best efforts to ensure the men's wellbeing, insisting they take precautions to prevent ailments, particularly scurvy.

Bligh soon found many of his crew were suffering from rheumatic complaints arising from the brutally cold climate, and fatigue meant men were being injured by the violent motion of the ship. The cook broke a rib and the ship's surgeon fell and dislocated his shoulder. It was amazing there weren't more injuries as the tempestuous seas were often so heavy they all but overwhelmed *Bounty*. The men on deck had to hang on for dear life and hope that the might of the waves did not carry them across the ship and over the side. 'The repeated gales seem now to become more violent,' Bligh wrote. 'The squalls so excessively severe that I dare scarce show any canvas to it. The motion of the ship is so very quick and falls so deep between the seas that it is impossible to stand without man ropes across the decks.'

Another log entry revealed more:

> The gale was very heavy and the weather cold with little or no intermissions of snow showers, until noon, when the sun shining very bright it cheered the spirits of all hands. To give the men a fresh meal tomorrow I ordered a hog to be killed, out of a half-dozen I have remaining. We had great abundance of poultry sheep and hogs but the weather for this month past has been so severe that we have now scarce any left.

As the battle with Cape Horn continued, physical exhaustion was beginning to affect the crew's ability to handle the ship. While their hearts remained strong the incredible hardships placed on everyone by the malevolence of the storms and the intense cold were proving to be too much. Despite round-the-clock efforts to claim precious progress to the west, Bligh's navigation calculations on 15 April again confirmed that they had made virtually no headway. Had more moderate winds prevailed, even from the same direction as they had experienced, then *Bounty* would have been able to claw her way to a point where she could safely clear the many islands scattered along the western side of Patagonia to then head towards Tahiti, some 4500 nautical miles to the north-west.

At five o'clock in the morning of 22 April the time had come. A simple entry from the captain in *Bounty*'s log said everything: 'At five the wind backing to the westward I bore away, it being needless to persist any longer.' He later added: 'It was with much concern I saw it improper and even unjustifiable in me to persist any longer in a passage this way to the Society Islands', and that the decision to head to Tahiti east-about was 'the surest way to accomplish the grand object of the voyage'.

Three days after altering course towards Cape Town, Bligh was convinced that his decision to turn back was the right one as the westerly gales persisted. He called on *Bounty*'s helmsman to steer north-east-by-east in the hope that on the way to Cape Town he might be able to confirm the latitude and longitude for the island of Tristan da Cunha, which Captain Cook, among others, had visited and explored. However, this mission was unsuccessful. Later it would be confirmed that the latitude Bligh had for the island was incorrect and as a result *Bounty* passed too far to the north.

The intensity of the weather was only matched by Bligh's resolve to retain good health among his crew. In one of his reports he described how he had not only opened his cabin to forward-sleeping crewmembers and their hammocks, he had other bedding brought in to be dried. He provided hot breakfasts 'of wheat with sugar, portable soup ... and a pint to each man of sweet wort a day, with their allowance of spirits, (very fine old rum) besides keeping them as dry as possible and clean is all that can be done'. The crew also had as much sauerkraut (for scurvy), mustard and vinegar as they wanted.

The raging seas continued to threaten *Bounty*'s safety, so every hatch had to be battened down. Conditions below were extremely claustrophobic as a result, which led to many of the sailors becoming violently seasick and incapacitated. Fortunately, though, there were still no symptoms of scurvy or any other disease among them.

In a bid to make life more bearable, fires were maintained below deck to dry the air and enable dinner to be boiled, but the downside of this was that eye-watering amounts of smoke spread through the ship. Bligh's notes at the time described how he wished he had installed a small cooking caboose on deck before leaving England.

One month to the day after *Bounty* abandoned the effort to round Cape Horn the crew rejoiced at the sight of land: the flat-topped Table Mountain, the magnificent backdrop to Cape Town. On approaching the coast, Bligh decided to heed the advice of other experienced mariners, that Table Bay was often an unsafe anchorage during autumn, so he opted for the more sheltered waters of False Bay to the south. Once there and at anchor, he and the crew could assess what work needed to be done to make the ship fully seaworthy again, and the supplies they needed before they sailed. There was no doubt that *Bounty*'s hull had to be re-caulked from bow to stern: it had been leaking so badly all the way across the Atlantic that the crew had to operate the pumps every hour.

By now, Bligh was realising that as captain he stood alone among his men. While he did everything possible to care for his crew's health and keep them happy on such a gruelling voyage, he always had to stand apart because, without any marines on board to support him, he had to retain a firm hand when it came to discipline and the safety of the ship. On the latter point he had no option while in False Bay but to deal a dose of six lashes to Able Seaman and Armourer's Mate John Williams, for 'neglect of duty in heaving the lead'; in other words he did not satisfactorily carry out orders to check the depth of the water with a lead-line, a duty designed to minimise the chance of *Bounty* running aground.

During this stopover, Bligh wrote a considerable number of letters which were to be delivered to England by ships heading that way. In one, to Duncan Campbell, he toyed with the notion of visiting the new British colony Captain Arthur Phillip was to establish on the shores of Botany Bay, if it wasn't going to interfere with the object of his voyage, but decided against it:

> I might wood and water at Botany Bay with little loss of time, and it may be imagined I will do so, but I cannot think of putting it in the power of chance to prevent my accomplishing the object of the voyage. I shall therefore pass our friends at that place, but could I have taken in any considerable supply it would have been for the good of the service for me to have done it. In the present case I can render them no service and Government will hear of them before any accounts could be brought home by me.

With all maintenance work completed and the stocks replenished, *Bounty* put to sea on 1 July, 38 days after arriving, bound for Tahiti. As she departed she fired a thirteen-gun salute in recognition of the Governor, and this was returned.

She cleared the Cape of Good Hope and sailed into the Southern Ocean, where she was confronted by the worst elements of a southern hemisphere winter – icy westerly gales and intense thunderstorms. It certainly wasn't the best time of the year to be there, but she made good speed until Sunday, 20 July, when she was on the northern edge of the Roaring Forties. Just after midday, and with only a foresail and a close-reefed main topsail set, the wind suddenly increased in strength to violent storm conditions. Before the crew could react and get the sails clewed up, *Bounty* surged down the face of an almost sheer Southern Ocean comber and kept going – down. As the bow was driven deep into the turbulent sea, the fo'c's'le disappeared beneath a mountain of white water. The helmsman managed to retain control and *Bounty* resurfaced unscathed from yet another incredibly dangerous situation. As the shout went out for the sails to be taken in, Bligh, who was standing on the exposed quarterdeck near the helmsman, ordered that the helm be turned and the ship put head-to-wind so she could lie-to and ride out the storm in relative safety.

Bounty remained this way throughout the night, until eight o'clock the next morning when the wind had eased to the degree where a reefed foresail could be set. She was then able to bear away to the east and resume her course. Just eight hours later the tempest returned, giving Bligh no option other than to once again order that they lie-to, and again *Bounty* remained that way all night. While this was considered the safest option, they were still in danger, as Bligh revealed in his log: 'By a violent blow from a heavy sea on the quarter the man at the wheel was thrown over and was much bruised.'

Bounty's course had been plotted to take her to St Paul Island, a small and desolate rocky outcrop which, due to its location, would later be used as a point of confirmation for navigators traversing the Southern Ocean. Bligh's aim was to verify through the use of his more modern navigation equipment the position of what was nothing more than a pin-prick on his chart. However, the chance of achieving this was being lessened by the poor weather. Visibility remained minimal and those on deck had to keep their wits about them. Still, there were no guarantees that Mother Nature couldn't, and wouldn't, deal a test that was beyond them.

Such a situation came on 25 July when a huge sea treated the 215-ton *Bounty* as a plaything, hurling her onto her beam ends so that she was all but knocked down. The crew on deck clung to whatever they could to avoid being lost overboard. Everything around them – equipment, the livestock and chickens cooped on deck – hurtled in every direction. Somehow *Bounty* suffered no damage, and as soon as she staggered back to upright, she was on her way once more as if nothing had happened.

At six o'clock in the morning of 28 July the weather had cleared to the point where the pinnacle of St Paul Island, which towers 900 feet above the sea, was sighted east-by-north of *Bounty* at a distance of 10 leagues. Striding the deck in uniform as always, Bligh changed their course to pass close to the shoreline, giving him the opportunity to use his modern navigation equipment and confirm that the latitude given for the island was incorrect. He later made the appropriate corrections to his chart.

For the next three weeks *Bounty* bullocked her way across the Southern Ocean, mostly driven by strong gales accompanied by snow and hail. With his crew having been punished so horrendously by the elements for seven weeks, the captain decided to seek shelter in the east-facing Adventure Bay, a short distance north of the southern tip of Van Diemen's Land. *Bounty* arrived there on 20 August 1788.

Once the ship was safely anchored, Bligh went ashore to look for the best locations to collect wood and water and also to search for any sign of islanders. Much to his surprise, there was no evidence of the indigenous people's presence for some time, but even more surprising was that there was no sign of any Europeans having visited the bay since *Resolution* and *Discovery* in 1777.

It could be seen as a tribute to Bligh that his men continued to retain a high level of respect for him after their torrid five-month passage through back-to-back winters from England, first to Cape Horn and then Van Diemen's Land. However, on arrival at Adventure Bay a significant sign of dissension emerged involving the ship's carpenter, William Purcell. Bligh explained:

> My carpenter on my expressing my disapprobation of his
> conduct with respect to orders he had received from me
> concerning the mode of working with the wooding party,
> behaved in a most insolent and reprehensible manner,
> I therefore, ordered him on board, there to assist in the general
> duty of the ship, as I could not bear the loss of an able working
> and healthy man; otherwise I should have committed him to
> close confinement until I could have tried him, the prospect of
> which appears to be of so long a date made me determine to
> keep him at his duty, giving him a chance by his future conduct
> to make up in some degree for his ill behaviour at this place.

But the problem didn't end there. When Bligh returned to the ship he was informed by his master, John Fryer, that Purcell had refused to assist in loading water barrels into the hold, stating that he would only 'do anything in his line'. Under normal circumstances on a larger ship the captain would have had no option but to commit him to some form of confinement, but Bligh needed every man in his small team to work as one, so he devised a tactic that would impose a form of discipline while at the same time bring the man to his senses. He declared Purcell was to receive no food or water and that any man in the crew who assisted him in any way would be dealt a most severe punishment. Much to Bligh's delight, it immediately produced the desired response from the carpenter: 'It was for the good of the voyage that I should not make him or any man a prisoner.' This particular incident would stand as one that demonstrated Bligh's ability to balance justice and compassion in a shrewd manner.

Bounty lay at anchor in Adventure Bay for nearly two weeks before there were any active signs of islanders: small camp fires were seen flickering among trees across the bay. Bligh knew from having been at Adventure Bay with Captain Cook that the indigenous people were timid, and it was no different this time. While it was obvious that they could see *Bounty* in the bay, they made no effort to make contact, so instead, Bligh went to them. This experience, along with what he and some of his crew had seen earlier on shore, led to the following observation: 'These people are an itinerant set and the whole dependence of their living is totally on mussels and other kinds of shell fish, as their resting places are always where those things can be gathered, which we easily discover by seeing heaps of shells wherever they have stopped.' Bligh was also curious about whether these people slept in the trees they hollowed out using fire, but concluded after the meeting that the 'wigwams' nearby were most definitely for sleeping, and the hollowed-out trees were merely fireplaces.

With there being no wind on the afternoon and evening of 3 September, Bligh took the opportunity to warp *Bounty* on her anchors away from the shore and into deeper water. At daybreak the next morning an offshore breeze prevailed, so the captain called for the ship's boats to be hoisted aboard and secured, then the rig readied for sailing, which came at midday. Soon *Bounty* was gliding across what is now known as Storm Bay and towards Tasman Island to the east. While on that course Bligh made two important observations of his surroundings, the first being: 'there is a remarkable high flat topped mountain to the NW by N' (Hobart's Mount Wellington); and the second: 'its western cape is exceedingly remarkable from the pitch of it being cut into a remarkable number of upright rock pillars of unequal heights' (the famous Organ Pipes on Cape Raoul). This confirms that Bligh discovered both these outstanding features of southern Tasmania. He also charted the existence of Tasman Island at the eastern entrance to the bay.

Within 24 hours *Bounty* was beginning to feel the surge of the swells in the Tasman Sea, from which point the captain set a course to the east-south-east that would take them to the south of New Zealand in following winds on what was the final stage of this voyage to Tahiti. Fortunately it was the final days of winter, but even so the men would have to endure extreme cold once more. They would be at an inhospitable 48 degrees of latitude when they cleared New Zealand's Stewart Island and headed into the South Pacific. The island hove into sight on Sunday, 14 September, and at that point the helmsman was called to steer east-by-north for what would then be a looping course to the final destination.

Five days after passing New Zealand, Bligh was to make another of his discoveries: a parcel of more than a dozen rocky islands which he named Bounty's Isles. On 9 October there came an emotional setback for all on board when one of the most energetic young able seamen, James Valentine, died from an asthmatic condition which it appears was brought on by complications following an illness he experienced while the ship was in Adventure Bay. On the same day it is recorded that Bligh clashed with both his surgeon, Thomas Huggan, who had neglected young Valentine before his death, and with his master, John Fryer, whose attitude towards Bligh had gone from being supportive to belligerent and troublesome. The first real sign that there were serious issues with the surgeon surfaced when some crew complained of rheumatic pain and were unable to dance in the evening as Bligh demanded. Huggan, who was himself suffering from alcohol-induced problems, diagnosed the supposed rheumatic pain as being a sign of scurvy. Bligh strongly disagreed, saying their symptoms were 'nothing more than prickly heat', and documented in the ship's log how the men's condition first became apparent: 'John Mills and William Brown refusing to dance this evening. I ordered their grog to be stopped with a promise of further punishment on a second refusal.

I have always directed the evenings from five to eight o'clock to be spent in dancing, and that every man should be obliged to dance as I considered it conducive to their health.'

As *Bounty* sailed into the higher latitudes, the hot tropical climate began affecting the crew, and Bligh believed this was the cause of an expanding sick list among his men. 'Several have complained of faintness towards midday,' Bligh observed. Accordingly, he insisted everything be done to maintain their health. This involved the widest possible range of food for them and a series of concoctions, which by today's standards are beyond comprehension: soup thickened with pearl barley, salt meat, a beverage made from Elixir Vitriol, 'thick barley gruel constantly for breakfast', vinegar, mustard and sauerkraut.

Soon there was another confrontation with the surgeon, and Bligh's frustration surfaced once more: 'The doctor's intoxication has given me much trouble these last five days ...'

Despite this, Bligh's log the following day reveals he tried desperately to reason with the surgeon in the hope he would 'turn sober again': 'I sent for the surgeon and in the most friendly manner requested him to leave off drinking, but he seemed not sensible of anything I said to him and it had little effect,' Bligh wrote.

When the surgeon was too drunk to get out of his bunk for four days. Bligh had no alternative but to order his cabin searched and all alcohol removed. Huggan soon emerged from his drunken hibernation and was back on deck in a sober state, much to Bligh's relief as he had an important task for him to carry out before their arrival in Tahiti:

As I have some reason to suppose the Otaheitans have not been visited by any ships since Captain Cook, I hope they may have found means together with their natural way of living, to have eradicated the venereal disease. To prove this and free us from any ill-founded suppositions, that we might renew the complaint, I have directed the surgeon to examine very particularly every man and officer and to report to me his proceedings. This was accordingly done and he reported every person totally free from the venereal complaint.

By now *Bounty* had swept up out of the Southern Ocean and was for the first time enjoying the influence of the south-east trade winds, and Bligh's navigation confirmed that the Society Islands would come into view within 48 hours. Accordingly, it became increasingly important for the ship's lookouts positioned in the rig to be even more vigilant, and they were. During the morning of 25 October the eagerly anticipated call came from aloft: the small volcanic island of Maitea (Mehetia), the easternmost of the Society Islands, had loomed over the horizon. Before long they were cruising past the northern shore of Maitea in such close proximity that the crew could see a small group of islanders on the shore waving large pieces of cloth. *Bounty* continued on a course to the west towards the northern side of Tahiti, which was a further 85 nautical miles away, and at six o'clock that evening it was sighted.

Early the next morning, as the well-travelled ship and its weary crew rounded Point Venus at the entrance to the expansive Matavai Bay, they were welcomed by a huge fleet of canoes. The arrival was as exciting for the Englishmen as it was for the locals, who were eager to clamber aboard and welcome their visitors. But first they had to be assured that these foreigners were friends and not foe, and establish that they came from 'Pretanee' (Britain), the home of their great friend Captain Cook.

With a rapport between the two sides then established, there was no stopping them: the islanders, men and women, came over the side en masse shouting words of welcome and celebrating *Bounty*'s arrival. Within ten minutes there were so many visitors that Bligh, who stood regal and proud in his full naval uniform, had trouble locating any of his crewmembers, and understandably so. They were surrounded by a plethora of exotic near-naked, caramel-skinned women, many exuding a beauty and allure beyond belief. They had discovered paradise – and it was obvious to Bligh that it was going to be too difficult and dangerous under the circumstances to move the ship any further into the bay. The captain had no option but to call for the anchor to be released. Within minutes the two sides were exchanging gifts and the *Bounty* crew knew that they were among friends.

When Bligh and his men did have time to reflect on what lay in the wake of the ship, they had every right to feel proud: they had sailed more than 27 000 nautical miles since leaving England – already the equivalent of circling the world at the equator – covering an average 108 nautical miles a day at a mean speed of 4.5 knots.

CHAPTER SIX

Tahiti, 1788

Seduction in paradise

Had the propagation of the breadfruit plant been better understood by Bligh and his botanists, they would have known before arriving in Tahiti that they were destined for a long stay. But the fruit was new to the British, so there was no real knowledge of it – except that it grew prolifically in the tropics and provided exceptional sustenance. As it turned out, *Bounty* could not have dropped anchor in Matavai Bay at a worse time for this venture. In late October, near the start of the southern hemisphere summer, the breadfruit trees were in fruit, which meant any juvenile saplings were not strong enough to be transplanted. The wet season, which started in January, was best, so that meant a stay of at least five months.

This news certainly didn't disappoint the crew, who were finding it extremely easy to settle into a warm and carefree South Pacific way of life. They were surrounded by magnificent tropical island scenery, starting with the azure waters that were surging in fine and long ribbons of white onto the black sand. These palm-fringed beaches were at the front line of a gently sloping coastal strip that swept up to breathtakingly lush and rugged volcanic peaks.

More interesting for the crew, though, were their immediate surrounds: they were overwhelmed by the entrancing natural beauty of so many of the Tahitian women. Suddenly all the hardship and pain from the attempts to round Cape Horn were forgotten; within days of their arrival it appeared that almost every one of them had acquired a *tyo*, a female friend.

Initially Bligh was welcomed to Tahiti by a number of subordinate chiefs, but he sought contact with Otoo, the chief of the region around Matavai Bay, whom he knew from having been to the island with Captain Cook aboard *Resolution* in 1777 – '63 moons' earlier, according to the Tahitian calendar. The captain was told that the chief was on another part of the island, but messengers had been sent to advise him that a ship carrying friends had arrived. Two days later Otoo and his wife, Iddeeah, arrived. When the chief came aboard *Bounty*, he welcomed the Englishmen, but advised Bligh that he had changed his name to Tynah, something that was customary on a number of occasions during a chief's life. He was a man of huge stature, around 6 feet 4 inches tall and proportionately robust.

As a symbol of friendship the islanders had brought to the ship a painting of Captain Cook done by John Webber when *Resolution* was there. However, the wooden frame had been damaged over the years, so they asked if it could be repaired. The master of another ship that had been there some months prior had informed the locals of Cook's death but not the cause, so Tynah pressed Bligh for information regarding the man they called *Toote Earee no Tahiti* – Cook, chief of Tahiti – but Bligh would not confirm Cook's passing. He had ordered his crew to do likewise for fear it might cause unnecessary disturbance among the Tahitians.

Bligh had also decided it was not prudent so soon after arriving to tell Tynah that the procurement of breadfruit plants was the purpose behind the visit. He thought it better to establish a relationship with the islanders, then plan an appropriate strategy. Regardless, he did send his botanist, David Nelson, and the latter's assistant, William Brown, to look for suitable plants around the bay, and they returned to report that it appeared their mission would be accomplished with relative ease.

Even so, Bligh decided to extend his search for breadfruit to Oparre, a 30-minute sail to the west of where *Bounty* was anchored, on the pretext that he wanted to visit Tynah's young son, Otoo, who was the *earee rahie* – the chief – of the village. During the short passage aboard *Bounty*'s cutter, Bligh told Tynah that he intended visiting other islands while in Tahiti. He also enquired as to what had happened to the cattle, sheep and other animals Cook had brought to the island. Tynah revealed that most had been slaughtered after a successful attack on Oparre by other islanders, adding that it had been hoped that *Toote* (which was how they pronounced Captain Cook's name) would return with a 'great ship' to avenge the loss. Bligh immediately saw an opportunity to raise the subject of breadfruit diplomatically: 'I told him that not only *Toote* but King George would be very angry at it [the slaughter of the animals], that he had many good friends in England, and when ships came again to Tahiti he would have other presents and good things sent to him. He was much pleased and satisfied.' Bligh then suggested that since King George III had sent many presents to Tynah, he should send something in return: 'he readily complied, enumerating the different articles he had, among which was the breadfruit ... I made a proper use of it, and [after] telling him the breadfruit was very good and that King George would like it, he said a great deal should be put on board.'

The deal was done. Bligh had his host, Tynah, at the point he wanted – they would get all the breadfruit plants they needed with the support of the locals. At this stage of the project, Bligh was understandably quite satisfied with its progress: 'I had now, instead of appearing to receive a favour, brought the chiefs to believe that I was doing them a kindness in carrying the plants, as a present from them to the *Earee Rahie no Britannee*.'

With the ship anchored in the superbly scenic situation in Matavai Bay, after his visit to Oparre, Bligh revealed he too was overwhelmed by the natural beauty surrounding him: 'These two places are certainly the paradise of the world and if happiness could result from situation and convenience, here it is to be found in the highest perfection. I have seen many parts of the world, but Tahiti is capable of being preferable to them all, and certainly is so considering it in its natural state.' Ironically, the profound beauty of this paradise would be one of the elements underpinning the collapse of his expedition months later when some of his men mutinied.

Eight days after *Bounty*'s arrival, Bligh ordered Fletcher Christian and a party ashore to erect a tent that would become the assembly point for the breadfruit plants before they were transferred to the ship. The crew knew the islanders were uncommonly accomplished thieves, so they established a line in the sand around the tent which the islanders were not permitted to cross unless invited.

Since they couldn't collect the breadfruit saplings at that time, the crew started preparing soil for the pots. Some breadfruit trees can be grown from seeds, but the variety in Tahiti had to be established from suckers growing as an extension of the tree's root system. Islanders would induce growth of these suckers by uncovering the root of a tree and cutting into it, and soon after a tiny shoot would emerge from that wound. However, before this new growth could be transplanted, it had to grow to a point where it had established its own life support system – an extensive network of roots.

Petty thieving became all too prevalent, so when the rudder gudgeon was removed from the stern of the large cutter and no perpetrator found, Bligh decided that he should punish the boatkeeper, John Adams (who had come aboard under the false name of Alexander Smith possibly because he was wanted by authorities in England for criminal activities), with a dozen lashes in the presence of the chiefs. This would allow Bligh to demonstrate to the chiefs how such offences were dealt with under the ship's law. There is little doubt this act was the harbinger of a degeneration of the relationship between the captain and some of his men. Already Bligh was aware that these particular individuals were becoming increasingly indolent towards their duties, their focus being more on developing a strong rapport with the island women, who were extremely generous with their favours. It was normal sybaritic behaviour for the women and heaven-sent for the visitors, who were becoming too easily intoxicated by seductive charms they could never have imagined back in England. No doubt Bligh knew if he stood between his men and their desires during this prolonged stay he would make life unnecessarily difficult for himself. His challenge was to maintain discipline as best he could: nothing would change until *Bounty* had weighed anchor for the homeward voyage.

The hospitality Bligh was experiencing with the islanders was considerably different to that of his men. From the outset it had flowed freely with Tynah and other chiefs on the island. When they were aboard the ship they drank wine, but while on shore Bligh had to contend with drinking ava, or kava as it is now known, something he found to be quite repulsive, but unfortunately an obligatory tradition he had to observe. He recorded one of his first experiences with this debilitating drink when he met Tynah's father, who was about 70 years old:

I found this old chief ... lying under a small shed and as soon as he saw me he seemed to be overjoyed ... he is a tall man with weak eyes and his skin is much shrivelled and dried by drinking of that pernicious root, the ava ... This ava is made from a strong pungent root which few chiefs ever go without – it is chewed by their servants in large mouthfuls at a time, which when it has collected a sufficiency of saliva is taken and put into a coconut shell. This is repeated until there is enough chewed – it is then squeezed and given to the principal men, each of them taking nearly a pint wine measure. What remains is mixed with water and again squeezed and strained, it is then delivered to the inferior chiefs or those of the highest class if they prefer it diluted.

While Bligh found the kava ritual close to vile, he was pleased when the islanders informed him that a *Heiva* – a traditional ceremony – was to be performed in his honour. It was by then late November 1788, and earlier in the month the *Bounty* crew, led by Bligh, had shared their own form of entertainment – a practical joke – with a large group of islanders aboard the ship, including the ever-present Tynah.

The ship's barber, Able Seaman Richard Skinner, had brought from London a lifelike hairdresser's model, a head used to show customers different hair fashions. Bligh suggested to Skinner that he prepare the model for some light-hearted fun, and he did this by styling the model's hair and forming a stick body for it which was clothed. That done, the Englishmen put word out to the islanders that they actually did have an English lady with them, and if they cleared the quarterdeck, she might make an appearance. Minutes later the 'English lady' was handed up to deck level by one of the crew standing on the boarding ladder suspended over the side of the ship. Another crewman then lifted her over the rail, and carried her across the deck to cries from the natives of '*Huaheine no Britannee myty*', meaning 'good woman of Britain'. Many believed her to be real and asked Bligh if this was his wife. One old woman was so convinced that she rushed to the mannequin's feet and laid down gifts of cloth and breadfruit. Others rubbed noses and kissed her. When the ruse was revealed the islanders saw the joke as being extremely funny and clever.

The day the *Heiva* was scheduled, 21 November, started extremely well when a local chief, Teppahoo, did as promised and found a bullock the captain could buy and have slaughtered for the crew's benefit. The purchase price was a hatchet, file, rasp, gimlet, knife, spiker nail and a shirt. The form of payment brought great excitement to the islanders observing the transaction: they had never seen such an array of highly prized currency.

Tynah and his family and friends, who rarely spent a day not in Bligh's presence, saw it as an honour to present the *Heiva* for the captain. Bligh had not previously seen such a ceremony, and it turned out to be an experience best left to him to describe:

> ... a great many people collected ... I was placed with Tynah, his wife and several chief women at the most conspicuous part of the ring and the performance began.
>
> Twelve men were divided into four ranks, three men in each one behind the other sitting on their heels, with two women in the front. Behind them all stood a man who was called a priest and who made an harangue which lasted about ten minutes that was listened to with some attention, during which Captain Cook's picture, that we had brought from the ship on purpose, was held beside me. The harangue being over I was clothed in a piece of white cloth and a small piece was wrapped round the

picture. The priest now spoke again, when an old man with one
eye came running up to me in a superstitious kind of manner, and
placed a piece of plaited coconut leaf at my feet. The same was
done to Tynah, and one piece was thrown under the picture. The
priest left off speaking and the Heiva began by the men jumping
and throwing their legs and arms into violent and odd motions,
which the women kept time with, and as they were conveniently
clothed for the purpose, their persons were generally exposed to
full view, frequently standing on one leg and keeping the other
up, giving themselves the most lascivious and wanton motions. As
this was for some time performed at the farthest part of the ring
from us, out of compliment the women were directed to come
nearer, and they accordingly advanced with their clothes up, and
went through the same wanton gestures which on their return
ended the Heiva.

In the course of this extraordinary performance the Queen
and chief women were highly delighted, and asked particularly
if we had no such Heivas in England.

At all times Bligh displayed a genuine interest in the islanders, their
lifestyle, traditions and welfare. He noted that there were around
100 000 inhabitants across the islands in this region and that they
were well aware of the problems associated with over-population,
which they dealt with through a brutal form of culling. He
demonstrated a remarkably realistic appreciation of the problem
and its solution, but that didn't stop him from suggesting an
alternative way of dealing with it. Incredibly his plan involved the
newly settled New Holland:

An idea here presents itself which, however fanciful it may
appear at first sight, seems to merit some attention: while we

see among these islands so great a waste of the human species that numbers are born only to die, and at the same time a large continent so near to them as New Holland, in which there is so great a waste of land uncultivated and almost destitute of inhabitants, it naturally occurs how greatly the two countries might be made to benefit each other, and gives occasion to regret that the islanders are not instructed in the means of emigrating to New Holland, which seems as if designed by nature to serve as an asylum for the superflux of inhabitants in the islands ...

December 5 and 6 were two days to remember for unfortunate reasons. A fresh gale had descended on Matavai Bay overnight and by morning the ship was rolling heavily and uncomfortably in the large swell. The gyrations were exacerbated by the vast amount of weight carried aloft: the masts, yards and rigging combined to create the effect of a giant, slow-moving pendulum. Bligh also had to contend with a problem with the previously recalcitrant carpenter, William Purcell. Some islanders brought to the ship a large stone that Bligh wanted shaped so they could sharpen the hatchets he had given them, but to the captain's astonishment Purcell 'refused to comply in direct terms saying "I will not cut the stone for it will spoil my chisel, and though there is law to take away my clothes there is none to take away my tools" ... I was under the necessity to confine him to his cabin. Although I can but ill spare the loss of a single man, but I do not intend to lose the use of him but remit him to his duty tomorrow.' Later the same day Able Seaman Mathew Thompson was dealt 'twelve lashes for insolence and disobedience of orders'.

Much to everyone's surprise the conditions they were experiencing deteriorated to a dangerous degree. This time of the year is today defined as the hurricane season, and Bligh's reports leave little doubt this is what they experienced. He indicated that the eye of the ugly storm blasting across Matavai Bay passed directly over them. Initially the wind came from the east-south-east, then later it came even more savagely from the opposing direction, north-west. The seas grew to such a height that the nearby Dolphin Bank, which had provided a natural barrier for the anchorage, was offering no protection at all. The waves broke over the ship and threatened to rip it away from the anchors. Bligh's log recorded that the situation was dire. Every part of the ship had to be battened down while all on board could do no more than place their trust in the anchors:

> In this state we remained the whole night with all hands up in the midst of torrents of rain, the ship sending and rolling in a most tremendous manner, and the sea foaming all around us so as to threaten instant destruction. However I did not strike yards and topmasts until eight in the morning when the wind increasing from the NW I gave up all ideas but riding it out, and made the ship as fit for it as possible. In this situation my friends on shore became very anxious for my safety.

The storm lasted more than 30 hours. On shore the prized breadfruit plants, which by then were starting to be collected and transplanted into the pots, were under threat from the salt spray brought in by the menacing seas. An additional threat to the campsite came with the torrent of water streaming down from the nearby mountains and carving its way across the beach like a river in full flood. Miraculously, the ship held true on its anchors, and the plants somehow survived the onslaught.

To Bligh's amazement, the moment the seas showed signs of abating, Tynah and his wife clambered aboard a canoe and battled their way through the still huge surf out to the ship, just so they could express their deepest concerns about what had happened. They and everyone else on shore were astounded that the ship had not foundered and been destroyed.

The following day an even more remarkable display of emotion and empathy over the immensity of the threat the ship had survived came when another native leader, Poeeno, and his wife reached the ship bearing a gift of fruit. No one on board was prepared for what followed: a customary but alarming display of sympathy shown by Poeeno's wife. 'The strongest and only established proof among these people of their sincerity on those occasions,' said Bligh, 'is the wounding of themselves on the top of the head with a shark's tooth until they bring on a vast profusion of blood, and having a knowledge of this I was prepared to prevent this woman from doing it, but I had no sooner come to her than the operation was performed before I was aware of it, and her face was covered with blood in an instant.'

Poeeno subsequently gave Bligh an assurance: 'You shall live with me if the ship is lost, and we will cut down trees to build another to carry you to Pretanee.'

Bligh needed no convincing that it would be unsafe for *Bounty* to stay in Matavai Bay any longer, and this was confirmed for him by the chiefs. He called for the ship to be readied for departure as soon as possible to a safer anchorage, but first they had to find that anchorage.

While that search was undertaken, work continued on the ship and its equipment, including the sails which were on shore. One of the tasks for the crew was to haul *Bounty*'s launch up the beach for maintenance, but unfortunately while this was taking place, a strapping young islander boy of around ten years of age injured himself when he fell under one of the wooden rollers being used to move the boat across the sand. There was immediate concern for him but he escaped serious injury.

On the same day it was the ship's surgeon who caused extreme alarm:

> About eight o'clock the surgeon's assistant made a report that the surgeon appeared in such a state that he thought it was necessary to remove him where he could have more air, and accordingly the cabin was got ready for him, but we had no idea of the dangerous state he was in. Mr. Fryer went with the people to get him up, when to his astonishment he found him on the deck totally senseless. Difficulty of breathing and a few slight exertions to discharge some phlegm, were the only appearances of life that he had by the time they got him to the cabin. An attempt was made to get him to swallow some coconut milk, but all to no effect and he died at nine o'clock.
>
> This unfortunate man died owing to drunkenness and indolence. Exercise was a thing he could not bear an idea of, or could I ever bring him to take a half-dozen of turns on deck at a time in the course of the whole voyage. Sleeping was the way he spent his time, and he accustomed himself to breathe so little fresh air and was so filthy in his person that he became latterly a nuisance.

Crew members cutting planks for the ship constructed a coffin for the departed surgeon while the captain arranged with Tynah for him to be buried on shore under a cairn. The captain then confirmed that Thomas Ledward, the surgeon's mate, would become the ship's surgeon.

After surveying a number of safe anchorages around Matavai Bay, Bligh brought great joy to his hosts when he announced he would be moving *Bounty* to the nearby harbour of Toahroah, just 3 miles to the west of where they were currently anchored near Point Venus. Everyone could continue their association with the ship, especially the women with whom so many of the crew had become familiar.

Before moving anchorage, the crew transferred 774 potted breadfruit plants by cutter from the beach to the ship. The next morning, Christmas Day, they weighed anchor and *Bounty* began the short passage to its new location. As a precaution Bligh sent the launch ahead to unload tents on shore then meet the ship at sea, from where it would show the way through the narrow channel leading to the lagoon. *Bounty* made her approach under topsails only while the launch, which was also under sail, rendezvoused at the designated point. Unfortunately, though, the wind faded to a whisper and the launch was suddenly becalmed. Inevitably, *Bounty* carried her way and sailed past, and in immediately recognising it was too dangerous to proceed any further, Bligh called his men to action – but it was too late: 'I now shortened sail and let the anchor go when to my astonishment the ship was aground, but she went on so easy I did not know it until the master came from the fore-yard and told me of it. I have been in many situations of this nature much more hazardous and I thought my precautions were abundant to carry me safe.'

With the hull suffering only superficial damage, Bligh called for two anchors to be set astern of the ship so it could be hauled off using manpower at the capstan and the windlass. The undertaking took less than an hour: at midday *Bounty* was floating free, much to the amazement of the islanders watching the salvage effort from their canoes and from shore, all certain she would not be refloated.

Once *Bounty* was safely at anchor, Bligh commanded the crew to begin preparing for departure and the next stage of the voyage –

to the West Indies. This included a rigorous and detailed check of every part of the ship – rigging, sails and hull. Provisions were also a priority: a number of hogs were slaughtered and the meat salted. The ship's butcher, Robert Lamb, was on the receiving end of twelve lashes 'for suffering his cleaver to be stolen', and while Bligh acknowledged to Tynah and other chiefs that Lamb was primarily at fault through negligence, the perpetrators would receive a similar punishment if caught (which they weren't).

In the final weeks of December, Bligh was informed that the supply of breadfruit had started to dwindle, but he was also assured this would change the following month. At the same time he was pleased to note that the islanders continued to provide the ship with a considerable amount of food – coconuts, plantains and fish in particular – which he purchased from them using the usual barter system.

Amid all this preparation the crew had to confront the sudden, and in some cases dreaded, realisation that departure was nigh, and with that the uninhibited and licentious lifestyle in paradise they had so easily and readily adopted was coming to a compulsory conclusion. It was a lifestyle which, before arriving in Tahiti, they could never have imagined in their wildest dreams. Soon it would be in *Bounty*'s wake while ahead loomed the drudgery of eighteenth-century England. For many, it was a troublesome thought gnawing at their minds. News of *Bounty*'s impending departure was also spreading across the islander population, and with that, obvious signs of sadness emerged in the form of an unprecedented outpouring of kindness towards the visitors. It confirmed they held a great desire for the Englishmen not to leave.

During the countdown to departure, reluctance to return to their mundane life was increasingly evident among some of the men and this, inevitably, led to more problems for Bligh. The first sign of trouble came in a most definite manner on the fifth day of the New Year, 1789. At four o'clock in the morning, it was discovered that the ship's small cutter was missing. Bligh immediately mustered the ship's company, and the ensuing roll-call revealed that three of his crew had deserted: the master-at-arms, Charles Churchill; Bligh's own steward and tailor, William Muspratt (who had received a dozen lashes twelve days earlier for neglect of duty); and Able Seaman John Millward, who had been on duty as the ship's sentinel between midnight and 2 am on the night. Also, because the mate-of-the-watch on deck, Thomas Hayward, was asleep on the job, the ship's arms chest had been raided and eight stands of arms and ammunition were stolen.

Bligh was less concerned about the men than he was about the cutter; it was vital to the operation of the ship and the safety of the crew. At first light he went ashore and secured the assistance of Tynah and other chiefs to initiate a search for the deserters. In no time word filtered back that they were headed for Matavai, so Bligh returned to *Bounty* and arranged for Tynah, two chiefs and the ship's master, John Fryer, to set off after them in another of the ship's boats. They were only a short distance to the east of *Bounty* when, much to their amazement, they spotted the cutter being rowed towards them. They discovered why: the five islanders on board were bringing it back to the ship, but minus the deserters.

Once the cutter was back at the ship Bligh duly 'rewarded the men for their fidelity', then much to his delight he learned that the islanders had full knowledge of the missing men's plans: on reaching Matavai they organised for islanders to take them by canoe to a village at Tetturoah, an island 30 nautical miles to the north. With this knowledge Bligh turned to Tynah, making it clear he was serious:

As the object now was to adopt means to get the people I told Tynah and the other chiefs that I looked to them for that service, and that therefore without delay they must proceed to Tetturoah and get them taken and brought back to me. That I would not quit the country without them, and that as they had always been my friends I expected they would show it in this instance, and that unless they did, I should proceed with such violence as would make them repent it.

Tough words, but it was language the islanders understood. Cook, along with Bligh, had been the first Europeans to make contact with the Hawaiians and Tahitians. Bligh, by his second voyage into the Pacific, would have had a working knowledge of the language, though not without misunderstandings.

The following morning two chiefs, Oreepyah and Moannah, were to set off in canoes bound for Tetturoah, well versed in the plan that Bligh had devised: 'the natives to collect round them as friends, and then to seize on them and their arms, and bind them with cords and to show no mercy to them if they made resistance'.

With the search underway Bligh had time to consider what might have caused the men to desert and also to contemplate the obvious and disconcerting change of attitude emerging among some of his men. They were becoming increasingly apathetic and lackadaisical – hardly surprising considering the casual and carefree nature of the South Pacific island society that embraced them. These and other circumstances were causing Bligh to feel the isolation that came with command. He and so many of the crew were worlds apart in upbringing, education (or lack of it) and attitude, yet he somehow had to bridge that divide if this expedition were to succeed – and it had to. He needed to retain control of his all-too-often wayward bunch, and to achieve this he needed to strike a delicate balance between leadership and camaraderie, while also being the judge, jury and disciplinarian when it came to punishment for any wrongdoing. How he must have wished at the time that *Bounty* had been that little bit larger so he would have been entitled to carry the small complement of marines he had wanted. They would have made his position as commander infinitely easier. Instead of having the marines support him and deliver punishment, it was crewman lashing crewman, which made life on board difficult. Each punishment was aimed at setting an example to the entire crew as much as it was to cleanse the offender.

The stability Bligh needed to maintain within his crew was never more apparent than at this time: he knew he had to keep corporal punishment to a minimum, even though he was dealing with some of the worst acts of insubordination defined under the Royal Navy's Articles of War. He had to decide how to achieve that balance while appropriately disciplining the deserters, should they be caught, along with the sleeping mate-of-the-watch. The deserters' crime was understandable. Hayward's crime, however, was unforgivable in that by being asleep he had failed to raise the alarm over the theft of the cutter. This dereliction of duty had also presented the absconders with the opportunity to arm themselves, so it was imperative that he be punished.

The log entry on the day regarding Thomas Hayward and the degenerating attitude of many of the crew provided fair evidence of Bligh's growing dilemma:

> Had the mate of the watch been awake no trouble of this
> kind would have happened. I have therefore dis-rated and
> turned him before the mast. Such neglectful and worthless
> Petty Officers I believe never were in a ship as are in this. No
> orders for a few hours together are obeyed by them, and their

conduct in general is so bad, that no confidence or trust can be reposed in them. In short they have driven me to everything but corporal punishment and that must follow if they do not improve.

Hayward's sentence was the most severe since *Bounty* departed England, but even so Bligh elected not to flog him. He ordered him to be put in irons, and he stayed that way until 23 March, eleven weeks later.

With the search for the deserters in its second week, the remaining crew continued to work on the ship. Things appeared to be going smoothly until 17 January when frustrating new evidence surfaced of a serious neglect of duty on the part of his officers. It came when Bligh ordered that all sails in the sail room be taken ashore to air, and he was infuriated by what he found:

> The new fore topsail and foresail, main topmast staysail and main staysail were found very much mildewed and rotten in many places.
>
> If I had any officers to supersede the master and boatswain, or was capable of doing without them considering them as common seamen, they should no longer occupy their respective stations. Scarce any neglect of duty can equal the criminality of this … To remedy the defects I attended and saw the sails put into the sea and hung up on shore to dry to be ready for repairing.

Heralded by gale-force winds and a booming tropical thunderstorm, word came to the captain that he had anxiously hoped to hear: the deserters, who had been gone seventeen days, had returned and were at Tettahah, a village about 5 miles from where *Bounty* was anchored. It was after five o'clock in the afternoon and darkness would soon push its way in from the east, so Bligh decided that despite the storm he would go after his men there and then. He ordered that the launch be immediately hoisted out from the deck, manned and readied to take him to the village.

The atrocious weather made for a difficult and dangerous passage through a series of reefs before the boat finally reached a beach near the village where it could be put ashore safely. This was still some distance from Tettahah, so Bligh then set out on foot along the beach, his destination being the home of his friend, the village chief, Teppahoo, where Churchill, Muspratt and Millward were said to be waiting. Much to Bligh's surprise the walk was not without incident. Suddenly a group of islanders emerged from the night to rob him of whatever they could. The threat disappeared as quickly as it came when Bligh fired a shot into the air, threatening at the same time to kill his would-be assailants.

As he approached the house he was surprised to see his men waiting for him outside, unarmed, unrestrained and ready to surrender. He talked with Teppahoo about the situation, then took the trio back to the beach. Bligh decided it was too late and too dangerous to return to the ship, so he opted to hold the deserters overnight in a shed on shore with two armed guards while the rest of his launch crew took shelter under cover aboard the boat.

When they arrived back on the ship the next morning the three offenders were thrown into irons, and a directive issued that no liquor of any kind was to be given to them. Their story to the captain was that after Oreepyah and Moannah had tried unsuccessfully to detain them at Tetturoah they decided it was best for them to return to their ship on their own accord and surrender. Bligh doubted this story; he believed that with their whereabouts known, and having been threatened and made unwelcome by the islanders at Tetturoah, they decided to move on to Moorea.

However, the bad weather had blown them off course to Tettahah. Bligh was also convinced that had their arms and ammunition not been rendered useless by water damage, the men would probably not have surrendered as they did.

Bligh's log for the following morning reads: 'Punished the deserters as follows – Charles Churchill with twelve lashes and William Muspratt and John Millward with two dozen each, and remanded them back into irons, for further punishment.'

To coincide with the first round of punishment for these men Bligh seized the opportunity to impress firmly upon the ship's company their obligations to the king, country and the mission by again highlighting the Articles of War, a 3475-word document created in 1749 listing regulations 'to be observed and put in execution, as well in time of peace as in time of war'. He explained his reason for doing this:

> As this affair was solely caused by the neglect of the officers
> who had the watch, I was induced to give them all a lecture
> on this occasion, and endeavoured to show them that however
> exempt they were at present from the like punishment, yet
> they were equally subject by the Articles of War to an adequate
> one. An officer with men under his care is at all times in some
> degree responsible for their conduct; but when from his neglect
> men are brought to punishment while he only meets with a
> reprimand ... an alternative often laid aside through lenity, and
> sometimes necessity as it now is in both cases, it is an unpleasant
> thing to remark that no feelings of honour or sense of shame is
> to be observed in such an offender.

All present no doubt gave thought to the deserters when the following part of 'Section XVI, Desertion, and Entertaining

Deserters' was declared: 'Every person in or belonging to the fleet, who shall desert or entice others so to do, shall suffer death, or such other punishment as the circumstances of the offence shall deserve, and a Court Martial shall judge fit.'

Immediately after the three deserters had received their first taste of punishment via the cat-o'-nine-tails for what Millward would later refer to as 'the former foolish affair', they wrote to their captain pleading for forgiveness and mercy on 26 January 1789:

> Sir,
>
> We should think ourselves wholly inexcusable if we omitted taking this earliest opportunity of returning our thanks for your goodness in delivering us from a trial by Court Martial, the fatal consequences of which are obvious; and although we cannot possibly lay any claim to so great a favour, yet we humbly beg you will be pleased to remit any further punishment, and we trust our future conduct will fully demonstrate our deep sense of your clemency, and our steadfast resolution to behave better hereafter.
>
> We are, etc.
>
> C. Churchill
>
> Wm. Muspratt
>
> John Millward

The plea of repentance fell on deaf ears. The promised 'further punishment' came on 4 February, and after that they were released from irons.

The reading of the Articles seemed to have the desired effect on all the men, except for Able Seaman Isaac Martin, who felt the lash a dozen times on the last day of January. He was found guilty of 'striking an Indian', and for this assault Bligh directed he receive two dozen lashes, a sentence no doubt influenced by the high value the captain placed on retaining a strong and friendly relationship with the islanders, then and in the future. Fortunately for Martin, Tynah and other villagers had pleaded with Bligh on his behalf prior to the punishment and the sentence was reduced.

With *Bounty*'s departure day drawing ever closer, work aboard the ship and the gathering of plants on shore accelerated. One never-ending problem was cockroaches: they were present in large numbers throughout the ship, so after being thoroughly cleaned, below decks was then filled with tobacco smoke in a bid to exterminate them. As an extension of this process all wooden chests were taken ashore and washed out with boiling water.

The accumulation and potting of breadfruit saplings was proceeding according to plan, and as time passed it became apparent to the botanist and his assistant that had *Bounty* been able to round Cape Horn and get to Tahiti earlier than she did, the result of the expedition would not have been anywhere near as successful. Bligh recorded in the ship's log how 70 of the plants were growing well as there had been so much rain, and about the general success of the exercise: 'In all these works I have natives to assist the gardeners and I have had the pleasure to keep all the principal chiefs with the greatest good humour and wish to serve us. Under these happy circumstances and the plants easily cultivated, the success of the voyage now only hinges on our passage home.'

While the surgeon had confirmed the entire *Bounty* crew was free of venereal disease before arriving in Tahiti, their ensuing promiscuity with the women of the island, who were constant visitors to the ship, unfortunately changed that. As a result the ship's newly appointed surgeon, Thomas Ledward, would have been a very busy man. The log gave a constant update on numbers:

Remarks in Toahroah Harbour

Monday 26th. January 1789: ... Six men in the Venereal List.

Friday 30th. January 1789: ... Five Venereals in the List.

Sunday 1st. February 1789: ... Three men in the Venereal List.

It has been estimated that at least one-third of the *Bounty* crew contracted the disease in Tahiti, and while no apparent evidence exists, it is suggested that many officers – including Fletcher Christian, who had the great benefit of being ashore most of the time, organising the gathering of the breadfruit trees – were among them.

Some weeks before *Bounty* was set to sail on the homeward leg of the journey a serious incident occurred, for which Bligh initially blamed the islanders, but in hindsight after the mutiny, considered it was possibly otherwise. An effort had been made overnight to hack through the mooring line securing the ship to the shore, and if it had been successful *Bounty* could easily have rotated on her anchor warp and been wrecked on a nearby reef, or stranded on the beach, beyond salvage. Understandably Bligh was furious:

> ... I am at a loss to account for this malicious act, for I found Tynah totally innocent of the transaction and also the other chiefs: however, as I threatened instant revenge unless the criminal was brought to me, they became all exceedingly alarmed. Otow in the midst of tremendous heavy rain with his wife moved off for the mountains, and also Teppahoo and his family. Tynah and Iddeeah only remained and expostulated with me not to be severe with them. He said he would do his endeavours to get the offender ...

With the cable spliced together and the ship again secure, the captain ordered the erection of a high structure on the fo'c's'le, 'so that the cables are immediately under the eye of the sentinel and a midshipman who take their watch there'.

Months later, after the mutiny, Bligh recorded an alternative theory on the incident:

> It has since occurred to me that this attempt to cut the ship
> adrift was most probably the act of some of our own people;
> whose purpose of remaining at Tahiti might have been
> effectually answered, without danger, if the ship had been
> driven ashore. At the time, I entertained not the least thought
> of this kind, nor did the possibility of it enter into my ideas,
> having no suspicion, that so general an inclination, or so strong
> an attachment to these islands could prevail among my people
> as to induce them to abandon every prospect of returning to
> their native country ...

It would be easy to question Bligh's notes and log of the voyage if he alone had maintained a record, but *Bounty*'s bosun's mate, James Morrison, had kept a daily journal documenting his version of the events that unfolded (from which he later compiled his account of the mutiny while in prison). While critical of Bligh and his fellow officers, and contradicting some of Bligh's log entries, it mostly supports the captain's sequence of events. Such was the case with the circumstances surrounding the three deserters, and also the cable incident. Here Morrison's note supported Bligh's latter theory:

> A little time after, two strands of a small bower cable were
> observed to be cut through at the water's edge, but as the cable

hung slack under the bottom it was not observed until a squall from the westward brought it to bear ahead, when we hove it in and spliced it before the wind became sufficiently strong to part it. This gave rise to many opinions and strict inquiry was made, but no person on board could give any account of it, though it was the private opinion of men as well as officers that no native had been so bold as to attempt it, though some supposed they had, as the buoy was sunk, thinking to be well paid for their trouble in diving after it ... However ... this remained a profound one [secret] and was not found out while the ship remained here ...

By now the worst of the weather had abated and Oreepyah finally returned from Tetturoah after his quest with Moannah to seize the three deserters and return them to their ship. He confirmed Bligh's belief that the deserters' account of what happened, and that they planned to surrender, was false. They had gone back to Tettahah because the weather forced them that way. Oreepyah said he and Moannah had done their utmost to detain the deserters and at one stage actually had them tied up; however, the trio convinced their captors to release them because they planned to return peacefully to the ship. Not surprisingly, once let loose they grabbed their weapons and escaped.

During the latter stage of the stay in Tahiti the ship's log reveals the highs and lows that Bligh experienced daily. One moment he fumes over an incident or set of frustrating circumstances, and the next he is expounding in great detail the pleasures of a particular social event on the ship or with the islanders. This tends to confirm George Tobin's view (who later sailed with Bligh on *Providence* in 1791) that Bligh's 'violent tornados of temper' were quickly followed with 'something like a plaister [sic] to heal the wound'.

Claims he was a cruel tyrant when it came to the treatment of his crew can be countered by ample evidence of his care for their health and conditions on board. Imbued in the rigid traditions of the Royal Navy since he was seven years old, it is easy to understand why he was so often filled with frustration when dealing with recalcitrant crew or slipshod work. Bligh was a highly intelligent perfectionist, an exceptional mariner obsessively dedicated to duty and detail, who struggled to understand why others could not show a similar devotion.

Compress these and all other elements of the expedition, including the lure of the Tahitian women, into one melting pot – a small, 90-foot-long ship with 44 men aboard – and you have an explosive formula, one that created so many trials for the commander who stood alone.

His tolerance was tested again in early March, this time by an islander who went to the tent on the beach and stole an empty water cask, part of an Azimuth Compass and the hammock belonging to gunner William Peckover, who was supposedly the lookout at the time. Bligh had done his utmost to ignore the majority of the locals' petty thieving since *Bounty* had arrived in Tahiti, but for this guilty party, should he be caught, there was promise of serious retribution. Bligh was so desperate to have this thief captured he sent word ashore to Tynah that there would be no further friendship between them 'unless the thief was produced, and that must be done in the course of the day'. The threat had the desired impact: within three hours the search party returned with some of the evidence – the cask – and the perpetrator held firmly in Tynah's grasp. 'There is the thief. Kill him,' Tynah declared to Bligh. Bligh then 'told him he had acted very properly and that he had secured my friendship and good will, and explained with much success how unjust it was and unfriendly to steal any thing from us, and the risk which they run in the attempt.' He added, 'That I punished my people for the most trifling offence against them, and that I would therefore insist on like punishment, on their side.'

The islander was then taken to *Bounty* and dealt 100 lashes 'severely given, and thence into irons'. There was relief for both sides to learn that the thief was not from the Matavai Bay area.

Bligh's plan was to hold the young man as a hostage in case of further thefts, but it was short-lived. At around four o'clock in the morning, five days after being put in irons, the young man managed to break the lock, free himself, then dive overboard and swim off into the darkness. Once again Bligh's fury had been fired by incompetence:

> I had given in written orders that the mate of the watch
> [Midshipman George Stewart] was to be answerable for the
> prisoners and to visit and see that they were safe in his watch,
> but I have such a neglectful set about me that I believe nothing
> but condign punishment can alter their conduct. Verbal orders
> in the course of a month were so forgot that they would
> impudently assert no such thing or directions were given, and
> I have been at last under the necessity to trouble myself with
> writing what by decent young officers would be complied with
> as the common Rules of the Service.

By now *Bounty* was in the final stages of being rigged and readied for departure, and undoubtedly that could not have come soon enough for the captain. After five months he would finally have his men and his mission back on course.

On 1 April, *Bounty* was ready to sail. On board were 1015 breadfruit plants in 774 pots, 39 tubs and 24 boxes, plus a number of other plants Sir Joseph Banks had suggested they collect.

Additionally Bligh recorded: 'My stock on board consisted of as much fruit as I could stow, 25 hogs and seventeen goats. Water on board, 47 tons.'

Bad weather – strong winds and thunderstorms – held *Bounty* at anchor for three more days. Then, on the evening of 4 April the ship was overwhelmed by islanders as they clambered aboard to say farewell – including Tynah and almost his entire family, and the female friends of the crew. There was also a sombre crowd on the beach: 'No mirth or dances on the beach as usual in the evenings. All sorrow at our departure,' Bligh logged.

One of the captain's final acts was to return to Tynah Webber's painting of Captain Cook, complete with repaired frame. It had been kept on board at the chief's request for the time they were in Tahiti. Then: 'At five o'clock,' Bligh reflected, 'we bade farewell to Tahiti, where for 23 weeks we were treated with the greatest kindness: fed with the best of meat and finest fruits in the world.'

CHAPTER SEVEN

Friendly Isles, 1789

A seditious plot

The wind was still strong when *Bounty* cleared Matavai Bay, and its direction suited the chosen course of north-west-by-north, one that would lead to the island of Huahine, 100 nautical miles away. Once there, Bligh's desire was to learn what he could of his friend Omai, a 'noble savage' who had freely left the island in 1773 with Captain Cook's second South Pacific expedition and travelled with him to England. As the first Polynesian to visit the country, Omai became a sensation in English society, to which he was enthusiastically introduced by a proud Sir Joseph Banks. Bligh had befriended Omai during his return journey to Tahiti aboard *Resolution*, on Cook's third expedition.

Once at the island Bligh decided it was best not to anchor. Instead he hoisted the Red Ensign to signal those on shore that the visiting ship they could see was British and friendly. He called for the ship's progress to be slowed to a near stop by systematically being hove-to then making sail, a procedure undertaken in the hope that the islanders would have time to make their way out from the shore in their canoes before the ship drifted too far away — and they did. However, the news they brought of Omai saddened

Bligh: he had died of natural causes '30 moons' after returning home.

While doing his best to hold his ship close to land, Bligh could not prevent *Bounty*'s slow drift out to sea – simply due to the considerable windage her hull-profile and rig presented. So it was no surprise that the islanders became anxious and quickly departed when they realised the distance between ship and shore was expanding. The call came for the buntlines to be eased and the sails to be clewed down, then, along with the headsails and spanker, trimmed to the wind angle – and with that the ship bore away to the west-by-south, on track to the Friendly Isles (Tonga), the first actual stop on a route that would eventually take them to the West Indies, more than half a world away.

Over the next few days the crew was kept busy with wet and squally conditions. 'Strong squalls with rain. Double reefed the topsails,' was an entry in the log; then a few hours later: 'Out all reefs fore topsail and loosed all staysails to dry.'

Despite the wet, it was solid sailing in a warm tropical environment, and *Bounty* claimed good miles. On the morning of 9 April, a sudden change came when a menacing, heavy black cloud rolled out of the east and headed for the ship. The crew readied themselves to reef the sails, then as they watched this ominous system close in, they were amazed to see a waterspout form and advance rapidly towards them. Knowing his ship could be seriously damaged should the twister hit, Bligh took no chances: he shouted an order to immediately alter course away from the waterspout, and for all sails to be taken in, except for the foresail, which would be enough to enable the helmsman to maintain steerage. Even so, the chance that the ugly vortex might hit *Bounty* remained real. The only thing the crew could then do was watch, wait and hope it would not make contact.

Those on deck were in awe as the spout continued on its deadly path; then as it came closer some took cover while others rushed down the companionway, seeking safety on the lower deck. The twister was almost frighteningly silent on approach – just a solid rustling sound – then it became a roar as it passed a mere 10 yards from the stern. Bligh, as was probably the case for everyone else, had never been so close to this type of maritime phenomenon, so he was pleased to be able to record his impressions of the dangers it posed: 'It is impossible to say what injury we should have suffered if it had passed directly over us. Masts I imagine might have been carried away, but I do not apprehend it would have endangered the loss of a ship.'

With *Bounty* sailing a route similar to that of previous voyages, there were no expectations of making any discoveries along the way. However, soon after sunrise on 11 April, there was great joy when an uncharted island was spotted about 15 nautical miles to the south-south-west. It was what is now known as Aitutaki, an atoll in the Cook Island group measuring about 25 nautical miles in circumference. Conditions were terrible at the time: from tropical thunderstorms delivering squalls – some that put the sails aback and others that called for all sails to be taken in – through to calms that glued the ship to the sea surface. So it was no surprise that it took 30 hours for *Bounty* to reach a position 3 miles off the southernmost point of the reef that encircled the many islands making up the atoll.

During the approach Bligh plotted the island's location on his chart and noted the dangers the reefs presented to navigators. He also observed that there was no sign of smoke from small fires, so it could be that the atoll was uninhabited.

From deck level he could easily see the white water being generated by the large ocean swells pounding on the reef. It was fair warning that it would be dangerous to take the ship much closer to shore, so he went aloft to survey the scene from the crow's nest: 'As I drew nearer to the southernmost key I discovered from aloft that there were a number of natives within the reefs, but as the sea broke dreadfully round them I imagined none were capable of getting through it to come out to us ... I was however agreeably surprised by a visit from four men in a single canoe.'

He also realised he had discovered a true South Pacific paradise. There was a huge lagoon behind the reef and islands with long strips of white sand on their edges. The background for these beaches comprised thousands of coconut palms swaying in the warm trade wind.

As the canoe came alongside, Bligh beckoned the men to come aboard, and when they did they showed no apprehension or surprise – except that they would not venture below deck. Both sides were able to communicate in a basic form as the men spoke the same language as Tahitians.

During this sometimes difficult but effective discourse it became apparent that the islanders knew of hogs, dogs and goats, but they had none of them on their islands, so Bligh took pleasure in putting a young boar and sow aboard their canoe along with yams and taro. He added to this booty a knife, a small adze, some nails and a looking-glass. He expected the men would then leave the ship, but instead, while two of them boarded the canoe, the other two remained on deck and proposed that they stay all night – probably because some of the *Bounty* crew were trying to negotiate for women to be brought from the island for their pleasure then taken back the next morning. It is astonishing that these crewmembers would take it upon themselves to enter into such negotiations without any consultation with the commander, but it wasn't to be: Bligh was already concerned for the safety of the ship, so to stop in such hazardous and uncharted waters overnight would have been unthinkable. He then told his visitors his predicament – that *Bounty* might be wrecked on a nearby reef should he choose to stay. On hearing this, the islander men decided to leave immediately.

The ship's log on that day contained one additional brief but interesting note: 'Punished John Sumner with twelve lashes for neglect of duty.' There were no other details but a few days later Sumner would be among the ranks of the mutineers.

Soon *Bounty* was under full sail again and being propelled into the night by a refreshing southerly breeze while heading towards Annamooka (in Tonga). At dusk the following day, 23 April, the easternmost of the islands in the group was sighted from the masthead, but unfortunately, with the wind as it was, the ship had to ply to windward for the next six hours for a gain of just 10 nautical miles before anchoring in the safe shelter of the roads. It was by then too dark and dangerous to continue sailing any further through the reef-strewn waters, especially after having had one close call during their approach: 'At two o'clock this afternoon in standing to the westward, we suddenly saw the bottom on which we had only at one time four fathoms. By direction from the lookout aloft we hauled to the northward and deepened in two minutes.'

In the morning *Bounty* was surrounded by canoes as it moved to the best anchorage at Annamooka, and while standing at the rail looking down on the friendly throng Bligh recognised a lame old man, Tepa, from when he was last there with Captain Cook twelve years earlier. Tepa was invited aboard, and soon after struggling up the boarding ladder from his canoe and being greeted on deck he was enquiring after Cook and others. He also told the captain that two chiefs Bligh had met there in 1777, Paulehow and Feenow, were at nearby Tongataboo and would shortly come to *Bounty*, but for some unknown reason they hadn't arrived by the time the ship departed.

With *Bounty* manoeuvred into place, the call was made to release and lower the anchor, and here Bligh once again had cause to vent his anger over the lethargic and indifferent attitude that seemed to be spreading like a cancer throughout the ranks. The bower buoy, which is used to mark the location of the ship's anchor, sank soon after the anchor had been set, and Bligh was adamant it was lost only 'for want of a little exertion in Mr Elphinston, the mate, in getting into a boat to get hold of it'. The anchor had to be hauled up again and the buoy replaced.

While that exercise was underway the captain chose to be taken ashore so he could organise the ship's wooding and watering requirements with the chiefs. About 300 people greeted Bligh when he reached the island. He was pleased to learn two things: that the convenient site Cook chose as a source of water remained the best, and the pineapples he had planted were proliferating.

Bligh took time to record in great detail the impressive and large 'sailing canoes' used by the islanders – the forerunner of the catamaran we know today. 'What we call the canoe is formed of two joined together by strong cross-pieces ... really a wonderful piece of art and contrivance, sailed with great swiftness and managed with much cleverness,' he observed. 'On the gunwale is erected a stupendous stage or platform strongly secured by lashings, and on this a hut or place of shelter, or sometimes a magazine for their provisions and valuable articles. In these vessels go whole families and a numerous attendance, and I have counted 90 passengers on board some of those that have already come to see us,' he wrote.

At daybreak the following day two parties were sent ashore, one comprising eleven men under the direction of Fletcher Christian to collect water; the other, which saw four men join William Elphinston, to gather wood. Bligh ordered Christian's party to be armed, but those arms were to remain in the boat, while Elphinston's men were unarmed. Both groups were also directed to remain 'unconnected with the natives', but within an hour the 'wooders' had allowed themselves to be surrounded by an 'amusing' group of natives, and while they were distracted an axe and adze were stolen – both extremely valuable tools for the expedition. Bligh commented in the ship's log after the incident:

> The men cleared themselves of the neglect as they could not comply with every part of their duty and keep their tools in their hands, and they therefore merit no punishment. As to the officers [referring to Fletcher Christian in particular] I have no resource, or do I ever feel myself safe in the few instances I trust to them. These islanders are a clever dextrous set of people, and would ever take advantages if they saw people negligent ... our iron utensils are jewels of inestimable value to them.

Later, with the assistance of Tepa, the axe was recovered, but not the adze.

Morrison's journal gave a somewhat different account of the incident, stating that the islanders became threatening and 'so troublesome that Mr Christian ... found it difficult to carry on his duty'. He added that Bligh damned Christian for being a 'cowardly rascal', asking him if he was afraid of a set of naked savages while he had arms. Christian replied: 'the arms are no use while your orders prevent them from being used ...'

By the end of Sunday, 26 April, the expedition commander felt he was being slated from two sides – the natives on the island, and a growing number of his crew who were becoming increasingly intransigent. He had earlier sent Fryer ashore to collect more water, and the botanist, David Nelson, to gather some interesting species of plants. As a consequence: 'these gentlemen both met with losses by the rabble. One lost the grapnel and the other a spade and met with some insults.' The spade was soon located but the grapnel had vanished, so with the principal chiefs, Paulehow and Feenow, not being present to command the islanders and insist the missing grapnel be returned, Bligh took the law into his own hands. He decided to set sail while holding two lesser chiefs, and all other islanders who were then on board, as hostages, until it was delivered to the ship. He recalled:

At one o'clock in the afternoon, unmoored and got under way. Many canoes about us. I now told the two Tubows, Latoomylange Qunocappo and another old chief, that I should keep them on board until the grapnel was returned. Vastly surprised, canoes were sent away for it, but they notwithstanding assured me it could not be brought tonight for it was not on Annamooka but some other Island. I however detained them until sun down, when they began to be very uneasy and beat themselves about their eyes with their fists and at last cried bitterly. I now told them I should not detain them any longer and called their canoes alongside to take them in, at which they were exceedingly rejoiced, and when I presented each of them with a present of a hatchet, a saw and several large nails, knives and gimlets, they fell into a degree of crying and showed such gratitude and thanks for my goodness that it affected all of us. I told them all English people were their friends and that thieving from them was what they always resented. They acknowledged it and embracing me with a flood of tears we parted.

Regarding the loss of the grapnel, Morrison's version contained some important points that possibly contributed in part to the mutineers seeing their act, which was less than 48 hours away, as being even more justified. He noted that, with the grapnel having been stolen and not recovered, Bligh had made prisoners of the chiefs and that the canoes alongside were ordered to cast off and stay astern of the ship. His journal reads: 'At this the chiefs seemed much displeased and were ordered down to the mess room where Mr Bligh followed them and set them to peel coconuts for his dinner. He then came up and dismissed all the men but two, that were under arms.' Morrison added that before the crew was dismissed the captain did not hold back in telling the officers and men 'that they were a parcel of lubberly rascals'. Morrison then states that during this dressing-down Bligh aimed a pistol at William McCoy and threatened to shoot him for not paying attention. William McCoy would be one of the most active of the mutineers, a man who would subsequently die a violent death on Pitcairn Island.

Having set sail on the evening of 26 April, *Bounty* was by noon the next day sailing west-north-west between the islands of Tofua and Agoodoo. Bligh's narrative relating to this part of the voyage, which was written some time after the event, concludes: 'Thus far, the voyage had advanced in a course of uninterrupted prosperity, and had been attended with many circumstances equally pleasing and satisfactory. A very different scene was now to be experienced. A conspiracy had been formed, which was to render all our past labour productive only of extreme misery and distress ...'

Interestingly, either because he didn't place any great emphasis on it or had no desire to record it, Bligh made no reference to one final incident aboard *Bounty* which Morrison recorded at length: 'In the afternoon of the 27th Mr Bligh came up, and taking a turn about the quarterdeck when he missed some of the coconuts which were piled up between the guns, upon which he said that they were stolen ...' Morrison reported that Bligh insisted this theft could not have taken place without the knowledge of the officers, but they denied all. According to Morrison:

> Mr Bligh replied 'then you must have taken them yourselves,' ... He then questioned every officer in turn concerning the number they had bought and coming to Mr Christian asked him. Mr Christian answered 'I do not know, sir, but I hope you don't think me so mean as to be guilty of stealing yours?' Mr Bligh replied 'Yes, you damned hound, I do. You must have stolen them from me or you could give a better account of them. God damn you, you scoundrels, you are all thieves alike, and combine with the men to rob me – I suppose you'll steal my yams next, but I'll sweat you for it, you rascals. I'll make half of you jump overboard before you get through Endeavour Straits.'
>
> He then called Mr Samuel and said 'Stop these villains' grog and give them but half a pound of yams tomorrow, and if they steal them I'll reduce them to a quarter.' The coconuts were carried aft and he went below. The officers then got together and were heard to murmur much at such treatment, and it was talked among the men that the yams would be next seized as Lieut Bligh knew that they had purchased large quantities of them and they set about secreting as many as they could of their own.

Virtually from this moment the embers that had ignited idle talk of a mutiny were now ablaze. Adding fuel to the flames was Bligh's short fuse, tongue-lashings and his motives for floggings – and finally the incident relating to supposedly stolen coconuts. These potentially violent and hardened seafarers were mostly from the lower ranks, contemptuous of discipline, and had had enough.

As embittered as they were, though, by Bligh's use of the lash, when compared with other Royal Navy captains, the revered Captain Cook included, Bligh was a restrained disciplinarian. Flogging was part of life in His Majesty's Britannic Navy during this century: it was approved in the Articles of War. The fact is that over a period of sixteen months Bligh brought out the lash on just seven occasions, yet while Cook has been lauded as a hero, Bligh has been reviled, maligned and damned through modern history as a merciless flogging captain. Sir Joseph Banks, who knew both captains extremely well, gave this insight into Captain Cook's management of his crew: 'Cook's sailors got more floggings than compliments ... they got drunk whenever they could get drink. They had tapped every cask of wine on board. They grumbled and growled and swore.' Also, while Bligh was known for his intolerance, sarcasm and anger towards his men, he mellowed as quickly as he exploded.

As night fell, *Bounty* sailed on while the conspirators counted those among them who would support a rebellion, and before long they knew an uprising against their captain could succeed: maritime history, beyond comprehension within the Royal Navy, was in the making.

During the early part of the night Bligh followed his usual procedure, first spending time at his desk below, checking charts then, with quill in hand, making entries in the ship's log, the final one being: 'Served fresh pork and yams as yesterday.' John Fryer recalled, 'I had the first watch, and between ten and eleven o'clock Mr Bligh came on deck, as he always did, to leave his orders for the night. At that time we were on speaking terms – but I am sorry to say that was but seldom.'

Bligh paced the deck while making observations of wind, weather, sea conditions and the trim of the ship. He also chatted with Fryer and the man at the helm. At midnight, after giving his final instructions to Fryer, he went below to his cabin and retired for the night.

For those on deck everything appeared very quiet. However, only yards away the conspirators were formulating the finer points of their clandestine and seditious plot.

CHAPTER EIGHT

Pacific Ocean, 1789

Mutiny!

It was a tick before six o'clock in the morning of 28 April 1789. The first hint of daylight was extending its way across the horizon after a night of light winds and a moon that was in its first quarter. *Bounty* was coasting along slowly and almost silently before a light east-south-easterly wind. The only regular sound came from the surge of the bow wave each time she breasted a gentle South Pacific swell, and the occasional creak from aloft as the masts, yards and rigging responded to new pressure caused by a subtle change in motion.

Fletcher Christian, the man Bligh looked upon as a friend from their merchant days, and whom he took aboard on strong recommendation as the master's mate for this voyage, had been listed as the officer-of-the-watch from four o'clock in the morning, but officer-of-the-watch he wasn't. Instead, he had been secretly orchestrating what Bligh would very shortly declare to be 'one of the most atrocious acts of piracy ever committed'.

While the captain and the majority of his crew slept peacefully, Christian sent word to rouse those supporting the mutiny – the men who most wanted to rid the ship of its captain, take control and return to Tahiti. They were to prepare for action. The plot was outlined from man to man in hushed tones on deck and below: where each rebel was to be stationed during the coup, and what their immediate role would be. They had to ensure that no one who might support Bligh became aware of the uprising and sounded the alarm. They would get only one chance at this, and the hit had to be perfect.

The signal was given that all was in readiness – the time was now. Christian grabbed a cutlass and strode purposefully to Bligh's cabin, bursting in and seizing him while he slept. He was backed by the master-at-arms, Charles Churchill, the gunner's mate, John Mills, and Able Seaman Thomas Burkett, while another three mutineers stood guard outside. 'On seizing me they tied my hands with a Cord behind my back and threatened me with Instant death if I spoke or made the least noise,' Bligh recalled. 'I however called so loud as to alarm every one, but the Officers found themselves secured by Sentinels at their Doors.'

Other mutineers acted swiftly and in unison throughout the ship, ensuring that none of the crew whom they thought might support the captain and go to his aid was able to do so. William Elphinston was tied to his berth; David Nelson, William Peckover, Thomas Ledward and the ship's master, John Fryer, were confined to their cabins, while on deck other rebels stood guard at the companionway amidships to ensure no officers 'put their heads above the hatchway'.

Once certain everything had gone according to plan and that his men had control of the ship, Christian and his supporters dragged the still shouting captain from his berth and forced him on deck clad only in his nightshirt. Bligh saw immediately that the mutineers had achieved easy access to the arms chest because the three men with Christian, and many other mutineers, carried muskets, bayonets and cutlasses.

Equally surprising for him was that none of his faithful had had any inkling trouble was brewing. Christian had plotted and executed the act so perfectly that even two of the men on morning watch, Thomas Hayward and John Hallett, only realised there was an uprising when they were confronted by men who, in addition to being well armed, were in control of the ship's weapons.

If Bligh took time to consider the magnitude and meaning of the circumstances confronting him it was only brief. Standing proud amid those supporting the insurrection he demanded to know the reason for this 'violent act'. The only response forthcoming was that he would be killed instantly if he did not hold his tongue. Around this time the bosun, William Cole, and the previously troublesome carpenter, William Purcell, were ordered on deck to assist the mutineers, and when they arrived they saw Bligh standing abaft the mizzenmast with his hands secured behind his back and under the close guard of Christian, who restrained him with a tether.

The mutineers were determined to maintain the momentum of their carefully hatched plan. Cole was ordered under the threat of death to immediately hoist the 16-foot jollyboat out of its chocks and over the side, but he was reluctant to do so. Sensing Bligh and some of the crew were to be put in the boat and abandoned, he demanded that the mutineers be aware that the jollyboat was leaking and unseaworthy. Christian then ordered that it be replaced by the larger and heavier launch. Once this boat was in the water Hayward, Hallett and John Samuel were then ordered to board it, a direction that prompted Bligh to demand why this was happening. The mutineers' response was little different from that given to his previous enquiry: 'Hold your tongue, Sir, or you are dead this instant.'

Regardless, Bligh remained steadfast in his bearing. He thought he might cause some level of uneasiness and instability in the ranks of the mutineers – that some might begin to consider their error of judgement and waver. At the same time he hoped that by continuing to make every endeavour to exert his authority over the scene he might rally support among his faithful so they could bring into effect a plan to attack the 'rascals' and change 'the tide of affairs'. He wanted the mutineers to realise the consequences of taking the ship when their actions were considered under the Articles of War.

Christian, who had by then swapped his cutlass for a bayonet, would have none of it. He pressed the cold steel blade against the captain and threatened him with instant death should he continue to be so vocal: he would run him through. Bligh recalled the chilling moment:

> The Villains round me had their pieces Cocked & Bayonets
> fixed, and particular People were now called upon to go in
> the Boat, and were hurried over the side. With these people
> I concluded of course I was to be set adrift. I therefore made
> another effort to bring about a Change by expressing myself in
> such a Manner as to be saluted with 'Blow his Brains out'. The
> Men under Arms round me had their Pieces cocked which so
> enraged me against those ungrateful Wretches that I dared them
> to fire and they uncocked them.

For a brief moment Bligh thought he might have found an ally among the rebels. Isaac Martin, one of those guarding him, appeared to have a change of heart – he showed signs of an inclination to assist him: 'As he fed me with shaddock, (my lips being quite parched with my endeavours to bring about a change) we explained our wishes to each other by our looks; but this was observed.' Martin was immediately stood down as a guard, and with that he declared he would join the men already in the launch, which he promptly did. However, following a barrage of threats and a tirade of abuse from his cohorts on deck, he realised he had no option but to return to the ship.

There was a second chance for retaliation and recovery of the ship, but it, too, fell short. When Bligh was being bundled out of his cabin and jostled towards the quarterdeck he had made eye contact with the master, John Fryer, whose cabin was opposite. In Fryer's cabin were two loaded pistols and ammunition, something Bligh desperately wanted the master to remember – with those he could probably retake the ship. 'I had ordered these pistols for the use of the Officer of the Watch following the desertion of three crew on January 24, in case of desertion in the Night. They were at first kept in the binnacle, but upon consideration that they might be stolen from there they were ever after kept in the master's cabin.' Unfortunately, though, Fryer was 'so flurried and surprised' by the mutiny he forgot that he had them; it wasn't until Churchill burst into his cabin and took them that he remembered they were there and what an asset they could have been.

Bligh would learn later that Fryer actually had devised his own plan to try to overthrow the mutineers: he would plead with Christian to be allowed to stay aboard and once that permission was granted he intended to muster support among the outlaws and resume control, possibly when the majority were drunk. But suddenly captain and master found themselves at cross purposes: Fryer obviously wasn't aware that Martin, who was then still guarding Bligh, was prepared to change sides and support the captain. Fryer quietly asked Bligh if he had any objections to him remaining with the ship, to which Bligh whispered, 'Knock him [Christian] down, Martin is good [for us].' Christian saw the communication and while not hearing its content, he sensed his mutiny might be about to unravel, so he ordered that Fryer be escorted back to his cabin. Bligh did not see the master again until he was forced aboard the launch.

The mutineers knew exactly who they were going to consign to the boat, in particular all the officers. One by one they were singled out and hustled to the side of the ship where they were made to climb over the bulwark before descending the side ladder into the launch. No one was allowed to have any contact or communication with their captain. 'I now unhappily saw that nothing could be done to effect the recovery of the ship,' he lamented. 'There was no one to assist me, and every endeavour on my part was answered with threats of death.'

When the majority had gone to the launch, Christian then further motivated his men by arranging what could only be deemed a mock celebration: he called for a slug of rum to be taken from Bligh's personal supply and served to each one of them so they could toast their success.

Morrison's account of the mutiny supports much of Bligh's version, but with a greater degree of colourful detail:

The night being calm we made no way, and in the morning
of the 28th, the Bosun came to my hammock and waked
me telling me to my great surprise that the ship was taken
by Mr Christian. I hurried on deck and found it true –
seeing Mr Bligh in his shirt with his hands tied behind him
and Mr Christian standing by him with a drawn bayonet in his
hand and his eyes flaming with revenge. Several of the men
were under arms, and the small cutter hoisted out, and the large
one getting ready. I applied to the bosun to know how I should
proceed, but he was as much at a loss as I, and in a confused
manner told me to lend a hand in clearing the boat and getting
her out which I did. When she was out, the small one was

got in. Mr Christian called to Mr Hayward and Mr Hallett
to get into the boat and ordered Churchill to see the master
and clerk into her. The Lieutenant then began to reason, but
Mr Christian replied 'Mămōō Sir, not a word, or death is your
portion.' Mr Hayward and Mr Hallett begged with tears in
their eyes to be suffered to remain in the ship, but Mr Christian
ordered them to be silent. The bosun and carpenter came aft
(the master and gunner being confined below) and begged for
the launch, which with much hesitation was granted, and she
was ordered out, while I was clearing her, the master came up
and spoke to Mr Bligh and afterwards came to me asking me if
I had any hand in the mutiny. I told him I had not, and he then
desired me to try what I could do to raise a party and rescue the
ship, which I promised to do. In consequence of which Jno.
Millward, who was by me at the time, swore he would stand by
me, and went to Muspratt, Thos. Burket and the bosun on that
score, but Churchill, seeing the master speaking to me ... came
and demanded what he had said. I told him that he was asking
about the launch, but Alex Smith who stood on the other side
of the boat told Churchill to look sharp after me saying 'tis a
damned lie Chas., for I saw him and Millward shake hands,
when the master spoke to them, and called the others to stand
to their arms, which put them on their guard.' As I saw none
near me that seemed inclined to make a push, and the officers
busy getting the boat in order, I was fain to do so too.

The bosun and others who were to go in the launch had collected
supplies they thought they would need to support what might lie
ahead – but in reality what that might be was unknown. They
gathered canvas, rope, sails to fit the launch's rig plus two water
casks, one of 8 gallons and the other 20. Purcell, despite his earlier

run-ins with the captain, was surprisingly ordered aboard the launch. Bligh had his theory as to why: 'It appeared to me that Christian considered keeping the Carpenter, but knowing him to be a troublesome fellow he determined he should go.' The upside to this was that he was allowed to take his carpenter's tool chest.

As the chest was passed over the side and handed down to the launch there was considerable jeering coming from the mutineers. Many didn't like it, some declaring amid profanities, 'Damn my eyes – he will have a vessel built in a month.' At the same time other mutineers were deriding those crammed aboard the launch, leaving them in no doubt as to the helpless situation they faced: 'They laughed at the situation of the boat, with it being very deep [in the water], and not having room for those who were in her.'

John Samuel, the ship's clerk and steward, made a valuable contribution by gathering a large amount – 150 pounds – of bread, some wine and rum, and most importantly a quadrant and compass for navigation. Much to Bligh's chagrin he was given no other navigational equipment. Bligh wrote in his account of the mutiny later:

> To Mr Samuel I am indebted for securing for me my journals
> and some ship's papers. Without these I had nothing to certify
> what I had done, and my honour and character would have been
> in the power of calumny without a proper document to defend
> it. All this he did with great resolution while being guarded and
> strictly watched. He attempted to save the time keeper and a
> box with all my surveys, drawings and remarks for 15 years past,
> which were numerous. Among these were my general surveys
> of the West Coast of America, East Coast of Asia, the Sandwich
> and Friendly Islands. But he was hurried away, being told, 'damn
> your eyes: you are well off to get what you have'.

Along with Bligh the following eighteen crewmen, 'the loyalists' who refused to join the mutiny, were crammed into the tiny 23-foot launch:

John Fryer	Master
Thomas Ledward	Surgeon
David Nelson	Botanist
William Peckover	Gunner
William Cole	Bosun
William Purcell	Carpenter
William Elphinston	Master's Mate
Thomas Hayward	Midshipman
John Hallett	Midshipman
John Norton	Quartermaster
Peter Linkletter	Quartermaster
Lawrence Lebogue	Sail Maker
John Smith	Able Seaman
Thomas Hall	Able Seaman
Robert Tinkler	Able Seaman
Robert Lamb	Able Seaman
George Simpson	Quartermaster's Mate
John Samuel	Clerk

There remained on board *Bounty* 'as Pirates and under Arms' the following:

Fletcher Christian	Master's Mate
Peter Heywood	Midshipman
George Stewart	Midshipman
Edward Young	Midshipman
Charles Churchill	Master-at-Arms

John Mills	Gunner's Mate
James Morrison	Bosun's Mate
Thomas Burkett	Able Seaman
Matthew Quintal	Able Seaman
John Sumner	Able Seaman
John Millward	Able Seaman
William McCoy	Able Seaman
Henry Hillbrant	Able Seaman
William Muspratt	Able Seaman
Alexander Smith	Able Seaman
John Williams	Able Seaman
Thomas Ellison	Able Seaman
Isaac Martin	Able Seaman
Richard Skinner	Able Seaman
Mathew Thompson	Able Seaman
Michael Byrne	Able Seaman
William Brown	Botanist's Assistant
Joseph Coleman	Armourer
Charles Norman	Carpenter's Mate
Thomas McIntosh	Carpenter's Mate

Of the 25 hands who would remain with *Bounty*, Coleman, Norman and McIntosh were held against their wishes (Heywood and Stewart would also claim this). Bligh wrote: 'they begged of me to remember that they declared they had no hand in the transaction. Michael Byrne, the fiddler who is half blind, I am told had no prior knowledge of what was done and wanted to also leave the ship.'

None of the mutineers were commissioned officers, and fourteen of the 25 were only able seamen. It wasn't until Bligh was finally ordered to leave the ship and board the launch that he could communicate with any of those going with him. He wrote:

They waited for me aboard the launch, and when the corporal informed Christian everything was in readiness he then told me 'Come, Capt Bligh, your officers and men are now in the boat and you must go with them. If you attempt to make the least resistance you will instantly be put to death.' Then, pushing me before him while holding me by the cord that lashed my hands, and while holding a bayonet, he urged me to the side of the ship, where, while surrounded by a tribe of armed ruffians, I was forced over the side.

As the captain went they untied his hands, and here he made this observation: 'Notwithstanding the rough treatment I received, the memory of past kindnesses by me appeared to produce some signs of remorse in Christian.' As the mutineers forced Bligh into the launch, the beleaguered captain asked Christian if this was fair considering the instances of friendship he had been shown. Bligh wrote that Christian 'appeared disturbed' by his question, and answered thus with 'considerable emotion': 'That, Captain Bligh, that is the thing: I am in hell. I am in hell.'

Once Bligh had joined the others in the launch, Christian ordered that it be moved to the stern of the ship and secured there, but before that Fryer was called on to return the pocket watch Churchill was adamant he had in his pocket. Knowing the great value the timepiece would be as a navigation aid, Fryer denied he had it, saying it was in his cabin. Churchill persisted, threatening that there would be trouble if he didn't return it. Fryer relented and handed up the watch.

With the launch abaft the ship, Bligh shouted to Churchill that he should be given two or three muskets for protection. The mutineers lining the taffrail responded with boisterous laughter and derisive taunts. 'Shoot the bugger,' one rebel shouted, while another was heard to say, 'See if he can live on half of a pound of yams.' Amid the abuse Churchill reminded Bligh that he was well acquainted with islanders in the region so he would not need the muskets. Eventually, though, Churchill relented – to a degree – and had four cutlasses thrown into the boat, along with a few pieces of pork and some unwanted clothing. All the time the mockery and humiliation heaped on the nineteen men wedged into the launch continued unabated.

Cole, the bosun, had been observing that drunkenness was taking hold of the mutineers and that they might, as he told Bligh at the time, 'certainly do some mischief if we stay much longer'. He strongly suggested to Bligh they should cast off and take their chances. Bligh readily agreed.

Fryer noted in his journal: 'There was very little wind and we out oars and pulled directly astern the ship which was steering WNW. We steered to the ESE, our reason for so doing being that we wanted to get clear of the ship as soon as possible so we were out of the reach of the guns.'

Soon they were more than 200 yards away – a somewhat safe distance – and with it they were also beyond the sounds of the raucous celebrations aboard *Bounty*. The only noise then, was the consistent thud that came each time the six oars that were slotted into the gunwale came under load. The conditions could not have been better for a 'settling in' period – there was virtually no wind and the seas were calm – and it appeared the weather would stay that way for some time. On Bligh's direction some of the men stationed at the bow raised the foremast and unfrapped its sail so it was ready should a breeze arrive. At that stage Christian and his rebels knew exactly where they were headed – Tahiti – while those on the launch, who remained in a state of total disbelief, knew nothing of their future. The absurdity of this situation was clear: one vessel of near 90 feet in length had a crew of 25 sailing in one direction, while a small boat a quarter of *Bounty*'s length was packed with nineteen men, floating barely above the sea surface, and moving away in the opposite direction.

By now Bligh, who was sitting near the tiller with some of his officers, had decided they should head for the nearest island, Tofua, and once that course was established using the compass they were fortunate enough to have with them, Bligh's mind then turned to those who had betrayed him:

> A few hours before my situation had been peculiarly flattering. I had a ship in the most perfect order, the voyage was two-thirds completed, and the remaining part to all appearance was very promising. Every person on board was in perfect health.
>
> I began to reflect on the vicissitudes of human affairs; but in the midst of this I felt an inward happiness which prevented any depression of my spirits ... I found my mind wonderfully supported, and began to hope – notwithstanding the calamity we had faced – that I would one day be able to recount to my King and country my misfortune.

His search within his mind for the principal reason for the mutiny was swift: the allure of the Tahitian women. That was the underlying trigger. The men hoped for a far more satisfying life among the Tahitians than what was guaranteed in England, and they were desperate to achieve it. He wrote that many of the mutineers 'were void of connections at home', so they were easily led to a new life on 'one of the finest islands in the world, where they need not labour, and where the allurements of debauchery are beyond belief'.

But why didn't the men simply desert in Tahiti, just as others had done from ships previously, rather than stage a mutiny? Bligh's theory on this was simple: deserters had always been captured and returned to their ships at the hands of island chiefs coerced by the ship's commander. This knowledge, plus the fact that *Bounty* was such a small ship, and that it carried no marines, meant a mutiny would be an easier and far more effective way to make good their escape to a new world and an idyllic life.

Regardless, Bligh was still mystified by how the rebels had managed to maintain such a high level of secrecy while fabricating their plan:

Thirteen of the party who were with me had always lived forward among the seamen; yet neither they nor the messmates of Christian, Stewart, Haywood, and Young, had ever observed any circumstance that made them in the least suspect what was going on. To such a close-planned act of villainy, my mind being entirely free from any suspicion, it is not surprising that I became a sacrifice. Perhaps if there had been marines on board a sentinel at my cabin-door might have prevented it; for I slept with the door always open so that the Officer of the Watch might have access to me on all occasions.

Additionally, the fact that Fletcher Christian was the mastermind was equally bewildering. Certainly, the previous day, Bligh and Christian had had stern words, as later reported by John Fryer. Christian was heard to reply to his captain, 'Sir, your abuse is so bad that I cannot do my duty with any pleasure – I have been [in] hell for weeks with you.' However, after the mutiny Bligh registered his thoughts towards Christian as being quite different: 'I was on the most friendly terms with Christian: that very day he was engaged to have dined with me, and the preceding night he excused himself from supping with me on pretence of being unwell; for which I felt concerned, having no suspicions of his integrity and honour.' He added, 'Here [with the mutiny] we may observe what height the baseness of human nature may achieve: not only is it ingratitude in its blackest dye, but eternal criminality against their country and connections.'

But enough of reflection on what is now past, thought Bligh. From that moment everything revolved around one word for his men and himself: survival. Initially this meant little more than staying afloat and reaching Tofua. Suddenly, though, all the men realised there was a lot more to survival than that – a large shark ripped its way across the surface of the ocean and, to their amazement, viciously attacked one of the oars before disappearing into the depths.

Within four hours of the mutiny, the mutineers aboard *Bounty* could no longer see the launch as it made its way towards Tofua. But the talk at the time was not so much about the fact that they had dispatched nineteen men in a small boat to what was almost certain death, but how little resistance there had been to the mutiny and how easily they had been able to take over the ship.

Morrison had said that when George Stewart and Peter Heywood were allowed on deck after the launch had been set adrift, Christian immediately went about explaining to them why he had been left with no option but to overthrow the captain and take possession of *Bounty*. He claimed he could no longer suffer the treatment he was receiving from Bligh, so the night before the mutiny he had decided to jump overboard and swim to shore to escape the abuse, a seemingly preposterous plan under the circumstances: *Bounty* was then 10 leagues – 30 nautical miles

– from the nearest island. Morrison says Christian had told three crewmen – Cole, Stewart and Hayward – of his plan and they then supplied him with some nails so he could construct a crude raft that would hopefully carry him to the shore. They also gave him a bag containing part of a roasted pig for food and some beads to trade with the islanders. However, while he apparently managed to assemble the basics of the raft and get it to the bottom of a boarding ladder on the side of the ship, the opportunity to make good his escape did not present itself – he had hoped those on watch would fall asleep, but they didn't. It was after three o'clock in the morning at that point, so Christian had no option but to sleep himself. A short time later, Stewart woke Christian and told him it was time for his watch. He also implored Christian not to abandon the ship and risk his life by swimming ashore, adding in a zealous tone, 'the people are ripe for anything'. There was already sufficient support from would-be rebels on board to seize the ship.

Back in England more than two years later, after some of the mutineers had been arrested and returned home for a court martial, Bligh strongly debunked the assertion that Christian had originally intended to abandon ship, saying *Bounty* was then so far from shore that he would almost certainly have drowned.

Immediately after the mutiny all the breadfruit plants were thrown overboard and the main cabin reclaimed for accommodation. By noon, when they could no longer see the launch from the masthead, the mutineers set *Bounty* on a new course to the south and divided the crew into two watches. As far as everyone was concerned, Tahiti was their ultimate destination, with Tubuai, one of the islands making up the Austral Group in French Polynesia, about 450 nautical miles south of Tahiti, being the first stop. But this was a plan that Christian held for only a few days. On contemplating the chances that a force would be sent from England to pursue and arrest them should news of the insurrection ever reach there, he devised another scheme.

The thud of the six oars and the splash from the blades stayed steady as the deposed seafarers rowed the launch north-east at a pace that was impressive considering the load it carried. Tofua was 30 nautical miles ahead, and it was important that they reached it before the weather deteriorated. Much to the oarsmen's delight, the surface of the glassy blue sea was soon being ruffled into darker hues by a zephyr that would prove to be a making breeze. Both masts were stepped through their respective thwarts then the lugsails hoisted and trimmed. It was easy going from then on, but in the launch's meandering wake lay what to this day is the best known and most ill-famed mutiny in maritime history.

CHAPTER NINE

New Holland, 1789

The incredible launch voyage

Having reached Tofua safely, then over the following four days managing to find only a meagre replenishment of supplies, Bligh and all but one of his eighteen men had made their incredible retreat from the island in the face of the cold-blooded horde of tribesmen – all of whom were intent on slaughtering them. Having just witnessed John Norton being brutally stoned to death on the beach, they knew there was no turning back, even though the heavily laden launch was already under threat of being overwhelmed and sunk by a strengthening gale and seas that were on the rise. The oarsmen continued to pull hard as the launch headed for the horizon and the sun descended. There was little talk, the atmosphere being one of stunned disbelief, shock and wonder.

They knew their only option was to attempt the extremely dangerous passage across the open ocean to Timor and the Dutch East Indies if they were to have any chance of making it to England. They were in the hands of the elements in what would be a perilous voyage of more than 3600 nautical miles. There was little going for them: Bligh had been grudgingly allowed the very basics of navigation equipment by Fletcher Christian – he didn't even have a chart to work from – so it would be his skill as a mariner and navigator, his scant knowledge of the northern waters of New Holland's east coast and the area around Timor, along with his leadership and the dedication of his men, that would get them through. In their favour was the prevailing wind at that time of year, a south-east trade wind, placing their destinations downwind. Still, this didn't guarantee safe passage. So many other circumstances could wipe them from the face of the sea: starvation, because of the miserable amount of food on board; rudder or rigging failure; and exposure to the extremes of wind, rain, sun and salt water. Beyond this, their ever-present and unwelcome companion would be the threat of capsize, or the boat succumbing to the ferocity of the wild weather and the breaking waves they would inevitably face. They were not deterred, however, as this was their only path to salvation.

Before nightfall, and with the glow of the volcano atop Tofua still evident in the east, the men took stock of their provisions: near 150 pounds of bread, 28 gallons of water, 20 pounds of cured pork, three bottles of wine, and 5 quarts of rum. There were also a few coconuts and some breadfruit, but the latter had been trampled and crushed while they were escaping from Tofua. Bligh did some calculations, then advised his men that what food they had would last eight weeks providing they rationed it to one-and-a-half ounces of bread and a quarter-pint of water – about a cupful – per man per day. The pork would be treated as a delicacy for as long as possible. The men accepted this decision 'with a great deal of cheerfulness'.

Bligh knew that despite the worsening conditions it was safer to head off shore immediately instead of holding a position in the lee of the island, his theory being that if they stayed close to shore the islanders could be lurking at first light and resume the pursuit. So, from that moment, what is today recognised as a near impossible and unparalleled voyage across uncharted seas, was underway.

It was eight o'clock. Bligh had already called for the smallest area of sail possible to be set – a deep-reefed fore-lugsail – and subsequently divided the men into watches: 'Our lodgings are very miserable and confined and I have it only in my power to remedy this by putting ourselves at watch and watch so that one half is sitting up while the other has no other bed than the bottom of the boat or upon a chest and nothing to cover us but the Heavens.'

It was baptism by fire, or more fittingly, flood, during that first night. Conditions deteriorated to the point where as many hands as possible were doing their best to bail water out as fast as it was delivered by the succession of waves bursting over the stern and cascading through the length of the boat. This water was particularly hazardous whenever the launch surfed down a large wave because it would flood to the forward sections, and its weight, combined with that of the men forced to sit at the bow, could easily cause the boat to nose-dive and submerge. If that happened, there would be no chance of recovery: eighteen wretched souls would be hurled into the ocean, all destined to perish.

This water also got to their food, as Bligh revealed: 'Our bread was in bags, and in danger of being spoiled by the wet: to be starved to death was inevitable, if this could not be prevented ... Fortunately the carpenter had a good chest in the boat, into which I put the bread the first favourable moment.' This comment, and the complete detail of the entire open-boat odyssey, was recorded dutifully by Bligh in a notebook he appropriated from Thomas Hayward soon after the mutiny. Somehow he managed to protect it safely from the elements ('kept in my bosom') for the duration of the voyage, and fortunately, by making his notes and sketches using indelible iron gall ink, it exists to this day. Among the entries are navigational recordings, rough sketch charts of some of the islands they passed, and a chart showing the launch's track through the

Great Barrier Reef and onwards. Its contents were subsequently used in the case against the ten mutineers who were eventually captured and returned to England.

As the tempest continued to rage, the men bailing frantically found their efforts frustrated by equipment lying in the bilge of the boat and washing around. Everyone recognised this as being another critical threat, so Bligh had no hesitation in ordering that each man retain only one spare set of clothing and that 'the rest be thrown overboard, with some rope and spare sails'. This move lightened the boat, which made it a little more manageable in the rough conditions.

They sailed through the night under the heavily reefed lugsail – just enough to hold them on course and provide sufficient speed to lessen the chance of their being pooped by a big breaking wave. The blazing red sunrise the next morning would soon confirm there was truth in the seafarers' adage 'Red sky in the morning, sailor's warning' because within hours the wind was blowing at gale force. There was no Beaufort scale back then, but this probably translated to around 30–35 knots: 'The seas ran so high that when we were between them the sail was becalmed then when we were on top of the sea it proved too much to be set, but I was obliged to carry it because we were now in very eminent danger of distress, the sea curling over the stern by then was obliging us to bail with all our might. A situation equally horrible perhaps was never experienced.' Having endured the full ferocity of this first night at sea, and with everyone then literally fighting to save themselves and their shipmates, Bligh felt it was appropriate to reward them: 'I now served a teaspoon of rum to each person, (for we were very wet and cold) with a quarter of a breadfruit, which was scarce eatable, for dinner.'

The captain also realised that the course they were holding towards northern New Holland might mean they would sight the rumoured islands of Feejee (Fiji). This was a long shot, though. The only indication of where this chain of islands was located, as Bligh recalled, came from the most basic information – that is, when islanders in Annamooka had pointed in a general west-north-west direction during Captain Cook's third voyage. Still, the thought of being the first European to discover them excited him. He and everyone else aboard the launch knew that after their close call with the islanders at Tofua, they would only land there in the most extreme of circumstances.

The conditions were not doing the men any favours: the tropics it was, but the weather was anything but balmy and benign, and the wind was no longer a gentle and refreshing trade wind. Forty-eight hours on from Tofua, they were still in the middle of a severe storm which, in addition to endangering the vessel, brought extreme levels of cold and fatigue to all on board: 'The nights were very cold, and at daylight our limbs were so benumbed, that we could scarce find the use of them. At this time I served a teaspoonful of rum to each person, which we all found great benefit from.' However, spirits lifted on this same day, 4 May, when they saw a small, flat island in the distance. During the next 24 hours other islands kept emerging above the horizon ahead and before long Captain Bligh and his men felt convinced they were the first Europeans to ever sight Fiji. As satisfying as this was, there was disappointment on board when the men realised some of the bread was already rotten. It was vital to their survival, however, so they decided it should be eaten.

To this point, Bligh's navigation had been little more than dead-reckoning based around the latitude and longitude of their departure point, the average course, and an estimation of their speed through the water. But now necessity became the mother of invention; using bits and pieces he'd found in the launch he made a crude form of a log which, if it worked, would provide a reasonably accurate reading on their speed: 'I had hitherto been scarcely able to keep any account of our run; but we now equipped ourselves a little better, by getting a log-line marked, and, having practiced at counting seconds, several could do it with some degree of exactness.' This makeshift log-line comprised a length of light rope with a series of knots tied in it at a given distance – in this case they probably used the overall length of the launch or an oar as a measurement guide. A block of timber, weighted so it was barely buoyant, was attached to one end of the line and lowered over the side into the water. This block would remain almost stationary in the water as the boat moved forward, and while one crew member counted the knots in the line passing through his hands another would count the time to fifteen seconds. Then, by knowing how much line had run out in that time, they were able to calculate how long it had taken the boat to cover a known distance. Using that figure for the conversion, they could determine how many nautical miles (1 nautical mile equaling 6076 feet) they were covering in an hour.

Bligh's resourceful seamanship came to the fore in this predicament. His judgement had to be perfect if everyone onboard was to survive. His superior seamanship and navigation, plus a rigid control of rations, were vital. However, *Bounty*'s master, John Fryer, would have you believe none of this judging by the narrative he wrote about the voyage following his return to England. His relationship with Bligh had been strained for much of the time since they arrived in Tahiti and after the mutiny he had become increasingly truculent. Once home, his sympathies turned towards the mutineers and the more rebellious of the men in the launch, so much so that after Bligh was lauded in England for his remarkable achievement, Fryer wrote, 'There was others in the boat – that would have found their way to Timor as well as Captain Bligh and made everyone with them more pleasant.'

Apart from the daily ration of bread, the men were, at this stage, receiving a quarter of a pint of coconut milk and two ounces of pork each day, and as paltry as this appeared, it was proving to be sufficient. One day, though, they thought for a brief moment they might experience a change of diet when they hooked a fish on a lure trailing behind the launch – 'but we were miserably disappointed by it being lost in getting into the boat'.

Their real concern was that unless heavy rain fell and they could capture it effectively their water supply might be exhausted before they reached New Holland. Up until now, there had been too much salt spray in the air when it had been raining heavily, so it was not drinkable. They knew they had the option to land on any of the islands surrounding them and search for food and water, but as Bligh explained, it was not worth the risk: 'I dared not to land, as we had no arms, and were less capable to defend ourselves than we were at Tofoa.'

The following day, 7 May, their voyage almost ended in disaster when they unwittingly sailed across a coral reef covered by little more than 3 feet of water. Fortunately, the depth stayed constant and they didn't run aground, so they made their way safely to the other side of the reef and deep water. Had they been in a much larger vessel, they would have grounded on this well-camouflaged hazard and possibly been wrecked.

While the launch meandered its way through this maze of spectacular and often rugged islands of 'Feejee', Bligh the marine cartographer came to the fore. He sketched the profile of many of the islands and also approximated their position by noting a latitude and longitude. As a result, Bligh created the first-known chart of the Fiji Islands – or Bligh's Islands as they were originally named.

Just hours after their first close call with a reef the launch went within yards of being swept onto one of the islands. A sudden change in the current forced them towards it, and they avoided being wrecked by rowing as hard as they could towards deep water. This relief was to be short-lived once more, as another threat emerged:

> We now observed two large sailing canoes coming swiftly after us along the shore, and, being apprehensive of their intentions, we rowed with some anxiety, being sensible of our weak and defenceless state ... Only one of the canoes gained upon us, and by three o'clock in the afternoon was not more than two miles off, when she gave over chase. Whether these canoes had any hostile intention against us is a matter of doubt; perhaps we might have benefited by an intercourse with them, but in our defenceless situation it would have been risking too much to make the experiment.

In John Fryer's recollection of events during the voyage, he agreed in general with what Captain Bligh had written in his narrative. However, this apparent threat from the canoes was one situation where there was some dissension among the crew: 'When the canoes were chasing us I was rowing and Captain Bligh was steering, and both Mr Cole and Mr Elphinston found fault with Captain Bligh's steerage, to the point where they were very much alarmed. When one of the canoes was gaining on us the Captain said, "Hurry my lads. If they come up to us they will cut us all to pieces."'

Fryer then claims that *Bounty*'s sailmaker, Lawrence Lebogue, challenged the captain, saying his decision to run was frightening everyone 'out of our wits'. He suggested they should stand and fight, and declared that Bligh was seen to be 'the first man

TOP CENTRE: A miniature portrait of Bligh (ca 1814), which was in the possession of Bligh's daughter Elizabeth. This miniature shows William Bligh in the uniform of either a rear-admiral or vice-admiral, ranks he achieved from 1814. CENTRE RIGHT: This miniature portrait of Mary Putland (nee Bligh) was painted the year before she accompanied her father to Australia where he took up the position of Governor of New South Wales. BOTTOM RIGHT: Bligh's signet ring with the motto 'finem respice': 'consider your end'. BOTTOM LEFT: A portrait of Elizabeth (Betsy) Bligh (nee Betham) by John Webber, who was the official artist on Captain James Cook's third voyage of discovery around the Pacific.

Courtesy NLA

Courtesy SLNSW

TOP LEFT: George Carter's 1781 painting of the death of Captain Cook in Hawaii.
BOTTOM LEFT: Bligh's telescope, thought to be the one he used from the time he
joined the navy until he returned to London following the *Bounty* mutiny.
TOP RIGHT: *In Adventure Bay, Van Diemen's Land* by George Tobin, HMS *Providence*'s
third lieutenant on Bligh's second breadfruit voyage. BOTTOM RIGHT: HMS *Resolution*
and HMS *Discovery* in the Arctic Sea, by Thomas Luny.

In Adventure Bay, Van Diemens Land 1788   Page 67.

TOP LEFT: Bligh and eighteen others are cast adrift from the *Bounty* in an open boat by Fletcher Christian and his fellow mutineers. BOTTOM LEFT: An aerial photograph of Bligh's passage in the Great Barrier Reef, 150 nautical miles south-south-east of Cape York. TOP RIGHT: Two pages taken from Bligh's notebook with his listing of the mutineers and their physical descriptions and a rough navigational sketch of the open boat's progress. CENTRE RIGHT: A smoothed, hollowed-out coconut shell used by Bligh during the open-boat voyage, inscribed 'W Bligh, April 1789' and 'The cup I eat my miserable allowance out.' BOTTOM RIGHT: Bligh and his comrades attempt to land on Tofua Island, depicted by Robert Cleveley. This was an unusual work for Cleveley who specialised in naval battles.

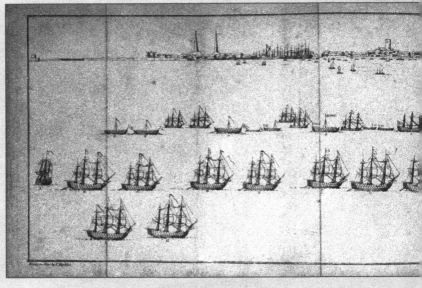

TOP: Bligh's depiction of Lord Nelson's attack on the Danish Line and City of Copenhagen, 2 April 1801. BOTTOM LEFT: Admiralty commission under seal papers appointing Bligh Commander of HMS *Falcon*, 1790. CENTRE RIGHT: *Action Off Camperdown*, 11 October 1797, by Thomas Sutherland. BOTTOM RIGHT: Identified as of Dutch origin, this sword is likely to have belonged to Admiral de Winter who surrendered his flagship *Vrijheid* to William Bligh at the Battle of Camperdown.

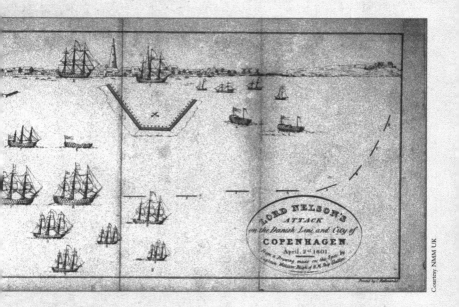

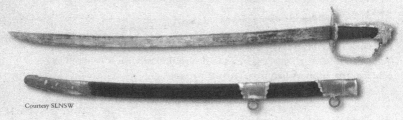

Drawings by William Bligh from his *Providence* sketchbook, Adventure Bay, Tasmania, 1792. TOP LEFT: A sketch and description of what is believed to be an echidna. TOP RIGHT: A heron. BOTTOM: A parakeet.

frightened'. Fryer stepped in, telling Lebogue, 'If you speak another word, I will come and heave you overboard ...' With that, the confrontation passed.

Bligh later reflected that these canoes were the same style as those of the Friendly Isles, confirming he was correct in not wanting to land on any of the islands. The similarity between designs left 'little room to doubt of their being the same kind of people'.

This exhausting day did finish on a high note, with a powerful thunderstorm allowing them to catch enough rainwater to increase their store to 34 gallons. It was the first time since they had begun their enforced voyage that they could completely quench their parched palates. But while their thirst was quenched, pain from the forced confinement was starting to wrack their bodies. Bligh wrote, 'Our limbs were dreadfully cramped, for we could not stretch them out, and the nights were so cold, and we were constantly wet, that after a few hours sleep we could scarce move.'

His effort to be fair to all in distributing the rations was made easier a week into the passage when he created a set of scales made from two coconut shells. Fortunately the men had found some pistol balls in the bottom of the launch, and in knowing 24 of these weighed one pound, Bligh used one as the appropriate counterweight to balance the ration of food for each man: 'I now served each person an ounce of the rotten bread and a gill [about half a cup] of water for their supper.' During the day he had also taken time to prepare his men for the worst. He knew there was no guarantee he or any of the crew would survive this ordeal, so he wisely decided to pass on his knowledge of the location and coastal environment of New Guinea and New Holland – thanks to his time with Captain Cook – so that they might be able to navigate their way there, and remain safe, should he not survive the passage. He also made some sketches for them.

While they continued to gain confidence in their handling of the launch they still held grave concerns about being swamped by the worst of waves during a severe storm, so they took the opportunity of fair weather to erect a 'weather cloth'. Using some canvas, and by rigging rope shrouds between the gunwales and the masts, they were able to create a 10-inch-high curtain around the boat that effectively increased the freeboard and gave them a better chance of keeping water out. Just hours later their handiwork was put to the test and it possibly saved them:

> About 9 o'clock in the evening the clouds began to gather and we had a prodigious fall of rain with severe thunder and lightning. By midnight we caught about 20 gallons of water. We were now miserably wet and cold. I therefore served to each person about a teaspoon full of rum to enable us to bear with our distressed situation ... The weather continued to be extremely bad and the wind increased. We spent a very distressing night without sleep in heavy rain. At daylight the only relief was the light itself. The sea was constantly breaking over us and we kept two persons bailing. We had no choice except to steer before the waves to avoid filling the boat.

Even in such atrocious weather Bligh did everything to plot their position as accurately as possible through dead reckoning: 'I observed the latitude to be 15° 17'S; course N 67° W; distance [covered] 78 miles; longitude made 10° W.' Maintaining this record every day was essential as the Great Barrier Reef, off New Holland's north-east coastline – a coral macrocosm standing as a natural fortress – was a near impenetrable barrier on which it would be all too easy to come to grief. It was vital to know when they needed to be on high alert.

Having left the islands of Fiji, Bligh set a course he hoped would see them leave the New Hebrides to their south – but it was only a guess because, without charts, they were all but sailing blind. In the following five days the eighteen seafarers endured a constant barrage of thunderstorms and gales: elements that combined to generate large and malicious breaking seas. Scant sail was set – only enough to provide some degree of safety and steerage – but it remained a white-knuckle ride. Each time the low-lying launch was picked up by the surge of a following sea it would shoot forward in a cumbersome fashion, rolling from gunwale to gunwale and copping a bellyful of seawater over the side at the same time. While two sailors were head-down in the bilge and bailing frantically, the anxious looks on the faces of the others said everything: they knew they were as close to the brink as they ever wanted to be. So much could go wrong; deep down the men prayed that the pintles and gudgeons, the hinges that attached the rudder to the transom, did not fail. If they did, the launch would immediately broach, lie beam-on to the seas, and water would overwhelm them. It would be the end.

Bligh's notes said everything:

Gales and very squally weather with a high breaking sea, so that we are miserably wet and suffer great cold in the night. In the morning at day break I served to every person about a teaspoon full of rum ... Our limbs being so cramped as scarce to feel the use of them. Our situation was now highly dangerous, the sea frequently running over our stern which kept us bailing with all our strength. At noon the sun appeared which gave us as much pleasure as in a winter day in England.

Then the next day: 'Having again experienced a dreadful night, the day showed to me a poor, miserable set of beings full of wants but nothing to relieve them. Some complained of great pains in their bowels, and all of having but little use of their limbs. What sleep we got was scarce refreshing being covered with sea and rain, and two persons were always obliged to keep bailing.'

Hour after hour, day after day, the gales and heinous conditions continued unabated, as did the suffering for the men. Since there was no chance of drying their clothes, Bligh told everyone to strip down and wring their clothes in the ocean: 'by which means they received a warmth which they wouldn't have enjoyed while wet with rain. It would assist them in being more exempt from catching cold, and violent rheumatic complaints ... constantly shipping water and very wet suffering much cold and shivering in the night ... constantly bailing.'

First light had barely presented itself at six o'clock on the morning of 14 May when, in the distance, stretching from the port aft quarter to the port forward quarter of the launch, there were four large and high islands, between 18 and 22 nautical miles away. During the next six hours they sighted two more islands, and more came within the following 24 hours. These were the New Hebrides, but Bligh remained uncertain because, without any charts, he had no way of confirming it. Like all European explorers venturing into this region, he knew of the existence of the New Hebrides: they had been discovered in 1602 by Spaniard Pedro Fernández de Quirós, a man who, unfortunately for him, was best remembered for being the least significant of all the great Portuguese and Spanish explorers over two centuries. Because the main island was so large, Quirós thought he had discovered the much searched for Great Southern Continent, so he named it *Terra Australis del Espiritu Santo* – the Southern Land of the Holy Spirit. Immediately after this discovery his sailors mutinied and forced him to sail home to Spain – so he didn't get to explore any of his find.

Reaching the New Hebrides meant that in two weeks these eighteen abandoned men had already defied an almost certain death and covered some 1200 nautical miles of treacherous open ocean at an average of 4 knots – and they were about halfway to the coast of New Holland. This should have brought them joy, but the constant hammering from the weather, the lack of food, and the sheer fatigue they were facing had every one of them wondering if they could go the distance. Bligh described this 'miserable situation':

> We are now but little better than starving with plenty [of islands] in view, but we could not risk going ashore to get relief – prolonging of life even in the midst of misery is preferable while we have hopes of surmounting all our hardships. For my own part I consider the general run of cloudy and wet weather to be a providential blessing to us. Hot weather would have caused us to have died raving mad with thirst, yet now, although we sleep covered with rain or sea, we do not suffer that dreadful calamity.

During the previous few days the wind had been significantly southerly in its direction, so Bligh was concerned they might be making too much leeway and they might be driven onto the coast of New Guinea, 'In which case most probably an end to our voyage would soon be the consequence.' So, with the gale still blowing and the seas literally breaking over the launch, he had to take the risk and insist that the course be held more to the south in a bid to avoid such a catastrophe.

From this point the men were confronted by nothing else but a 1200-nautical-mile open expanse of ocean. There would be no point of refuge until they were safely inside the Great Barrier Reef.

Everyone was starting to look emaciated – they were starving – and while Bligh would have liked to distribute larger portions of food, he stood steadfastly by his original plan, except for the odd occasion when he decided to include one ounce of pork with each serving.

By now the magnitude of their plight was unimaginable. Incredibly, while bailing to keep the boat afloat was originally looked upon as an exhausting and unpleasant chore, it was now considered to be their only form of exercise. If there was another pleasure to be had, it was the rum: 'The little rum I have is of great avail to us, when our nights are peculiarly distressing I issue a teaspoon full to each person, which brings joyful tidings when they hear of my intentions.'

After sixteen days at sea the men would have been forgiven for thinking they had survived everything nature could throw at them, but on this day it was obviously the devil who was dealing: at midday a waterspout came whirling across the sea surface and almost scored a direct hit. It was yet another miracle escape.

Bligh had now plotted a course he hoped would see the launch reach New Holland well to the south of what is now Cape York. This tactic would allow him to sail north along the eastern edge of the Great Barrier Reef, for some distance if necessary, in search of an opening to the protected water inside the reef. From there they could easily reach shore and search for food before starting the next stage towards Timor. But would they even get to New Holland? On 19 May, Bligh's log revealed some serious concerns: 'Constant rain and at times a deluge. Always bailing. At dawn of day some of my people half-dead. Our appearances were horrible. Extreme hunger is now evident, but thirst no one suffers. What little sleep we get is in the midst of water, and we wake with severe cramps and pains in the bones.' A few hours later things were looking up: 'At noon the sun shone out and revived everyone.'

But the following day the worst weather had returned, and they were beginning to wonder how much more torture they could bear before surrendering:

> Our distress is now extremely great – we are covered with so
> much rain and sea breaking over us that we can scarce see or
> make use of our eyes. Sleep, although we long for it, is horrible:
> for my part I seem to live without it. We suffer extreme cold
> and every one dreads the approach of night. About 2 o'clock
> in the morning we experienced a most extreme deluge of rain.
> It fell so heavy that we were afraid it would fill the boat, so
> we were obliged to bail with all our might. It continued until
> dawn, when I served a large allowance of rum.

The following two days were even worse:

> Our situation today highly perilous. If ever men experienced
> the power and goodness of divine providence we have done
> so this day. Several heavy seas broke over us and almost filled
> the boat. Obliged to carry sail yet tremble every minute for
> losing the mast. Our present situation would make the boldest
> seaman tremble that ever lived. We are obliged to steer a course
> running directly before the waves, which are breaking all over
> us. We must steer with the utmost care, as the least error with
> the helm would immediately bring our destruction.

Yet, even in such threatening conditions, Bligh also noted that he had, with great difficulty, made a sun observation at noon using his quadrant. He plotted a dead-reckoning position which put them about 200 nautical miles south of New Guinea's easternmost island and 500 nautical miles from the outer edge of the Great Barrier

Reef. They had been averaging an impressive 100 nautical miles each day during the gales.

If these desperate men, wedged shoulder-to-shoulder in this small, over-burdened boat, thought they had by now seen and survived the worst of it, they were mistaken. The following day, 23 May, came from hell, and Bligh later wrote of his great concern that some of his men wouldn't make it through the night. 'Everyone complained of severe bone aches – all of which were cured to some measure by about two spoonfuls of rum. After that, having wrung our clothes and taken our breakfast of bread and water, we were a little refreshed.'

After a further 24 hours came the first signs of real relief from the appalling weather in more than two weeks. The sun broke through with enough warmth for the scrawny, unkempt men to strip off their threadbare clothes and hang them out to dry. Bligh then had to make an extremely difficult decision. He took stock of the amount of bread remaining: at the current rate of consumption there was enough to last 29 days, but if they were unable to source any additional food on the coast of New Holland and forced to sail all the way to Java without replenishing supplies, then the bread would have to last six weeks. He was left with no alternative but to advise his men that if they wanted to ensure their survival, with there being no guarantees that other food would be found, each man would receive only $1/24$ of a pound of bread for breakfast and dinner, and none for supper. For Bligh, telling the men of the revised rations made him feel as though he was robbing them of life, but he assured them that should their situation improve, he would immediately increase the allowance.

Incredibly, within 24 hours of this decision came this entry: 'Providence seems to be relieving our wants in a very extraordinary manner. At noon we caught a Noddy [by hand], about the size of a small pigeon. I divided it with its entrails into eighteen portions and by the method of "Who shall have this?", it was issued, bones and all, with the allowance of bread for dinner. We used salt water for sauce.' They then caught the first of two boobies, birds which, much to their delight, are generally found in close proximity to land. 'Many of those flying about us almost landed on our heads. This bird is as large as a good duck. I directed it to be killed for supper and the blood was given to three of the most distressed for want of food. I divided the body, entrails, beak and feet into eighteen shares, and with an allowance of bread we made a good supper.' To their great delight the stomach of the second booby contained several small flying fish and squid. These were kept as a treat – tiny morsels that they were – to be shared by all for dinner.

These birds were a positive signal that land was near, because soon after came more encouraging signs: they sailed past tree branches, some of which were encrusted with barnacles while others showed signs of not having been in the water for long. Bligh then brought a rise in spirits among the men when he declared they must be in close proximity to 'the reefs of New Holland'. He ordered for the launch to be steered due west until the reef was sighted.

It was then 25 days since they had escaped with their lives from Tofua, and finally it appeared that the incessant gales were on the decline. As promising as that might have appeared, however, it created a different level of discomfort for the weather-weary sailors: 'The weather is now serene but unhappily we feel we are not able to bear the sun's heat, many of us suffering a languor and faintness which gives an indifference to life.' For the majority there had been little to do since departing the island, unless it was their turn to bail the boat, which even in moderate conditions was a requirement that came every ten minutes. For those not engaged in bailing they could only hang on, try to contain their fear, and pray that they would some day see Mother England once more.

That afternoon, 27 May, Bligh became increasingly convinced that land was not far ahead: 'The clouds stayed so fixed in the west that I had no doubt we were near to New Holland and every person, after taking his gill of water before supper began, enjoyed conversation on the probability of what they would find.'

At one o'clock the following morning came the sound every man had so desperately wanted to hear, even though it was a portent of danger. John Fryer told the story:

> I had been asleep in the forward part of the boat and relieved
> Mr Peckover as lookout at 12 o'clock. About an hour later I said
> to the man that was steering the boat, 'Don't you hear a noise
> like the roaring of the sea against the rocks', and the man said,
> 'Yes sir, I think I do'. I then stood up against the mast for some
> time, and at last I saw the breakers ahead. I immediately woke
> Captain Bligh and told him that the breakers were in sight.

Bligh saw the line of breakers pounding on the reef just a quarter-mile to leeward – dangerously close. He called for the aft lugsail to be lowered immediately, and as soon as he did a number of the men located amidships scurried to meet the order. Simultaneously, he changed the course to the north-north-east while calling on others to man the oars and pull hard away to ensure they escaped what he felt was imminent danger. Suddenly the aches, pains and stress of being at sea in such an abysmal environment for a month seemed to be forgotten. There was an air of elation; men found strength, and after little more than ten minutes of effort they could no longer see or hear the breakers. Fryer later noted that he did not interpret the danger to be as great as Bligh saw it, but even if Fryer was correct, it was still the captain's call: his job was to ensure the safety of the launch and all on board. This was another situation where there was no second chance.

By reaching the coast around 300 nautical miles south of the northernmost point of New Holland, Bligh had maximised his chance of finding a safe passage through the reef and reaching the shore. The search for that channel began at first light when, with sails again set, the launch bore away to the west – and into yet another perilous position. By nine o'clock the reefs were in sight once again. 'The sea broke furiously over every part,' Bligh later wrote. 'I had no sooner got near to them, and beyond them we saw the water so smooth that every person already anticipated the heartfelt satisfaction he would receive as soon as we could accomplish my intention.' But, unannounced, the wind changed direction and they realised the launch was then trapped in the crescent-shaped bay the reef formed; they could not clear either end of the long, curving reef, even by tacking and sailing as close to the wind as possible. Worse still, they were being blown to leeward towards the massive surf breaking onto the coral. Bligh continued: 'Our situation was now dangerous. I expected but little from the men on the oars because they had no strength to pull them, and it was becoming more and more probable by the minute that I would have no option and I should be obliged to take the reef.'

The size of the pounding surf left no doubt that the chance of successfully executing such a manoeuvre – surfing down a wave without broaching, then hopefully finding enough water covering the coral so they could sail across it and into the smooth water – was beyond calculation. The boat would almost certainly be wrecked, with fatal consequences. Seaman that he was, Fryer realised the dangers they faced so hastened to the stem of the boat and stood as high as he could, holding on to the luff of the foresail for security while he scanned the long stretch of white water to leeward and ahead, looking for a break in it. From the stern Bligh called to him, 'Mr Fryer, do you see anything?' to which Fryer responded, 'Yes sir. I see a place where there are no breakers.'

Bligh scrambled his way forward, between men and over thwarts, and quickly confirmed the sighting about one mile ahead, as well as an island in the same direction that was obviously inside the reef. With that he gave the helmsman the course to steer, and the two sails were trimmed to suit.

Initially it appeared to be a very narrow gap in the coral, but still there was no certainty it would lead to the sheltered leeward side of the reef: it might have just been an indentation that led to nowhere. However as they approached they realised it was a lot better than that. 'When we came in to it we found that providence had guided us into one of the finest harbour mouths that possibly could be,' Fryer wrote in his narrative. 'I will leave the reader to judge what feelings a set of poor fellows must have had at such a time as this as I do not have words to express myself.'

Within 30 minutes the launch had entered the channel and was heading west with the aid of a strong following current. They were safe. Every man had survived against the most implausible odds. 'We now returned God thanks for his gracious protection, and with much content took our miserable allowance of $1/24$ lb of bread and a gill of water for dinner.'

CHAPTER TEN

Great Barrier Reef, 1789

Desperate days

The moment the launch changed course to the west and entered the narrow, coral-lined channel nature had carved through the Great Barrier Reef, a spirit of euphoria and reprieve overwhelmed all eighteen men. Life had been pumped back into their veins, no matter how weak they were. The Grim Reaper no longer beckoned from beyond death's door. Every yard they covered as the launch pressed deeper into the passage, the closer they came to a safe haven – for the time being – and before they had gone little more than one nautical mile they were in a new world. Suddenly the seas that had threatened them for so long were nonexistent: the surface of the water was as smooth as glass. It was 28 May 1789, and the gap they had just found in the reef would become known as Bligh's Boat Entrance.

Their first desire was to replenish their food supply, and the most expedient way to do that was to try their hand at fishing on the inner edge of the reef. But the strong tidal current, which was on the flood to the north, was so powerful they could not get the anchor to hold in the deep water. Upon that realisation, Bligh then stood by his promise to have them in a secure anchorage and on shore at the first suitable spot they could find. He called for sails to be set and the oars to be manned as they headed for islands they could see close to the mainland, and with that, 'all our past hardships already seemed to be forgot'.

Ironically, on the very same day Bligh and his fellow outcasts reached New Holland, the mutineers made landfall for the first time since abandoning their former shipmates. But it wasn't in Tahiti, which Bligh and his men believed was the destination when *Bounty* disappeared into the distance, it was Tubuai, one of five islands in the Austral group, about 450 nautical miles south of Tahiti. Captain Cook was the first European to discover this beautiful tropical archipelago when he visited the island of Rurutu in 1769 during his first expedition into the South Pacific. On his third voyage to the region he recorded a sighting of Tubuai, but did not go ashore.

Morrison recalled that during his passage to these islands he and others aboard who were not comfortable with being associated with the mutineers gave consideration to a counter-attack in the hope they might retake the ship. The thought was that on the night *Bounty* set her anchor in Matavai Bay, 'we could easily get rid of those we did not like by putting them on shore and that in all probability our design might be favoured by an extra allowance of grog'. Morrison suggests that Christian somehow got wind of the scheme, but as he wasn't sure who might be involved, he took every possible precaution to prevent it happening – including arming himself at all times with a pistol, and having one of his staunchest allies, Churchill, guard the arms chest.

Christian had already decided Tubuai, and not Tahiti, would be the new home for the mutineers. It was a logical plan because anyone who might come searching for them in the future would only expect to find them in Tahiti, and not on a remote island hundreds of miles to the south which offered virtually no safe anchorage for a ship of *Bounty*'s proportions. He knew if he were to have the ultimate chance of achieving this goal he would have to impress the islanders from the outset, so he went to the extreme of having crew uniforms made from old canvas studding sails in the hope that the locals would sense the Englishmen had considerable authority and therefore make them very welcome.

That wasn't to be the case: the Tubuaian welcome was hostile, not convivial. No sooner had the mutineers landed than they were attacked by spear-carrying warriors and by the time they retreated to the ship and eventually set sail, twelve islanders were reportedly dead and many more wounded. The situation was so bad that Christian named the magnificent tropical lagoon in which they were anchored Bloody Bay.

This far from friendly reception did not deter Christian. He was convinced Tubuai was the ideal location for their secret colony, so he decided to sail north to Tahiti, collect as many hogs, goats and chickens as possible, then return and literally try to bribe his way into the community with an overwhelming display of generosity and kindness. If that didn't work he would use force.

On the passage to Matavai Bay, Christian exerted considerable authority over his lowly lot, insisting that no one mention their plans for Tubuai to any Tahitian. He also stated unequivocally that should anyone desert while they were there, they would be shot immediately upon recapture.

Understandably, the Matavai Bay islanders were as much surprised as they were overjoyed when *Bounty* reappeared on 6 June, just two months after departing. They hurried down the beach, launched their canoes and headed out en masse to where the ship was anchored, and once there they began clambering up the ladders and onto the deck, eager to welcome their English friends back to their paradise. Just as quickly, though, they were overcome by puzzlement: where was *Brihe* and other members of the crew, and what had happened to the breadfruit plants? Christian, Morrison wrote, was well prepared for the inquisition, telling them they had been met by Captain Cook, and he had taken Captain Bligh plus some of the crew, as well as the plants and the launch, aboard his ship while sending *Bounty* back to Tahiti to get hogs, goats and chickens for a new colony the king had ordered be established in New Holland. 'This being made known to the natives, none of us dared to contradict what Christian had said,' Morrison added. 'We knew that if they said anything contrary it would soon reach Christian's ears, because the Tahitians are not remarkable for keeping secrets.'

Meanwhile, Bligh and his men reached an island close to the coast just after five o'clock in the afternoon. It had a bay and a sandy point on its north-western side, both of which were well protected from the south-easterly trade wind.

I landed to examine if there were any signs of the natives being near us, but although I discovered some old fire places I saw nothing to alarm me. It appeared that we would be safe for the night. Everyone was anxious to discover something to eat, and soon oysters were found on the rocks, but as it was nearly dark only a few were gathered. We had to wait until morning before deciding where we would proceed to next, so I consented that one half of us should sleep on shore and the other in the boat … we took our rest for the night which happily was calm and undisturbed.

It was the first time in a month that they had been able to stretch out and sleep in a calm environment.

When the men stirred from their sleep around dawn Bligh was pleased to see that their spirits had lifted simply through being on land. Maybe, just maybe, everyone might retain the strength to overcome the inevitable suffering that would confront them during the remaining miles to Timor. With no signs of indigenous people in the vicinity he directed some men to search for food and water and others to carry out maintenance on the launch. This work took on a new meaning overnight when the rudder had separated from one of its hinges – a gudgeon attaching it to the transom had worked free and disappeared. Bligh and his men were profoundly lucky this breakdown happened near land. 'If this had happened at sea it would most probably have been the cause of our perishing as the control of the boat would have been lost,' Bligh wrote. 'It appears therefore a very providential circumstance that it has happened here where it was in our power to remedy the defect.'

When the men searching for supplies returned to the bay, there was more cause for elation – they had found plenty of oysters and fresh water. Using the heat of the sun and the small magnifying glass he had carried with him to read the divisions on his sextant, Bligh started a small fire. Equally fortunate under the circumstances was that one of the men had managed to grab a copper pot and take it with him when forced into the launch by the mutineers. Bligh used it to cook a stew comprising the oysters, pork and bread, then he served each man a pint of it. Everyone was extremely grateful, except the bothersome master, Fryer, who was adamant that water should have been added to the mix to create even larger portions. 'He showed a turbulent disposition until I laid my commands on him to be silent,' wrote Bligh.

Apart from the challenge of trying to reach Timor, the captain's priority continued to be the health of his men: 'The general complaints of disease were dizziness, great weakness of the joints and violent tenesmus [extremely painful constipation] as most of us had not had an evacuation since we left the ship. I constantly had a severe pain at the pit of my stomach, but none of our complaints were alarming.' Bligh also insisted that whenever they were on shore no man was to expose himself to the heat of the sun in the middle of the day; each was to find a shaded area under a tree or bush and rest during that period.

But even under these conditions, Bligh the explorer was ever present. Apart from logging the latitude and longitude of conspicuous islands and interesting topographical features on the mainland, he continually made notes of his general observations, including signs of native people and wildlife:

I found evident signs of natives having been to this Island, for besides fire places I saw two miserable wigwams having only one side covered. We found a pointed stick about three feet long with a slit in the end of it to sling stones with. It is just the same as the natives of Van Diemen's Land use. The track of some animal was very conspicuous on the land, and Mr Nelson agreed with me it was a kongorro [kangaroo], but how this animal can get from the mainland I know not, unless brought over by the natives to breed and render a supply of food certain to them.

Concern mounted when some of the men defied their captain's directive that they should not eat any of the fruits or berries found on the island for fear they might be poisonous. After gorging themselves on three different types of berries, the resulting stomach cramps and pains were so severe they thought they might die. However, as time passed and the symptoms eased, it was realised that the fruits were actually wholesome: they had simply over-indulged. Beyond that, their hunt for food on this island was frustrating because, while it was home to a wide range of parrots and other birdlife, they had no way of bringing them down without a firearm.

Before departing and heading towards the northern tip of this coastline which, thanks to Captain Cook's notes, they believed to be about 125 nautical miles away, Bligh decided that because he and his castaways had seen 'fresh life and strength' restored to them, and that the same day was the anniversary of the Day of Restoration of King Charles II, he would name it Restoration Island.

That evening there were grumblings from the master and the carpenter, Purcell, over not having a bread ration included with the pint-and-a-half of stew Bligh had made using the inner part of palm-tree tops and oysters they had collected. These protests caused a growing concern within the group as it appeared that Purcell and Fryer were trying to create disorder and gain support from those who were the most vulnerable, those who were weaker both physically and emotionally.

As the launch was their lifeline to Timor, Bligh once again took the precaution of having some of the crew sleep aboard that night while the rest slept around a small fire on shore. The following morning the weather and wind confirmed it was time to move on, so while some men went out to collect oysters and water others prepared the boat. Another stew was planned for dinner and as it had been discovered that all but two pounds of the pork had been pilfered by 'some inconsiderate persons − but everyone most sacredly denied it', the decision was made to put what pork remained in the pot with the oysters and see to it that everyone got their fair share.

What came immediately after this meal was little short of a mini mutiny. Just before noon Bligh gave an order to gather oysters for the journey as his plan was to sail in the afternoon. Full after the meal of stew, the men were distracted from this task, and some maintained they were too weak to collect oysters. Others thought it more important to get underway than to collect oysters. Bligh rejected their conduct and declared that they would pursue the voyage as he directed. The men were also advised there was sufficient bread to last 38 days if each person was limited to $^1/_{24}$ pound for breakfast and dinner each day.

At four o'clock on the afternoon of Sunday, 31 May, they were ready to leave the newly named Restoration Island. As they were about to board the boat they saw twenty spear-carrying islanders running down the beach on an opposite shore shouting and beckoning to them. But, on seeing the heads of other islanders peering over a hill above the beach, Bligh thought better of making contact with them, especially if they had canoes. It was high time to depart.

The course away from Restoration Island was north-by-west towards Fair Cape, which was about 16 nautical miles along the coast. With a strong tide and a south-easterly wind in their favour they were making good speed under sail. The decision was to travel through the night, and at three o'clock in the morning it was ever-vigilant eyes that again saved the day on what was an uncharted coastline, besides some scant hand-me-down knowledge from Cook's visit. The men sighted low-lying land not far ahead so Bligh instantly changed the course to the north-east, then soon after made the call to backtrack as they were trapped in a bay with no passage north. By daybreak they were again in safe water and on course, and as the sun began to illuminate the land Bligh was surprised by what he saw: 'The appearance of the country was all changed, as if in the course of the night I had been transported to another part of the world, for I had now a miserable low sandy coast in view with very little verdure or anything to indicate it was at all habitable to a human being.' Further on, as they passed between some small and scenic islands to the north of Fair Cape, they spotted seven islanders, some of whom they believed to be making hostile gestures towards them. Bligh took the launch close to the shore to observe them, but not one would come closer than 200 yards.

Obviously, there was no desire to land there. Instead, Bligh chose another island a few miles to the north, and no sooner were they there than more dissension broke out, principally between the troublemaking master and carpenter and Bligh, which had the potential to be an overthrow of his authority. It came after the captain had divided the men into three parties, two to go out in different directions in search of food, and the other to stay by the boat as a precaution against attack and a need for a swift escape. Having issued these directives Bligh became aware of mutterings among the men, some declaring they would rather go without dinner than look for food. It was nothing short of a challenge to their captain. Purcell was 'insolent to a high degree', telling Bligh he was 'as good a man as I was'. Concerned about how this behaviour might escalate, the captain chose to 'strike a final blow to either preserve my command or die in the attempt'. He grabbed a cutlass and challenged Purcell to defend himself. Purcell backed down, but with the support of only the botanist, Nelson, Bligh was outnumbered. Events did indeed escalate, as Bligh reported:

> ... the master very deliberately called out to the bosun to put
> me under arrest, and was stirring up a greater disturbance, which
> I declared if he interfered when I was in the execution of my
> duty to preserve order and regularity, and that in consequence

any tumult arose, I would certainly put him to death the first person. This had a proper effect on this man, and he now assured me that on the contrary I might rely on him to support my order and directions for the future. This is the outline of a tumult which lasted about a quarter of an hour. I saw there was no carrying command with any certainty or order but by power, for some had totally forgot every degree of obedience I saw no one openly scouting the offenders although they were known, and ... I was told that the master and carpenter at the last place were endeavouring to produce altercations and were the principal cause of the murmuring there. Such is generally the case under such disastrous circumstances as mine. I now took a cutlass determined never to have it from under my seat, or out of my reach, as providence had seemed pleased to give me sufficient strength to make use of it.

Following this incident Bligh took time to declare the names of the ten men who supported him and recognised his position as the leader of this extraordinary undertaking. They were Nelson, Samuel, Hayward, Peckover, Ledward, Elphinston, Hallett, Cole, Smith and Lebogue. This meant there were seven who were essentially opposed to him: Fryer, Hall, Lamb, Linkletter, Purcell, Simpson and Tinkler. Still, divided as they were, all then worked towards gathering food and water for the next stage of the voyage, and by the time they were ready to set sail they had an abundance of oysters, clams and small fish – which they had collected from rock pools – stored on board, along with a significant amount of fresh water.

While the men were procuring the supplies, Bligh climbed to the highest point on the island hoping to plan his overnight course to the north, and while he realised he was more distant from the mainland than expected, he decided they should try to reach the coast by nightfall and stop there. He believed there was less risk to their wellbeing by doing this than staying on the island and running the risk of being attacked by islanders, whom he was certain knew of their presence. The fact that they had found an old canoe measuring 33 feet overall and half buried in sand on the beach reinforced Bligh's theory that the natives on the mainland could have easy access to the island. However, going by the description he gave of the canoe, it might not have had its origins with the local inhabitants: it could well have been washed up from an island in the Pacific.

Before leaving, Bligh named this place Sunday Island. It is located about 3 nautical miles north of what is now Cape Grenville, which boasts a spectacular series of bleached-white sandhills and beaches. 'Milk white sand hills very conspicuous,' the captain logged as the launch sailed away from the cape on a west-by-north west course downwind towards a series of islands they could see close to the distant shoreline. They reached there at six o'clock in the evening: 'I got to it just at dark, but found it so surrounded by a reef of rocks that I could not land without a risk of staving the boat, and therefore I came to a grapnel for the night.' Bligh also noted with concern that the men were still complaining of 'sickness at the stomach and dreadful tenesmus'.

They spent a rough night at anchor, and with the wind increasing in strength from the southeast at first light, it appeared likely that the grapnel would not hold for much longer, so they decided to beach the boat on the ebb tide to ensure it remained safe.

Once on the beach the men saw turtle tracks in the sand and a profusion of birdlife, so they made plans to stay there overnight in the hope of catching turtles, bringing fresh meat to their supplies for the first time since the mutiny. They still initiated a search for food, but it brought little success. Then, just before noon, Nelson caused alarm in the camp when he returned supported by two others: he had suffered sunstroke. Bligh brought out the one medicine he had with him – wine: 'I gave it to him in very small quantities with some small pieces of bread soaked in it, and having pulled off his clothes and laid him under some shady bushes he began to get better.'

Still fearing that they might be attacked by natives from the mainland or nearby islands, Bligh insisted that their camp fire remain small after dark so it could not be seen: 'I was strolling about the beach to observe if I thought it could be seen from the mainland and I was just reconciled that it could not when all of a sudden the cay appeared ablaze and the fire seen at a more considerable distance. I therefore ran to know the cause of such an open violation of my orders.' The cause of the problem was again the master, Fryer, who had insisted on having his own fire for the evening, and in doing so managed to set alight the grass around the camp. As a result Bligh and most of his men had a near-sleepless night, staying alert in case islanders arrived on the scene, not that they had enough strength to fight off such an attack. Even so, while this fear loomed, two men went out at eight o'clock that evening searching for turtles while three others went after birds. The bird party returned at midnight with only twelve in hand – the small catch a result of Lamb apparently causing the flocks to take flight when he went off alone to snare his own birds. He caught only two, and ate them raw there and then. Of this incident Bligh wrote: 'Thus all my plans were totally defeated for which on the return of the offender I gave him a good beating.' There was further frustration when the men hoping to catch and kill turtles returned at three o'clock in the morning with nothing to show for seven hours of searching.

After a fitful night's sleep Bligh decided it was time to move on towards Timor: 'I tied up a few gilt buttons and some pieces of iron to a tree for any natives who might come after me, and happily finding my invalids much better for their night's rest, I got everyone into the boat and departed at dawn of day. Wind at SE course to the NBW.'

Within a matter of miles from the island the men realised they were heading back into dangerous territory. For the first time since sailing through the entrance to the Great Barrier Reef they were in exceptionally rough seas – probably due to converging currents and the fact that they were now beyond the protective barrier of the reef to their eastward side. Incredibly, while every one of the eighteen was still facing a fate unknown, Bligh's dedication to duty saw him continue to make navigational notes that he hoped would benefit other seafarers traversing this region in the future. He even went to the extreme of apologising for his shortcomings: 'I am sorry it is not in my power to speak of the depth of water, that would create trouble and delay, but as every other remark and observation that can be made falls upon myself, I can only say that a ship may pass wherever I omit representing danger, as far as a man's judgement can be relied on that is formed from appearances.'

They were now rounding the northernmost tip of the coast of New Holland and steering to the north-west. As they proceeded a group of large and bold islands came into view, which included what is now known as Horn Island, near Thursday Island. As there were so many Bligh named the area the Bay of Islands. That night they took shelter behind a sandy isthmus which Bligh would subsequently name Turtle Point because of the surprising number of turtle bones and shells his men found on shore: evidence of islanders feasting there, but not of late.

These islands represented the end of their coast-hopping experience and the start of another major trial – the long passage to Timor – and, as if the inherent dangers confronting these men weren't enough, another problem emerged: the captain's already difficult task of navigating them safely across an open sea was made even more complex. The watch the gunner had brought with him had stopped, and now noon, sunrise and sunset were their only markers of time.

All along, Bligh had continued to apply place names to points of interest until the launch emerged from the western shores of these islands to the north of Cape York. It was 4 June, and he noted: 'Here terminated the rocks and shoals of the north part of New Holland, for I could see no land to the westward of south.'

For most of the previous six days they had enjoyed some degree of respite following their remarkable passage from Tofua. Now they were back to open ocean sailing with nowhere to hide from extreme weather. Just five hours after clearing the land they were again subject to their pitiful conditions, but the captain could not help but notice that his men, despite their grossly weakened state, took it in their stride. None revealed any sign of despair: 'whoever had despaired would have been dead before I got to New Holland. I now gave everyone hopes that eight or ten days might restore us to a land of safety, and after praying to God for a continuance of his most gracious protection I served an allowance of water for supper and kept my course to the WSW to counteract a gale from the southward ...'

The sea state and wind strength were such that the crew rotated through stints of constant bailing, knowing that if they didn't the launch would founder and inevitably take them with it. In the evening some boobies began soaring around the boat and Bligh managed to grab one. The blood was drained from it and served to the weakest men for nutrition, while the carcass provided dinner the next day when it was served according to the usual way. Later there was disquiet upon the discovery that some of the clams hung to dry had been taken, but everyone denied it.

By now conditions were again appalling. It was a constant battle to keep water out of the boat and hold a safe and proper course down the face of the incessant and steep waves looming up from behind and breaking over the boat. By this time the men were so weak that the cold and wet were having a far greater impact on them than at any other stage of the voyage. Many were being sapped of energy and the desire to continue.

> Monday 8th June, 1789 – This day the sea run very high and we were very wet, suffering much cold in the night. I now remarked that the surgeon Mr. Ledward, and an old hardy seaman, Lawrence Lebogue, giving way very fast. I could only assist them by a teaspoonful or two of wine at daylight. Amongst most of the others I observe more than a common inclination to sleep – a symptom of nature being almost reduced to its last effort.

This was also to be a day of note for an all-too-different reason. Having covered around 3000 nautical miles they had their first catch on the lure they were trolling – a small dolphin fish. Each man was immediately served 2 ounces of the catch, including the offal, and the remainder saved for dinner the next day. The weather was still bringing fresh gales from the south-east, and while this ensured the launch made good speed there was no denying that the men on board would have given whatever they could if they were offered a reprieve from the constant battering. Their eyes were little more than red slits, their skin was salt-caked and raw from exposure to wind, sun and water, and even though they were in the tropics, within just 600 nautical miles of the equator, their wasted bodies shivered mercilessly from cold.

Yet, while life was being sapped from them, all of them somehow remained alive. Bligh's journal entry for the next day confirmed this: 'in the morning, after a miserable night, I began to see an alteration for the worse with more than half my people whose looks rather indicated an approaching end to their distresses. They received bread and water for breakfast and dinner.'

One more day brought them new hope, but there were also further signs of distress:

Birds and rock weed show us we are not far from land, but
I know such signs must be here, as a long string of islands
stretch to the eastward from Timor towards New Guinea,
I however hope to fall in with Timor every hour, or else I have
scarce a hope but I shall lose some of my people. An extreme
weakness, swelled legs, hollow and ghastly countenances, great
propensity to sleep and an apparent debility of understanding,
give me melancholy proofs of an approaching dissolution. The
bosun, when I was rallying him today, very innocently told me
that he really thought I looked worse than anyone in the boat.
The simplicity however with which he uttered such an opinion
diverted me, and I had good humour enough to return him a
better compliment.

Bligh's noon sighting brought 'universal joy and satisfaction'. They were then 33 leagues – about 100 nautical miles – from the eastern tip of Timor, and at their current rate of knots they should sight land within 24 hours. It was less than that because at three o'clock the next morning they could make out the distinct profile of a landmass: 'With an excess of joy we discovered Timor bearing WNW to WBW.' To ensure they remained a safe distance off shore Bligh had the helmsman change course to the north-north-east until daylight, then they bore away and ran down the south-east side of the island.

The level of elation among the men was fathomless. Bligh's notes read: 'It is not possible for me to describe the joy that the blessing of seeing the land diffused among us. Indeed it is scarce within the scope of belief that in 41 days I could be on the coast of Timor in which time we have run by our log 3623 miles, which on a medium is 90 miles a day.'

However, their joy was a little premature. Hell hadn't quite finished with them. They would soon face another epic battle against an ocean that seemed determined to consume them.

Bligh knew a Dutch settlement existed somewhere on the island, but he wasn't sure exactly where. Instinct told him it was most probably towards the south-west corner, so he elected to sail to the west along the southern shore. As they progressed they spotted some huts obviously belonging to Malays, but because the sea was running so high it would have been too dangerous to try to go ashore, so they continued on their course. That evening one of the crew managed to snatch a booby that came too close to his lightning-quick hand and it was instantly destined to be dinner at noon the next day. But this effort by Bligh to stretch supply out and ensure they would have something to eat until they reached land, where they could get more supplies, brought nothing but contemptuous complaints from Fryer: 'I had some difficulty stopping the master's muttering because I would not serve it for breakfast, for this ignorant man conceived he was instantly in the midst of plenty.'

After sailing along the coast for 25 miles that day, 12 June, not gaining any clues as to the whereabouts of the Dutch outpost and being desperately worried they would pass it, they hove-to for the night under a reefed lug foresail. Apart from the man designated as officer-of-the-watch, everyone did the best they could to sleep in their extremely overcrowded environment. That opportunity came to an end at two o'clock in the morning when Bligh opted to wear ship and run downwind towards the shore so they would be well placed to resume their search for the outpost. Fortunately, they had drifted only 6 nautical miles to leeward during the night.

One more day, and it was another day of fruitless searching along the mountainous coastline. With each day passing, Bligh could only watch as the weakest of his men took another step towards death. Again, that night, the launch went hove-to – 'that I might not commit a blunder in the night by running past any settlement'. By morning there was another strong gale blowing, but the troubled leader had no option but to push on in search of liberation from their hideous experience.

The heat of the day made the atmosphere extremely hazy, making the task more difficult. Even so, Bligh believed he could make out a gap between the coastline to which they had been sailing parallel, and land he could see in the distance, which he opted to sail towards. When the launch reached the shore they confirmed it was a large island, and on entering a sandy bay where they anchored, they assessed what lay around them and which way they might head in search of the settlement. As soon as they stopped, the master and carpenter again began stirring up trouble, this time complaining that they should be allowed to land on the shore and search for supplies. Bligh thought otherwise. While he had seen both smoke from fires and cleared land in the distance, he was not comfortable about landing there; he wanted to press on. But, having had enough of the sneering comments from the pair, he confronted them once more: 'I gave them the leave to quit the boat.' However, on realising they had no support from anyone else on the launch, they quickly decided to stay.

Bligh didn't hesitate following this showdown. The grapnel was brought aboard and the sails set for a course that would take them back towards what they then knew was the western end of Timor, just 15 nautical miles away. But almost as soon as they ventured onto the open water they were pounded by what was possibly the wildest weather they had experienced since leaving Tonga. A deadly fast-flowing current, which was running over a shoal and against a gale of wind, created a death trap for the launch: the closely formed waves were as steep as church spires and the launch struggled to climb above them. Torrents of white water cascaded over the gunwales and into the bilge, adding even greater weight to the already barely buoyant boat. It was in danger of literally being sucked under the surface of the sea.

Weak as they were, every man did what he could to return the water from whence it came. '... at this time I was steering the boat we were nearer being swamped than at any time,' was Fryer's recollection of this terrifying moment that came when they were – unknowingly – almost within sight of the Dutch settlement.

Somehow these desperate men again managed to win what was a fight to the end. The launch cleared the shoal and continued on a course towards the land ahead. Bligh wrote:

> At two o'clock this afternoon we discovered a spacious bay
> with a fair entrance about two or three miles wide. I now
> conceived hopes that my voyage was nearly at an end, as no

place could appear more eligible for shipping, and of course, likely to be the Dutch settlement. I therefore bore up and came to a grapnel on the east side of the entrance in a small sandy bay where we saw a hut, a dog and some cattle, and I immediately sent the bosun and gunner [Cole and Peckover] away to the hut in order to discover the inhabitants.

This mission was successful. They returned with five Malay men to where the dilapidated launch and its decrepit-looking occupants waited, and for the first time since the mutiny they knew they were close to surviving. Through animated sign language they were left in no doubt that the Dutch settlement where the governor resided was some distance along the coast to the north-east. The two words Bligh could decipher were *Bassar*, which he believed to be the governor's name, and *Coupang*, which was the name of the port. Through a continuation of their elementary sign language and a promise of financial reward, Bligh convinced one of the men to join them aboard the launch and guide them to Coupang – Kupang as it is today. To the profound joy and relief of the castaways, the Malays brought with them some cobs of corn. In addition there were some dried pieces of turtle, but these needed to be soaked in hot water before eating.

Fortunately their newly found pilot was eager to get underway, so the two lugsails were hoisted and soon the launch was making its way along the eastern shore of the channel between the two islands. This progress continued until early evening when the wind died to a whisper, so from there it was a call to man the oars. The men rowed until around ten o'clock, when it was obvious the tide had changed and they were making little or no progress against it, so the only option was to drop the grapnel and wait. For the first time since this amazing voyage began, Bligh felt confident they would achieve their goal within a matter of hours, so he rewarded his men with a double allowance of bread and some wine. The nightcap had the desired effect, for the next day the captain logged: 'At one o'clock in the morning, after the most happy & sweetest sleep that ever men had, I weighed and continued.'

Before daybreak came the most exciting sound imaginable for these desperate men – the sound of cannon fire – and while they could not see the source of the report, they knew they were within earshot of deliverance from their hell. Soon after, there were some shadowy but unmistakable profiles to be seen in the distance: 'Before day we discovered two square-rigged vessels and a cutter at anchor to the eastward,' the captain wrote, before elaborating on how the torment continued right to the end.

> I endeavoured to work to windward but we were obliged to take to our oars again having lost ground on every tack, and having kept close to the shore we continued rowing until four o'clock when I brought to a grapnel and gave another allowance of bread and wine to all hands. Being refreshed we again rowed until half an hour before day, when I came to a grapnel off a small fort & town called Coupang.

Incredibly, though, while they had survived this extraordinary voyage, there was no immediate rush to go ashore. Instead, Bligh did as expected of any eighteenth-century Royal Navy captain and followed protocol: 'When the bosun left the ship [*Bounty*], among the things he had thrown into the boat was a bundle of signal flags. These I had in the course of this miserable voyage converted into a small Jack, which I now hoisted in the main shrouds as a signal of distress, for I did not for very evident reasons choose to land without leave.'

With the distress flag aloft and flapping almost listlessly in the rigging in the morning breeze, the captain and his men sat humbly and patiently aboard the launch while their eyes scanned the shore, all the time searching for a sign of life and a signal that they were welcome. And one hour later it came: 'Soon after daybreak a soldier hailed me to land, which I instantly did.'

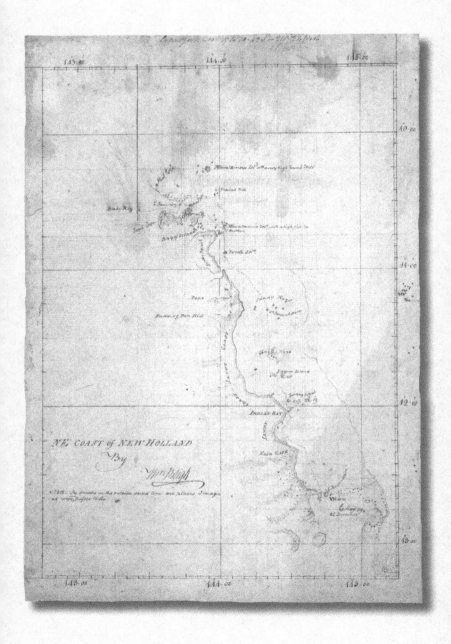

NE COAST of NEW HOLLAND
By

PART III

Captain Bligh

CHAPTER ELEVEN

Timor, 1789

From hell to home

When Bligh set foot on the shore in Coupang on Sunday, 14 June 1789, the abhorrent voyage of the damned was all but complete. By any standard it would have been considered a challenge of incomprehensible proportions, and unachievable, but it turned into a 47-day, 3618-nautical-mile crusade against often barbaric weather and an horrendously challenging sea. For nearly half the time he and his seventeen miserable men were out there, they were fighting everything the elements could fashion as a weapon – winds that blew a gale, menacingly savage and large foaming seas that threatened to overwhelm their small boat at any moment, and torrential rain. Their defence was simply an impoverished yet determined will to survive, and a captain who represented the ultimate embodiment of a great seafarer, skilful navigator and resolute leader. Now, after averaging between 100 and 110 nautical miles on most days, they were in Timor, and every one of them was alive, though barely.

Inevitably there would have been an air of amazement and disbelief when Bligh and his seventeen skeletal men were seen from the shore, all weather-beaten and bedraggled in a battered and worn-out vessel. Where had they come from in such a small boat, was the immediate question. Why so many men? Why were they in Coupang?

With the tattered remnants of the captain's Royal Navy uniform flapping in the early-morning breeze it would have been apparent to the Dutch soldier that he was looking at the commander of the group, and Bligh presented himself accordingly, with full naval procedure. As luck would have it, one of the first people to emerge from the inquisitive 'crowd of Indians' that had gathered on the shore – mainly Malays and Chinese – was an English sailor, from one of the ships anchored in the shelter of the narrow road between Coupang and the large island of Semau only a couple of nautical miles to the west. In the discussion that followed, Bligh learned that the governor of the settlement was seriously ill, so he made a request to be introduced to the English ship's captain, Captain Spikerman, who he was mistakenly led to believe was the second most senior person in the town.

The welcoming faces of the people and their surroundings were heaven sent for Bligh and his survivors. The launch, with the men still aboard, was immediately in front of Fort Concordia, which the supremely powerful Dutch East India Company (*Vereenigde Oost-Indische Compagnie*, or VOC) built after the colony was established in Coupang in 1630, a move that effectively brought about the end of Portuguese dominance in the region. VOC was by the standards of the day a company of gargantuan proportions, and the spice trade to Europe it was developing in these 'Spice Islands' was destined to make it considerably larger. It had been established as a chartered company in 1602 and quickly became the most remarkable organisation of the era – the world's first multinational corporation and the first to issue stock. Between 1602 and 1796 VOC sent nearly one million Europeans to work in Asia, while its charter saw it holding quasi-governmental powers that gave it the right to negotiate treaties, wage war, coin money and establish colonies. VOC was dissolved in 1800 after succumbing to corruption and massive debt. Its then territories became known as the Dutch East Indies.

It was extremely fortunate for Bligh and his men that this settlement existed. If it hadn't, there would have been few, if any, alternatives where they might secure the opportunity to be repatriated to England. They could have tried to get to Captain Arthur Phillip's newly established colony at Botany Bay, in New Holland, but in doing so they almost certainly would have perished through being so much more vulnerable to extreme weather. Apart from that destination, and Coupang, there was little else on offer.

Bligh was received 'with great humanity' by Captain Spikerman, who immediately ordered that the men be received at his own home. 'I now desired everyone to come on shore, which was as much as some of them could do, being scarce able to walk,' Bligh recalled. 'They, however, got at last to the house, and found tea with bread and butter provided for their breakfast.'

The look of joy and the recognition of deliverance by the men presented Bligh with the opportunity later that day to pen very effectively what he had seen and experienced at this time, a time when he was able to compare his horribly ravaged men with the healthy individuals who were their hosts:

> The abilities of the most eminent artist perhaps could never
> have more brilliantly shone them in a delineation of two groups
> of figures that at this time presented themselves, and where
> one might be so much at a loss to know which most to admire,
> whether the eyes of famine sparkling at immediate relief, or
> their preservers horror struck at the spectres of men. For anyone

to conceive the picture of such poor miserable beings, let him
fancy that in his house he is ... giving relief to eighteen, whose
ghastly countenances, but from the known cause, would be
equally liable to affright as demand pity; let him view their
limbs full of sores and their bodies nothing but skin and bones
habited in rags, and at last let him conceive he sees the tears of
joy and gratitude flowing over their cheeks at their benefactors.
With the mixture of horror, surprise and pity ... were the
people of Timor on giving us relief.

There was no rest for the captain this day. At eleven o'clock the
governor, William Adrian Van Este, who was dying from an
incurable disease, took leave from his sickbed and welcomed him.
Bligh would note later that on hearing of the almost inconceivable
magnitude of their trans-ocean voyage, Van Este 'considered
it as the greatest blessing of his life that we had fallen under his
protection'. The governor also advised him that his son-in-law,
Mr Timotheus Wanjon, was second-in-charge of the settlement
and would assist in every way. This took effect immediately
because by late morning arrangements were completed for Bligh to
be accommodated in a large, unoccupied house, which he insisted
he share with his men, who had by then received new clothes and
had their medical problems attended to by the town's surgeon.
After that Bligh watched all seventeen of them enjoy their first
'meal of plenty' in almost two months before he then dined with
his host, Wanjon, 'but I found no extraordinary inclination to eat
or drink, or did I find my stomach able to bear anything ...'

By mid-afternoon Bligh and his men were exhausted, and
most, including the captain, took time to rest. It was the first
time since the mutiny they had enjoyed any form of bedding and
reposed with any degree of comfort. Even so, many of them,

including Bligh, could not sleep: 'I found my mind more disposed to reflect on the sufferings I had gone through, of the failure of my expedition, but above all of the thanks due to Almighty God who had given me power to support and bear such heavy calamities, and to enable me at last to be the means of saving eighteen lives which would never otherwise have been thought of.'

His notes from that day revealed the distress he had felt in having to rigidly control the distribution of rations, and the emotional grief from having to refuse requests for more food. He never deviated from the agreement that he made with the men on setting out from Tofua:

The consequence of this care was, that at our arrival we had still remaining sufficient for eleven days, at our scanty allowance: and if we had been so unfortunate as to have missed the Dutch settlement at Timor, we could have proceeded to Java, where I was certain every supply we wanted could be procured.

The quantity of provisions with which we left the ship, was not more than we should have consumed in five days, had there been no necessity for husbanding our stock. The mutineers must naturally have concluded that we could have no other place of refuge than the Friendly Islands; for it was not likely they should imagine, that, so poorly equipped as we were in every respect, there could have been a possibility of our attempting to return homewards ...

When I reflect how providentially our lives were saved at Tofoa, by the Indians delaying their attack, and that, with scarce anything to support life, we crossed a sea of more than 1200 leagues, without shelter from the inclemency of the weather; when I reflect that in an open boat, with so much stormy weather, we escaped foundering, that not any of us were taken off by disease, that we had the great good fortune to pass the unfriendly natives of other countries without accident, and at last happily to meet with the most friendly and best of people to relieve our distresses; I say, when I reflect on all these wonderful escapes, the remembrance of such great mercies enables me to bear, with resignation and cheerfulness, the failure of an expedition, the success of which I had so much at heart, and which was frustrated at a time when I was congratulating myself on the fairest prospect of being able to complete it in a manner that would fully have answered the intention of His Majesty, and the honourable promoters of so benevolent a plan.

With respect to the preservation of our health, during a course of 16 days of heavy and almost continual rain, I would recommend to everyone in a similar situation the method we practiced, which is to dip their clothes in the salt water, and wring them out, as often as they become filled with rain; it was the only resource we had, and I believe was of the greatest service to us, for it felt more like a change of dry clothes than could well be imagined. We had occasion to do this so often, that at length all our clothes were wrung to pieces: for, except the few days we passed on the coast of New Holland, we were continually wet either with rain or sea.

The path to full health over the ensuing days was more rugged for some than others: even Bligh was suffering, but he still insisted on overseeing their welfare and recovery. Those who were capable were ordered to bathe before sunrise each day in a beautiful freshwater river nearby, and everyone had to make regular visits to the hospital so their progress could be monitored. Five days after their arrival at Coupang the captain recorded: 'Every person is now beginning to recover except myself. Great weakness and fever still hangs about me which keeps me confined. A little sago is the only thing my stomach can bear.' Three days later there were more encouraging signs: 'I began today to feel my health returning to me and my living is changed to a use of more solids. Some of my company have become unwell from having eaten too much. The sore feet and legs of some are troublesome to heal, they are however getting tolerably on and begin to lose their ghastly meagre countenances.' The fact that Bligh's health was improving saw him take up the governor's offer of the use of a horse, something that led him 'to take a small ride into the country' so he could appreciate and log details of the land around the settlement. Of the settlement itself he wrote: 'The town consists of about 150 houses including Malays and Chinese. Its situation is perhaps peculiarly desirable on account of the road and a fine river, and to the latter we may without error attribute the great share of health that the inhabitants enjoy.'

Half a world away, Fletcher Christian and his *Bounty* renegades were not finding it as easy as they would have liked when it came to establishing their South Pacific utopia. After being forced to sail to Matavai Bay following their unfriendly reception at Tubuai, the mutineers were beginning to question their leader and show signs of general dissent.

Christian retained his determination to return to Tubuai, while some others were thinking otherwise. It was vital that he gained the absolute support of the islanders if he was to secure the animals and other supplies necessary to establish his new community. Having convinced the Tahitians that Bligh and some of the *Bounty* crew had gone with Captain Cook to the new settlement in New Holland, which he said was named *Whytootackee* (Aitutaki – the name given to the South Pacific island discovered by Bligh with

Bounty) and was waiting there for *Bounty*'s return, Christian then added as an enticement that Cook had confirmed he would return to Matavai Bay once the colony was established.

The islanders' support for Christian was immediate and immense. The cargo that went aboard included 460 hogs, 50 goats, the bull and cow Captain Cook had left them, and some chickens, dogs and cats. They also discovered they had some unexpected guests after they departed for Tubuai – the nine men, eight boys, ten women and one female child who were aboard included some stowaways.

When they arrived at their destination on 23 June, their welcome was far friendlier than the previous time. Christian went ashore immediately to find a site for the fort he intended to build, and the moment he departed from the ship unrest broke out among the mutineers. Some defied his orders and also went ashore, where they stayed the night. Inevitably, Christian was starting to experience the disrespect and contempt of authority these men had previously shown towards Captain Bligh.

No sooner had work started on the construction of the fort than there were disturbances with the islanders. Quarrels erupted and as a consequence, Christian shot one islander dead and burned down the home of a chief. The unrest continued through to 10 September, when Christian called all his men together to discuss the situation, and their grievances, the principal one being a lack of female companionship. The vote that followed saw sixteen in favour of returning to Tahiti and nine against. The majority ruled.

Their departure from Tubuai was not as simple as the men hoped. While collecting their animals and other equipment to load the ship, they were trapped in an ambush by 700 hostile islanders. Serious bloodshed followed and before *Bounty* was able to set sail, a considerable number of islanders were killed and wounded and some of Christian's men had been brutally beaten.

When *Bounty* arrived back in Matavai Bay 48 hours later, the crew immediately split, sixteen leaving the ship to establish a life there, the remaining eight opting to stay with Christian and travel to a destination which was yet to be decided. Only James Morrison's journal gave any indication of what Christian's plans might be:

> It being late before everything was landed, Mr Christian told us that he intended to stay a day or two and hoped that we would assist him to fill some water, as he intended to cruise for some uninhabited island where he would land his stock (of which the ship was full, together with plants of all the kinds that are common in these islands) and set fire to the ship, and where he hoped to live the remainder of his days without seeing the face of a European but those who were already with him.

Come morning and *Bounty* had vanished. Christian had apparently surrendered to his beliefs that some of his supporters may change their mind if they stayed in Tahiti any longer, or that his presence might be discovered through the arrival of another ship. He was also convinced that should Bligh somehow, miraculously, find his way back to England, the Royal Navy would most certainly send a ship to the South Seas in search of the traitorous crew.

Unbeknown to everyone except himself at that stage, *Bounty* was heading to Pitcairn Island, a destination Christian believed would not be considered by anyone searching for the ship and its crew. His theory proved to be correct because it wasn't until nineteen years later, in February 1808, that the American sealer *Topaz*, under the command of Captain Mayhew Folger, stopped at Pitcairn Island and solved for the world the mystery of what became of Fletcher Christian and the last remnants of the *Bounty* mutineers.

On 24 June, ten days after Bligh and his waif-like outcasts from *Bounty* reached Coupang, the captain declared his next plan:

> My intentions being to leave Timor as soon as possible, that
> I might be enabled to leave Batavia [Jakarta, in Java] before the
> sickly monsoon sets in, my opinion being that if I remained
> here until the vessels that were in the road were ready to sail,
> I might not get to Batavia before the beginning of November,
> and thereby lose the opportunity of the Dutch Fleet that sails in
> October for Europe – in which case I must remain until January
> for our own China ships that then pass through the Straits of
> Sunda; a length of time in the sickly season that I should avoid
> by every means in my power.

Bligh knew he would be pushing luck to the absolute limit if he continued towards Batavia aboard the launch, even though it had carried him and his men a great distance across precarious oceans – 'it would be unjustifiable to proceed in her any farther' – so there was only one solution: to purchase or hire a vessel suitable for transporting them to Batavia. The money for this came through an agreement with Timotheus Wanjon, in which Bligh could draw the necessary bills on the British Government.

A week later he had purchased on behalf of His Majesty's Service a 34-foot schooner that had been built in Java. The cost – 1000 rix-dollars – was the lowest he could find for any vessel capable of completing the mission, and she came 'complete for sea', with sails, rigging and two anchors and cables. She was immediately renamed HMS *Resource*. Within days the carpenter, assisted by some Chinese workers, set about repairing and preparing *Resource* for the planned 1200-nautical-mile passage. This purchase meant that the Royal Navy now had a ship it didn't know about, and it also didn't know it had lost one – but the Admiralty certainly would know the moment these men, or the mail, reached England.

On the same day as the purchase of *Resource*, Bligh presented the governor with an account of the loss of *Bounty* and the names and all relevant details of the mutineers. He demanded 'in His Majesty's name that orders might be sent to all their settlements to take the pirates if they came there'.

The description of the mutineers, which he compiled in consultation with the crew who were with him, gave an interesting insight into the individuals, especially how young they were, and the distinctive 'marks' they bore. At age 40, or thereabouts, Thompson, Mills and Coleman were considered to be middle-aged. The majority were aged between twenty and 28, while Heywood and Ellison were only seventeen. Most had been tattooed extensively while in Tahiti.

These were some of the descriptions delivered to the governor:

Fletcher Christian / Aged 24 years – 5ft 9in / Complexion: Dark and very swarthy / Hair: Blackish or very dark brown / Make: Strong / Marks: Star tattooed on the left breast and tattooed on the backside. His knees stands a little out and may be called a little bow legged. He is subject to violent perspiration and particularly in his hands so that he soils anything he handles.

Edward Young / Aged 22 years – 5ft 8in / Complexion: Dark and rather bad /Marks: Lost several of his fore teeth and those that remain are all rotten.

James Morrison / Aged 28 years – 5ft 8in / Marks: Has been wounded in one of his arms with a musket ball.

William Mickoy [McCoy] / Aged 25 years – 5ft 8in / Strong /
Marks: A scar where he has been stabbed in the belly.

Henry Hillbrant / Aged 25 years – 5ft 7in / Strong / Marks:
His left arm shorter than the other having been broke. Is
Hanoverian born and speaks bad English.

William Brown / Aged 27 years – 5ft 8in / Marks: A
remarkable scar on one of his cheeks which contracts the
eyelid and runs down to his throat.

Later, Bligh left a copy of this list in Batavia and subsequently
forwarded copies – with a brief explanation of the mutiny – to
the governor-general of India, Lord Cornwallis, and to Governor
Phillip in New South Wales.

In the seven weeks it took to ready *Resource* for sea, the
majority of the men had regained their full health. However, Bligh
registered some sad news on 20 July: 'I had the misfortune to lose
Mr. David Nelson: he died of an inflammatory fever. The loss of
this honest man I very much lamented.' The funeral, supported by
twelve Dutch officers dressed in black, took place the next day and
his body was interred behind the settlement's small chapel.

In this period leading up to their departure, Fryer continually
frustrated and challenged Bligh through insolence and by persistently
disobeying orders. At one stage he encouraged his brother-in-
law, Robert Tinkler, to 'stick his knife into the bosun' following
a confrontation. Fryer's 'vicious and troublesome disposition'
saw Bligh repeatedly recording complaints against him, but their
predicament in Coupang prevented him from taking stronger
action. This would come later. The intractable and problematic
carpenter William Purcell also fell into this category.

On 19 August, the day prior to weighing anchor and sailing for Batavia, Bligh attended to his correspondence, which would be sent to England as mail on the next ship heading to Europe from Coupang, though just when that would be was unknown. This was the day that he wrote his famously affectionate letter to his wife, Betsy, breaking the news of the mutiny, his misfortune and his whereabouts. Chances were that this letter would not reach its destination before he did, so it is without doubt that he wrote it to ensure she had his personal account of the mutiny should he die during his efforts to reach home. There is also no doubt that by writing this letter to his beloved he would have brought considerable relief to his own mind.

> Coupang in Timor,
> August 19th 1789
> My dear Betsy
> I am now in a part of the world that I never expected, it is,
> however, a place that has afforded me relief and saved my life,
> and I have the happiness to assure you I am now in perfect
> health. That the chance of this letter getting to you before
> others of a later date is so very small, I shall only just give
> you a short account of the cause of my arrival here – what an
> emotion does my heart and soul feel that I have once more
> an opportunity of writing to you and my little angels, and
> particularly as you have all been so near losing the best of
> friends, when you would have had no person to have regarded
> you as I do, and you must have spent the remainder of your
> days without knowing what was become of me, or what
> would have been still worse, to have known I had been starved
> to death at sea or destroyed by Indians – all these dreadful
> circumstances I have combated with success and in the most

extraordinary manner that ever happened, never despairing from the first moment of my disaster but that I should overcome all my difficulties. Know then, my own dear Betsy, I have lost the *Bounty*.

... on the 28th April at daylight in the morning Christian having the morning watch. He with several others came into my cabin while I was asleep, and seizing me, holding naked bayonets at my breast, tied my hands behind my back, and threatened instant destruction if I uttered a word. I however called loudly for assistance, but the conspiracy was so well laid that the officers' cabin doors were guarded by sentinels, so Nelson, Peckover, Samuels or the Master could not come to me. I was now dragged on deck in my shirt and closely guarded – I demanded of Christian the case of such a violent act, and severely degraded for his villainy but he could only answer – 'not a word sir or you are dead.' I dared him to the act and endeavoured to rally someone to a sense of their duty but to no effect ...

The secrecy of this mutiny is beyond all conception so that I cannot discover that any who are with me had the least knowledge of it. Even Mr. Tom Ellison took such a liking to Otaheite that he also turned pirate, so that I have been run down by my own dogs ...

My misfortune I trust will be properly considered by all the world – it was a circumstance I could not foresee – I had not sufficient officers and had they granted me marines most likely the affair would never have happened – I had not a spirited and brave fellow about me and the mutineers treated them as such. My conduct has been free of blame, and I showed everyone that, tied as I was, I defied every villain to hurt me ...

I know how shocked you will be at this affair but I request of you My Dear Betsy to think nothing of it – all is now past and we will again look forward to future happiness. Nothing but true consciousness as an officer that I have done well could support me ... give my blessings to my dear Harriet, my dear Mary, my dear Betsy and to my dear little stranger [Bligh's unborn fourth child] and tell them I shall soon be home ... To you my love I give all that an affectionate husband can give – love, respect and all that is or ever will be in the power of your ever affectionate friend and husband

Wm Bligh

As a precaution against him failing, through accident, to reach England, Bligh also wrote a letter to the Lords of the Admiralty to ensure they knew what had happened with *Bounty* and how he came to be in Coupang.

While *Resource* was being prepared for the journey the refugees had become aware of an additional threat they could face between Coupang and Batavia: pirates! Consequently, Bligh arranged for the Dutch authorities to loan him suitable arms which could be carried aboard *Resource*. These included swivel brass cannons, fourteen muskets, fourteen bayonets, plus ammunition.

On the morning of 20 August the seventeen *Bounty* discards hoisted the sails on the little schooner *Resource* and departed Coupang, bound for Batavia. The launch – their already legendary lifeboat – was in tow, and as the ship moved directly and slowly away from the shore on a course to the north-west-by-west, booming rounds of cannon fire resounded across the water. First *Resource* saluted the fort with thirteen rounds, then came the same number in response; there was a nine-gun salute from Captain Spikerman's ship, to which Bligh replied, and in a final farewell the fort let go with another seven.

It was downwind sailing before a pleasant south-east trade wind, but due to the fullness of the design of the vessel and the speed-sapping drag that came from the launch, progress was slow – generally between 1 and 4 knots.

The course set for *Resource* was almost direct to the western end of the island of Flores, where, according to the Dutch map they had been given, they should turn north and sail through 'the Streights of Mangaryne' then change course to the west. When they reached the straits, Bligh decided the passage appeared too narrow and dangerous to negotiate, but he was left with no option but to go through – the only other alternative to get to the north proved impassable because of contrary winds and hellish swirling currents. It was ten days after leaving Coupang that they were finally clear of the straits and heading west. The track was then along the northern shore of the island of Sumbawa, then across the northern side of Bali and on to Surabaya, where they were scheduled to be joined by a pilot and three small prows, which would act as escort vessels and help protect *Resource* should there be an attack by pirates between there and Batavia.

Soon after *Resource* reached Surabaya on 12 September, there was another major confrontation between Purcell and Fryer and their captain. Some crew were found drunk below deck and this brought about direct challenges to Bligh's authority. The infraction was the last straw for Bligh: he decided to pursue and punish the perpetrators of 'these disgraceful things'.

Bligh ordered the master and carpenter to be held as prisoners and taken to shore, 'for I now no longer found my honour or person safe among these people'. When the captain reached the shore with them he wrote to the governor of Surabaya, Anthony Barkay, requesting he 'inquire into the cause of this tumult'.

Sourabya [sic], 15 Septr, 1789

This is to certify that I have solicited (in the name of the King of Great Britain) the premier of this place to cause to be detained under an arrest and from hence to be immediately sent to Batavia and there to be ready to embark with me on my arrival for Europe, two officers, under the names of John Fryer, master, and Wm Purcell, carpenter, who have acted tumultuously on board His Britannic Majesty's schooner, *Resource*.

Also to cause three others, Thomas Ledward, acting surgeon, John Hallett, midshipman, and Wm Cole, boatswain, to be brought on shore and examined, they having declared that they could witness against their Commander, who on that account as a British Officer, to prove his honour request that a public enquiry may be made.

Wm. Bligh.

At the court hearing the following morning Ledward, Hallett and Cole appeared before three local senior military officers, and upon examination none could register any serious complaints against their captain. 'The examination being over I dismissed these wretches and ordered them on board,' wrote Bligh.

By now the two prisoners, Fryer and Purcell, understood that they had gone beyond all reason in challenging their captain's authority and would almost certainly face a court martial on returning to England, so Fryer in particular went to great lengths to beg forgiveness. Bligh would have no part of it, and instead of having them aboard *Resource* for the remainder of the passage to Batavia, consigned each one of them to an escorting prow.

On 17 September, *Resource* set sail from Surabaya with the pilot on board and the prows in support, heading for Batavia, which was 400 nautical miles to the west. They reached their destination on 2 October, and within hours of going ashore Bligh was struck down by a violent fever brought on by the oppressive heat and humidity, an ailment later diagnosed as malaria. It was so severe that the surgeon-general there advised him to leave Batavia for England as soon as possible, but he should also know that all ships heading to Europe were grossly overcrowded. Bligh took this advice and initiated plans to depart. Two days later *Resource* was auctioned off for a disappointing 295 rix-dollars and, much to his regret, the launch was also sold: 'The services she had rendered us made me feel great reluctance at parting with her; which I would not have done, if I could have found a convenient opportunity of getting her conveyed to Europe.' This same day Bligh lost another of his men – the third since the mutiny. Thomas Hall, a cook who had been seriously ill since arriving in Timor, passed away.

With placements for passengers to Europe at a premium, Bligh quickly set about organising his passage to England and that of the remaining crew. The first opportunity was three berths aboard the Dutch packet ship *Vlydte*, which was sailing on 16 October, and he assigned those places to himself, his clerk, John Samuel, and John Smith, who was acting as his servant. The ship's ultimate destination was the Dutch town of Middelburg – which today, ironically, is on the edge of Bligh Bank in the English Channel. *Vlydte* was scheduled to stop in England on the way.

Two months after leaving Batavia, *Vlydte* anchored in Cape Town's Table Bay, and once there Bligh penned a letter to his great friend and mentor Sir Joseph Banks, detailing the circumstances around the loss of *Bounty*. It read, in part:

> In this you will see Sir the misfortunes of a man who pledges
> his honour to you, could not be foreseen or guarded against,
> whose conduct will bear the test of the minutest enquiry and

who only regrets that you should see him so unsuccessful. But although I have failed in the completion of my undertaking, I had accomplished most assuredly, the most difficult part of it. My sufferings have been very great, but through the whole, that no dishonour could be reflected on your recommendation I have endeavoured to make the remaining part of my voyage of some avail. Even in my distressed situation, I went in search of Fidgee [Fiji] Islands and discovered them, or a number of others through which I sailed, and have made a decent survey of them with respect to their situation. I have also done the same on the coast of New Holland from the latitude 13° south, and passed to the northward of Captain Cook through the Prince of Wales Islands in latitude about 10° 30'S. I was fearful having no arms to go near to New Guinea, otherwise I would have determined how far Endeavour Straits was an eligible pass for shipping, but that perhaps is already done. I have been very ill and am still an invalid, but I hope to see you in the month of April, if I can persuade a terrible old fellow of a Dutchman [the ship's captain] to carry sail.

After sailing from Table Bay on 2 January 1790, *Vlydte* anchored off the Isle of Wight, on the southern side of the Solent, on 14 March. It had been two years and three months since Bligh had seen the coast of England – a sight he had thought so many times he might never again experience.

When the anchor was confirmed as being secure, a small boat from the Isle of Wight rafted alongside the ship and soon after Bligh went aboard carrying what few possessions he owned. He was then ferried across the Solent to Portsmouth where, after he stepped ashore in this famous naval town, he reported his arrival to authorities.

In signalling the end of this almost inconceivable chapter in his remarkable life, Bligh wrote soon afterwards:

Those of my officers and people whom I left at Batavia were provided with passages in the earliest ships; and at the time we parted were apparently in good health. Nevertheless they did not all live to quit Batavia. Mr. Elphinston, master's mate, and Peter Linkletter, seaman, died within a fortnight after my departure, the hardships they had experienced having rendered them unequal to cope with so unhealthy a climate as that of Batavia. The remainder embarked on board the Dutch fleet for Europe, and arrived safe at this country, except Robert Lamb, who died on the passage, and Mr. Ledward, the surgeon, who has not yet been heard of [he was lost at sea when the Dutch ship he was aboard foundered between Batavia and the Cape of Good Hope]. Thus of nineteen who were forced by the mutineers into the launch it has pleased God that twelve should surmount the difficulties and dangers of the voyage and live to revisit their native country.

CHAPTER TWELVE

London, 1790

Trial, fame and infamy

When 35-year-old Royal Navy lieutenant William Bligh came ashore at Portsmouth early in March 1790 he could have been anyone. There would have been little, if any, evidence of his original naval uniform: while the mutineers did throw some clothing into the launch when they abandoned their shipmates, it is highly unlikely anything would have survived the rigours of the voyage to Timor. It is more likely he would have been dressed in civilian clothing given to him after the ordeal.

Also, while it was a slow process, his health was improving. Not a tall man, he was showing signs of the slightly corpulent proportions he carried when he set sail aboard *Bounty*. What he didn't realise as he walked through the streets of his homeland and refreshed memories of times past was that the relative anonymity he was experiencing would be short-lived. Before long Lieutenant William Bligh, RN, would be one of the best-known names in England, and he would be hailed a hero for guiding his seventeen remaining crewmen From Tofua to Timor without the loss of another life.

Within days he was back in London for a reunion with Betsy and his 'little angels'. They were exciting times. After more than two years at sea he reacquainted himself with Harriet, Mary and Elizabeth, and got to know the twins who were by then almost two years old. Jane and Frances had been born three weeks after he had changed course towards Cape Town having been forced to abandon his determined effort to round Cape Horn. As news of his homecoming spread, along with details of the circumstances surrounding his return, so the number of visitors grew, each one of them eager to hear his incredible story. All this must have seemed overwhelming for Bligh: suddenly, after years of being aboard a small ship and in an isolated, far-flung part of the world, he was confronted by the bustle of everyday life in London, a city very much in flux due to the influence of the French Revolution, which had started only months earlier.

Within weeks, as news of the mutiny and its consequences spread, the name William Bligh became known from London to Lancaster, Portsmouth to Plymouth. He was praised in newspaper reports, some suggesting he deserved every reward possible. The accolades came from far and wide in recognition of his most incredible trans-ocean voyage, which history would hail as one of the greatest-ever feats of survival. His bravery, daring, leadership and skill as a navigator put him at the pinnacle of public prominence.

It was several months before Bligh's companions from the longboat voyage reached England and returned to their families. Because their stay in Batavia was prolonged through the lack of berths aboard ships making return passages to Europe, they'd simply had to wait their turn.

In the interim Bligh's priority was to follow standard naval procedure and present himself to the Admiralty with his account of the loss of *Bounty*. Captains returning from sea were required to lodge all documents relating to the voyage, the most important of which was the ship's log detailing all aspects of the voyage, including destinations, the chosen course and observations. By doing this, Bligh was able to discuss with officials his immediate future in the Royal Navy, and much to his relief he was advised that he would retain his commission as commander of *Bounty* because its fate was unknown. At the same time, the Admiralty decided to make use of him being home by having him serve as a relief commander on naval ships on a number of occasions.

Regardless of this work, Bligh became increasingly preoccupied with the failure of the voyage and the loss of his first naval command to mutineers. His concern was what impact the loss of *Bounty* might have on his career, and his relationship with his great supporter Banks, whom he was certain would have been disappointed and embarrassed by this failure. Bligh promptly wrote to him apologising, but he need not have worried: Banks was by then even more impressed by the man he had so readily endorsed prior to the departure of *Bounty*.

Losing a ship was not a simple matter as far as the Admiralty was concerned, however. The all-powerful Lords were acutely conscious of the potential embarrassment for the Royal Navy as a consequence of one of their commanders losing his ship to a bunch of seafaring ruffians. Right then that commander, Bligh, was a national hero, but there was no guarantee that fickle public sentiment would stay that way. They decided the right course of action would be to pursue the perpetrators of this act and deliver them home to England to face justice. After consultation with the Admiralty, His Majesty's government announced that a ship, HMS *Pandora*, would be readied to sail to Tahiti so the *Bounty* rebels could be hunted down and arrested. It sounded like the perfect, face-saving solution at the time, for both the Royal Navy and Bligh, but the result it would deliver was unexpected and tragic.

Innocent though he was, under naval law Bligh was obliged to face a court-martial inquiry in which his actions and those of the crew relating to the insurrection and subsequent loss of his ship would come under close scrutiny. That trial began on 22 October 1790 aboard HMS *Royal William*, moored at Spithead, with Bligh's old commander from Gibraltar, Admiral Samuel Barrington, presiding.

According to protocol, Bligh was the first witness. When proceedings commenced, he advised the court that the only objection or complaint he held against any of the officers or men who were with him on the launch voyage was with the carpenter, William Purcell. Following this declaration all survivors present then swore that they held no grievance against their captain. Even John Fryer went on record as saying the captain did everything in his power to recover the ship. Regardless, it is surprising that Bligh hadn't lodged a complaint against Fryer at the start of this court martial, but his decision could have been tied to the possibility that the mutineers might still be arrested and returned to England, whereupon they would face their own court martial. If that happened he would need all the support he could muster when it came to defending his honour.

The proceedings in the court were remarkably brief. Only a short time after Bligh and his men were asked to retire, they were ushered back in to hear the verdict. Immediately Bligh was relieved to see that on the table he stood before, it was the hilt of the president's sword, not the blade, pointing towards him. This was, in the annals of the Royal Navy, the traditional sign indicating a verdict of not guilty. The officers then verbally delivered their decision: that *Bounty* was 'violently and forcibly seized' by Fletcher Christian and his supporters, and that Lieutenant William Bligh, and those tried with him, could not be held responsible for the loss. All were honourably acquitted. The court then turned its attention to the charges against Purcell, and after hearing the evidence, declared that the allegations had been proved in part and that he should be reprimanded.

The acquittal, coupled with the publication of Bligh's *Narrative of the Mutiny, On Board His Majesty's Ship Bounty; And The Subsequent Voyage of Part of the Crew, In the Ship's Boat*, which he had written since his return, further fuelled the public's fascination with his odyssey into an unknown and exotic world. By now his distinction in English society was such that he and Betsy were presented to King George III at Buckingham House under the escort of Sir Joseph Banks.

Bligh's exoneration also led to the Admiralty promoting him to the position of commander and giving him the commission of the fourteen-gun sloop HMS *Falcon*, with the rank of captain. Favours from the Admiralty came again in December when the Lords decided to overrule the traditional requirement of three years' additional service, and appointed Bligh post-captain to HMS *Medea* for rank only.

For the next four months he went onto half-pay while waiting for a command, and he spent much of this time at his desk penning a more detailed and graphic account of his experiences on the South Seas. In March 1791 he received an intriguing direction, which had been orchestrated by Banks, and just one month later his new posting was confirmed. It was beyond his highest expectations.

CHAPTER THIRTEEN

South Pacific, 1791

Pirates and Pandora

It was the First Lord of the Admiralty, John Pitt, 2nd Earl of Chatham, who, five months after learning of the mutiny, initiated *Pandora*'s mission to capture the culprits and bring them to trial. This decision was not because of Bligh, but rather because a Royal Navy ship had been taken without any authority. There were compelling reasons for these wanted men of *Bounty* to be found and punished: they were in breach of the Articles of War to the highest degree; and further, as England spread its influence across the oceans of the world, it had to be demonstrated to all Royal Navy sailors that any violation of these Articles, even half a world away, would bring retribution.

Pandora was a 24-gun, 500-ton frigate launched at Deptford in 1779. She went into service immediately on the English Channel as a precaution against a threatened invasion by the combined French and Spanish fleets. Four years later she was laid-up and stayed that way until being recommissioned for this assignment.

The captain the Admiralty appointed for the task, 48-year-old Edward Edwards, held the reputation of being an autocrat. He was depicted by the nineteenth-century judge and author Alfred

McFarland as being more suited to the protection of the Black Hole of Calcutta than being captain of a Royal Navy ship. This reputation was built on the fact that in 1782 Edwards had mercilessly put down a mutiny aboard HMS *Narcissus*, of which he was commander. Apart from the sailors who died in the confrontation, six others were hanged and two were flogged so badly they died.

Edwards' brutal reputation would become all too evident on this mission to Tahiti, when he had the infamous '*Pandora*'s Box' built on the ship's deck: a despicable cell-cum-cage designed to hold the prisoners. However, his defence for this monstrosity could have been that he was simply following, to the letter of the law, his orders from the Admiralty: 'You are to keep the mutineers as closely confined as may preclude all possibility of their escaping, that they may be brought home to undergo the punishment due to their demerits.'

The broad order on departure was to sail to Tahiti, and if the mutineers were not found there then he was to visit as many islands as possible in the Society and Friendly groups in search of them. To assist in identifying the reprobates, Edwards included two of *Bounty*'s acquitted midshipmen – Thomas Hayward and John Hallett, the last of whom had been the youngest officer in the crew – in the complement of more than 130 men aboard *Pandora*.

After departing Portsmouth on 17 November 1790, *Pandora* reached Tahiti on 23 March 1791. Even before she came to anchor, an islander had paddled out in a canoe and climbed aboard, and within minutes he revealed to the captain that some of the mutineers were still on the island, but *Bounty*, with Christian and nine of his supporters, was long gone to a place unknown. He also told Edwards that Christian had said Captain Bligh was now living in a new colony named *Whytootackee*, in New Holland, with Captain Cook.

Still before the anchor was lowered, another visitor arrived; the *Bounty* armourer, Joseph Coleman, swam out to the ship, clambered up the boarding ladder to the deck and immediately surrendered. He then revealed the whereabouts of the mutineers on the island and advised that Charles Churchill and Mathew Thompson had been murdered by islanders. Beyond this, one can only imagine the look on his face when he saw former shipmates Hayward and Hallett aboard *Pandora*. Next to come to the ship were Peter Heywood and George Stewart, and they too surrendered. Their claims of innocence – that they were forced to stay aboard *Bounty* against their will, and that they had not sided with the mutineers – fell on deaf ears.

On hearing that the remaining mutineers were living at points across the island, Edwards ordered they be hunted down. At the same time, after Burkett, Sumner, Muspratt, Hillbrant, McIntosh and Millward got word of the reason for *Pandora*'s arrival at Matavai Bay, they took to the mountains. It would prove to be a wasted effort: a squad of 27 armed men from *Pandora* were sent after them and soon all were in custody.

Knowing the impact the natural appeal of Tahiti had on Bligh's expedition, Edwards had to be on full alert when it came to his own men going ashore. He feared the same thing could happen to his crew during this search and recovery mission. Even so, this 'inhumane' captain showed considerable leniency when he allowed the wives of the prisoners to visit the ship. They were permitted to visit daily and bring their children with them to see their fathers. Indications were that six children had been born to these couples in the time since *Bounty* first arrived in 1788 – two boys and four girls. Some of the women at this time were mothers-to-be.

Just five weeks after *Pandora* arrived in Tahiti all fourteen mutineers remaining there had been arrested, locked in irons and crushed into *Pandora*'s Box – known as the poop or roundhouse to the *Pandora* crew. On 8 May the order came to weigh anchor: Edwards' planned search of other South Pacific islands for Christian and his cohorts was underway.

This ongoing mission was soon shattered by tragedy. The ship's jollyboat, carrying five crewmen – including the son of *Pandora*'s bosun – disappeared without trace while they were searching the Cook Islands for the mutineers. Then, not long after this terrible loss, there was another confounding yet highly remarkable incident. A small schooner named *Resolution*, which had been built by the mutineers in Tahiti and subsequently commandeered by Edwards for *Pandora*, was assisting in the search when it disappeared with nine hands on board in extremely savage weather when they were north of Samoa. After a two-day search for survivors Edwards abandoned the effort, believing all had been lost. But amazingly, after *Pandora* had been wrecked and Edwards and his survivors arrived in Semarang, to the east of Batavia, some weeks later, this stout little vessel was discovered there lying at anchor.

In what had been another incredible story of survival, the crew of *Resolution* had safely navigated their way there after giving up hope of finding *Pandora*. In circumstances distinctly similar to those Bligh and his men had faced in the first stage of the launch voyage, they came across the island of Tofua – and went ashore. After trading nails for food and water they suddenly found themselves facing the threat of violent attack, just as Bligh had experienced there two years earlier. Fortunately, though, they had guns, so were quickly able to repel their attackers. Then, as was also the case with Bligh's launch voyage, the nine men reached what to this day is an unidentified Dutch settlement in the Dutch East Indies, but as soon as they arrived the governor became suspicious of them. He believed they were probably *Bounty* mutineers, simply because they could not produce any identification papers and their vessel was made of 'foreign' wood. As a result he placed them under guard and sent them aboard *Resolution* to Semarang, so they could be interrogated. Fortuitously, Edwards arrived soon after and identified them as his crew.

Captain Bligh had expressed strong concerns about the risks of *Pandora*'s voyage after she had sailed for Tahiti. He asserted on many occasions that Edwards would not get his ship home safely because he lacked knowledge of the treacherous waters between New Holland and New Guinea. Truer words were never uttered. In fact, it was well before he reached this region that careless navigation and impetuosity, in the form of a compelling desire to accelerate progress towards home, brought about Edwards' undoing. First, he went close to driving *Pandora* onto the vast Indispensable Reef, south of Rennell Island in the Coral Sea. Then, soon after, when he thought he was sailing through the Louisiade Archipelago, he was in fact off the coast of New Guinea – a 200 nautical mile error.

Until this time Edwards had applied prudent seamanship in the interests of safety in dangerous and uncharted waters. He was ordering the ship to lay-to each night so it was virtually stopped, but then his impatience took over and *Pandora* was sailing through the night. By late afternoon on 28 August, Edwards had his ship heading south, parallel to the outer edge of the Great Barrier Reef, while he and others searched for an opening in the coral bastion that was large enough to allow them to sail to the west and on towards Endeavour Strait. At seven o'clock, after darkness had descended, the captain had *Pandora* lying-to when a check of the lead-line caused concern. It showed a depth of 50 fathoms, whereas only a short time earlier they could not find the bottom at 110 fathoms. The wind was then near gale force from the south-east, and the reef, which was disguised by darkness, became a dangerous lee shore *Pandora* was being blown towards. Edwards had only one option: to call 'make sail' so they could claw their way back to deeper water. But it was already too late. Within minutes it was as if every ounce of gunpowder in the ship's magazine had exploded, causing a horrendously violent eruption. *Pandora* had smashed onto the near-vertical edge of the reef at considerable speed and was mortally wounded. The heavy timbers of the forward sections were no match for the impact: the planks had opened up so severely that an absolute torrent of water was flooding into the cavernous hull. Worse still, with the sails set and a considerable swell running, the ship was being pounded harder and harder onto the coral and was starting to list alarmingly to one side.

When daylight came, it was clear nothing could be done to save her: she would soon sink. *Pandora*'s boats had been launched during the night and secured to the bulwarks in readiness for the call to abandon ship. It was then a case of saving as many men as possible, but not necessarily the mutineers. Here Edwards' reputation as an inhumane individual shone through when, having sent some of the mutineers to the pumps during the night in a futile bid to save his ship, he ordered others he had freed to be put back into irons and into the cell. As *Pandora* began her final death throes Edwards still showed no mercy towards his prisoners. Ignoring their shouted pleas to be released, he simply jumped overboard and swam to a pinnace.

By then the deck was awash back to the mainmast and *Pandora* was going down rapidly. With the captain gone the bosun's mate, William Moulter, could no longer cope with hearing the men crying for help, so before leaping into the sea he clambered atop the box, released the bolt securing the hatch and flung it open. That was all he had time to do.

'Among the drowned were Mr Stewart, John Sumner, Richard Skinner and Henry Hillbrant, the whole of whom perished with their hands still in manacles,' wrote James Morrison about his experiences as a prisoner aboard *Pandora*.

About 4 miles downwind from where the ship foundered, there was a small sandy cay, to which the survivors made their way. Many had been picked up by boats after clinging to wreckage for some time. Later, a headcount concluded: '89 of the ship's company and ten of the pirates ... were saved, and that 31 of the ship's company and four pirates were lost with the ship.'

The survivors remained on this small islet for a few days while the boats were prepared for the 1200-nautical-mile journey to Coupang. During that time Edwards kept the prisoners isolated from his crew and refused them any shelter from the blazing sun. Despite their best efforts to protect themselves by covering their bodies with sand each day, their sunburn became so severe that they were red raw.

By 15 September all the survivors and prisoners had arrived in Coupang. Some months later they were transported to Cape Town; then on 18 June 1792, HMS *Gorgon* reached Spithead with, among others, the ten surviving *Bounty* 'pirates' aboard.

With Tubuai off the agenda as a suitable site for Christian and his men to establish their South Pacific hideaway, and Tahiti being a far-too-obvious destination, Fletcher Christian knew he had little time to find an alternative.

It appears that not long after arriving in Tahiti for the second time, Christian learned that a plot to take the ship was brewing among the mutineers who had elected to stay there, so he immediately set about quitting the island under the cover of darkness. Such was his haste that he didn't even take time to raise the anchor: he had his men simply hack through the cable. He also refused to allow any of the nineteen islander women who were still on board *Bounty* to disembark before setting sail, for fear they would raise the alarm. Even so, one of them leapt overboard when the ship was about a mile outside the reef and, in pitch-darkness, started swimming back to the bay. The following day, when the ship sailed close to another island, Christian is said to have allowed a further six of the women to board a canoe that had come out from the shore.

Remaining aboard *Bounty* with Christian were Edward Young, John Williams, Isaac Martin, John Mills and William Brown, along with the man they referred to as 'Reckless Jack', Alexander Smith (whose real name was John Adams), and two others, William McCoy and Matthew Quintal, who were considered to be the 'bad men' among the crew. Also aboard were eighteen Polynesians, twelve of them women, and a baby girl.

No actual record, including a log or narrative from Christian, was ever found, so there is some level of speculation as to how he came to decide on Pitcairn Island. However, with nearly four months having elapsed between the day *Bounty* left Matavai Bay, 23 September 1789, and her arrival at Pitcairn Island, which was only 1200 nautical miles east-south-east of Tahiti, it is safe to assume Christian cruised through the region in the hope he might find a suitable deserted island, but it was proving a fruitless mission. It has been suggested that one day during this quest he found a book aboard *Bounty* titled *Voyage Round the World*, by Captain Philip Carteret. In it the author gave an account of the discovery of Pitcairn Island when he was sailing HMS *Swallow* through the South Pacific on a circumnavigation that took place between 1766 and 1769. Carteret's description of the island matched Christian's parameters for a perfect refuge: it was off the main track followed by ships when traversing the South Pacific; it was only accessible in relatively calm weather; it had a fresh water supply, and coconuts, fish and seabirds were in abundance. Additionally, the volcanic soil was ideal for the cultivation of tropical fruit and vegetables. Most importantly of all, it was secure, as its existence was all but unknown to the outside world.

When *Bounty* arrived at the latitude and longitude Carteret had given for Pitcairn Island, there was nothing to be seen but wide blue ocean. Christian could then only guess that the captain had noted the wrong longitude, so in the hope that this was the case, he set the ship on a zigzag course along the line of latitude, and sure enough, the man aloft scanning the horizon soon saw the jagged, dome-shaped profile of the 1100-foot-high island – the pinnacle of a volcanic eruption countless centuries earlier – becoming defined in the haze ahead. Telescopes quickly locked onto the object and the sighting was confirmed. They had found their island. The date was 15 January 1790.

For the next three days, rough weather prevented them from going ashore so Christian had no choice but to cruise around the island, a distance of only 5.2 nautical miles. When the bad weather abated he, along with Brown, Williams, McCoy and three Tahitians, went ashore, and in a very short time all knew they had found their nirvana. Pitcairn Island was beyond their wildest dreams when it came to being totally isolated from the rest of the world – in fact, unbeknown to them, they were about to establish one of the most remote human habitats on earth.

Bounty was then guided into the relatively calm waters of what is now known as Bounty Bay, and from there all the livestock, plants and equipment plus personal possessions were transported to the rocky and rugged shore and moved to safe ground. With that done they decided they should sever all ties with civilisation by scuttling the ship – a decision influenced by their firm belief that if they left it at anchor, there was a chance that a passing vessel would one day recognise it and stop there. This was a risk they could not afford to take.

CHAPTER FOURTEEN

Tahiti, 1791

Second chances

In March 1791, as *Pandora* surged down vivid blue South Pacific swells towards Tahiti with her canvas sails stretched taut by a perfect south-east trade wind, Bligh was at home in England and about to receive some gratifying news, which would confirm once more that he remained very much in favour with Sir Joseph Banks and the Admiralty regardless of the loss of *Bounty*.

It was a time when the English were enjoying an extended period of peace, a circumstance that gave Banks the opportunity to again champion the cause for the transfer of breadfruit plants from Tahiti to the West Indies, a project that still retained the endorsement of the king. The good news for Bligh was that he was still the chosen man for the job.

The communiqué from Banks advised Bligh of this and confirmed that a 107-foot sloop-of-war, HMS *Providence*, which was still under construction at the Blackwall Yard on the Thames, had been purchased one month earlier specifically for the task of completing the voyage the *Bounty* mutineers had terminated two years earlier. Better still, in being given a second chance to complete his original mission, Bligh would be promoted to captain, a posting which was confirmed when *Providence* was launched in April. He saw the name of this new ship as being quite auspicious: it defined the new expedition perfectly, as he viewed its completion as being an essential part of his destiny in the Royal Navy.

Apart from directing Bligh to deliver the breadfruit plants to the West Indies, the Admiralty also commissioned him 'to make a complete examination of Torres Strait', a shallow, reef-strewn and dangerous stretch of water between the northern tip of New Holland and the southern coast of New Guinea. He had been through this region once before, aboard *Bounty*'s launch with his seventeen loyalists, but they had traversed waters well to the south of Torres Strait. Should an accurately recorded safe channel be found through the strait, then ships returning to England from the Pacific region – especially those servicing the new penal colony in New South Wales – would no longer have to sail through the treacherous Southern Ocean to reach home. Instead they could sail west-about through the strait, across the top of New Holland into the Indian Ocean, then enter the South Atlantic via the Cape of Good Hope. It could prove to be an invaluable shortcut for shipping.

With the directive to chart these unknown waters, Bligh decided that for safety reasons he would need a smaller support vessel. He detailed this desire in correspondence to Banks: 'A small vessel with about 30 men would be of use and may enable me more effectually to render the navigation of Endeavour Strait less hazardous ... an expeditious help for ships home from Botany Bay.' With his request recognised, Bligh chose the brig *Assistant* as the tender for *Providence* and appointed Lieutenant Nathaniel Portlock as captain. *Assistant*'s proportions were, in Bligh's estimation, most suitable for a support vessel: 51 feet overall, a displacement of 110 tons, and a crew of 27. Lieutenant Portlock was a friend of Bligh's; he had been master's mate aboard *Discovery*, the support vessel for *Resolution* on Cook's final voyage. In the reshuffle of officers that came after Cook's death, Portlock was transferred to *Resolution* and served as master's mate to Bligh.

Bligh was equally happy with *Providence*, which was fitted out under his directions at Deptford. She was only 9 feet longer overall than the 90-foot *Bounty*, but twice the tonnage, at 420 tons. The size of *Providence* pleased Bligh for many reasons, none more so than the fact he would now be entitled to have marines aboard to support him; his entitlement allowed him to secure the services of a lieutenant, a sergeant, two corporals, a drummer and fifteen marines from Chatham Barracks.

Among the crew of *Providence* were two very familiar faces for Bligh: *Bounty* crewmembers Lawrence Lebogue, the sailmaker, and steward John Smith. The fact that both had agreed to join *Providence* for this second sojourn into the South Pacific is seen by many as confirmation that Bligh's persona was nowhere near as bad as many people have suggested: there is no way they would have signed on for a two-year voyage with the captain had he been the tyrant he was supposed to be.

This second breadfruit voyage would establish a triumvirate with a direct correlation to the establishment of the convict colony in New South Wales. It comprised Captain James Cook, Captain William Bligh and the seventeen-year-old midshipman Matthew Flinders. Cook was Flinders' hero; Bligh had been Cook's sailing master; and now Flinders, who would become one of Australia's greatest maritime explorers, joined the crew of *Providence* for the expedition to Tahiti. The conduit between all three was Sir Joseph Banks. Just two years after Flinders joined the Royal Navy, and in circumstances Bligh could relate to, Banks recognised the young seafarer's talents and had no hesitation in recommending him for a position as midshipman aboard *Providence*. Initially, Flinders was hesitant about sailing under Bligh because he was well aware of his reputation as a hard and excessively demanding taskmaster, but friends who knew Bligh convinced him otherwise.

Bligh was not disappointed by Banks's recommendation, so not surprisingly Flinders enjoyed a similar mentoring experience under his captain aboard *Providence* as Bligh had with Cook aboard *Resolution*. Bligh's talents as a seafarer, navigator and cartographer had been honed under the astute eye of Cook, and now Bligh would do likewise for Flinders.

Flinders would later pioneer the exploration of much of the Australian coastline. In 1798 he proved there was a strait between the mainland and Van Diemen's Land, and in 1803 he successfully completed a voyage of discovery around the entire coast of the mainland. When he returned he stood staunchly as the voice calling for the continent to be named Australia. Unfortunately, it was an innocent circumstance this same year that saw Flinders incarcerated in Ile-de-France [Mauritius] for almost seven years. When Flinders had arrived there by boat he was unaware Britain and France were once again at war, but his ignorance of this fact didn't help him: the island's governor, General Charles De Caen, deemed his passport to be invalid: that could only mean Flinders was an 'imposter' – an English spy, so he was detained. Flinders had until then been sailing the 29-ton schooner *Cumberland* back to England from Sydney when he was forced to divert to Mauritius as hull planking had opened up and she was in danger of sinking. De Caen, a most faithful servant of Napoleon, would have no part of this explanation from Flinders. He was imprisoned. There is no explanation as to why he was detained for so many years, despite attempts in England and France to secure his release. Not even Napoleon could have him freed. The Emperor gave his approval on 11 March 1806, but De Caen ignored the directive, saying

Flinders – who was then on parole and staying in a residence – was a dangerous man. It was not until 14 June 1810 that Flinders was free to sail for England.

Providence's crew also included two gardeners, James Wiles and Christopher Smith, whose job was to supervise the collection of the plants in Tahiti and then tend them until they reached the West Indies. Bligh chose as his first lieutenant his 26-year-old nephew, Francis Bond. With memories of the problems he faced with *Bounty*'s crew still raw in his mind, Bligh went to great lengths to ensure he had the men he wanted this time, right down to an artist to accurately record all points of interest during the voyage. Much to the captain's disappointment, however, the man who was Bligh's choice was forced to withdraw through illness not long before the ship was due to leave. With no suitable replacement available, Bligh decided he and *Providence*'s third lieutenant, George Tobin, would combine their talents and fulfil the task. 'This obliged us all to work with our pencils as well as we were able,' wrote Tobin, but he was actually being overly modest. The pair were well recognised for providing much of the rich illustrated record of the voyage.

Fully provisioned and fitted-out for their extended voyage, *Providence* and *Assistant* weighed anchor and set sail from Spithead on 3 August 1791, bound for Tahiti. Soon the two ships were sailing in company down the English Channel and into the Atlantic, and as they did neither Captain Bligh nor anyone else in England had any idea of the success or failure of *Pandora*'s mission to arrest the mutineers who had overrun *Bounty* more than two years earlier. At the time, *Pandora*, with the criminals crammed in the infamous cage, was making her way home across the Pacific. Just three weeks later, as *Providence* and *Assistant* sailed south towards the equator, *Pandora* was wrecked on the Great Barrier Reef.

As was the case with the *Bounty* voyage, the first stop on this passage was Tenerife, and when *Providence* and *Assistant* anchored there 25 days after departing England, Captain Bligh was struck down by an acute fever, possibly a recurrence of the malaria he had contracted in Batavia. This time the problem was compounded by severe headaches, probably migraines.

He was no better when the expedition departed Tenerife after staying a week. Their course would take them to the south via the Cape Verde Islands, but there was no plan to stop there. However, they began to think otherwise when Bligh's condition deteriorated to the degree where he was increasingly bedridden and soon incapable of handling the day-to-day operation of the ship as commander. He was even beginning to think he might die. He registered in the ship's log: 'unsure how long I might survive'. He had no choice then but to direct Lieutenant Portlock to transfer from *Assistant* to *Providence* and take charge.

Portlock and his officers were sufficiently concerned for their captain that they elected to anchor *Providence* overnight in the hope they might be able to get him ashore so he could rest in greater comfort, but the heat and humidity at that time of year was so extreme it was decided to abandon that plan.

Sick as he was, Bligh was determined to write, as a loving husband to Betsy and a devoted father to his children, a letter that could be delivered to her by the next passing ship returning to England. But as he prepared to put quill to paper he realised he did not have the physical strength or mental ability for the task, so he called upon Edward Harwood, the surgeon aboard *Providence*, to write it for him. The actual letter has been damaged over the years, but even so, affection and emotion shine through:

Snt. Iago, Septr 13th, 1791.

My dear Betsy,

I beg you will not be alarmed at not seeing my own writing.
Am vastly recovered since my ... you from Tenerife – but as
my ... is of a nervous kind, Mr Harwood thought it improper
from me to attempt writing. I anchored here today to procure
a little fruit, and shall leave it by midnight, as I find it an
unhealthy time of the year. I am now taking the bark and feel
considerably stronger; so that hope before we reach the Cape to
be perfectly re-established in my health; from thence shall give
you a full account how I have proceeded – I am confident it is
ordained for us once more to meet, you may therefore cherish
your dear little girls in that happy hope ...

My blessing to them all and with that affectionate esteem
and regard you have ever known me,

I remain,

Your sincere and affectionate husband

Wm Bligh.

God bless you, my dear love and my little angels

Slowly, as *Providence* sailed into cooler and less humid climes,
Bligh's health began to return. However, it wasn't until the two
ships had almost reached Cape Town, on what was an otherwise
uneventful passage, that he recovered to the extent that he could
again walk the deck as commander.

As they sailed deeper into the southern hemisphere so the
following winds strengthened, all the time pressuring the ships
into higher speeds. It was and had been smooth sailing since they
had farewelled England. The only problems involved a human
element: Bligh was forced to order that the quartermaster, John
Letby, receive 30 lashes from the cat-o-nine-tails for refusing to

follow orders and assaulting the bosun's mate on 30 October, six days before Cape Town hailed into view. This would prove to be one of the few times any crewmember was flogged. No doubt the presence of marines helped maintain discipline, but even so Bligh remained reluctant to flog his men; he believed it was far from the best way to maintain order.

On the approach to Cape Town, Bligh's mind would have inevitably turned to the titanic struggle he and his men had endured in the bid to get *Bounty* around Cape Horn and into the Pacific at the height of a callous southern hemisphere winter. This time, much to his relief, there was no such requirement from the Admiralty, even though the warm summer months were approaching – the season of less wild weather.

Determined to ensure he was back to full health before leading the expedition into the Southern Ocean for the next stage, Bligh took leave of the ship and travelled 30 miles inland to the beautiful village of Stellenbosch, where he intended to rest and regain his strength. Bligh was well aware Stellenbosch was the perfect place for him to relax and escape the rigours of shipboard life – because when he was sailing master aboard *Resolution*, Captain Cook had sent a scientific mission there to gain an appreciation of the attributes of the picturesque town, which Cook noted 'stands at the foot of the range of lofty mountains'.

Providence and *Assistant* remained at anchor in Cape Town for two months and during that time Bligh met Captain John Hunter and the remainder of the crew of HMS *Sirius*. They were returning to England aboard a Dutch ship after *Sirius* had been wrecked on Norfolk Island, off the coast of New South Wales.

Bligh spoke at length with Hunter – whom ironically he would follow fourteen years later as governor of New South Wales – about the new penal colony and the problems it confronted. Subsequently, as a practical man who was always looking for logical solutions to problems that his and other missions faced, he decided it was important to advise Banks of his thoughts and theories regarding the situation in New South Wales. Bligh wrote to Banks saying he believed the poor nature of the soil at the colony, which was affecting the growth of crops, 'might be remedied if Government would send them cattle and they could make manure'. He suggested the quickest and simplest solution would come if every ship leaving England for New South Wales carried at least six head of cattle, adding, 'Until this is done there will be eternal discord and little returns'. Of his own mission Bligh added that he hoped he would discover the much-needed safe passage between New Holland and New Guinea on the return voyage.

During the layover in Cape Town both ships were refitted for the next stage of their passage to Tahiti, the 5500-nautical-mile leg to Van Diemen's Land, which began on 23 December. It was a remarkably easy passage – especially when compared with Bligh's experiences in this part of the world with *Bounty*. This was clear in a letter Third Lieutenant Tobin wrote to his brother:

> For myself, James, I began to feel at home in the charge of
> a watch, nor without considering my appointment to the
> *Providence* as a very flattering one, particularly as she was the
> first ship in which I made my debut as a commissioned officer.
> In her commander I had to encounter the quickest sailor's
> eye, guided by a thorough knowledge of every branch of the
> profession necessary on such a voyage. He had been master
> with the persevering Cook in his last voyage in 1776, and as
> has been already noticed, commanded the *Bounty*, armed ship,
> when the first attempt was made to convey the breadfruit tree
> to the West Indies. It is easy of belief that on first joining a man

of such experience my own youth and inferiority were rather busy visitors. They were, but we had by this time crossed the equinoctial and were about doubling the Cape together and I had courage to believe that my Captain was not dissatisfied with me. Of this surely enough – even to you.

Even so, Bligh's 'quick sailor's eye' was often matched by an equally quick temper, though it was short-lived. Bligh was a perfectionist who had no time for incompetency or slack attitudes among his men, but whereas other commanders would easily address such acts with a liberal dose of the lash, Bligh tended to lash with his acerbic tongue rather than the cat-o-nine-tails. Interestingly, his outbursts often coincided with the recurrent fevers and acute headaches that plagued him for much of the entire voyage.

It was a seven-week, mostly downwind and often rollicking passage from Cape Town to Van Diemen's Land. The two ships, which benefitted from the powerful following seas of the Southern Ocean, averaged an impressive 5 knots for the distance. When they rounded the southern tip of Van Diemen's Land and tracked north towards Adventure Bay, Bligh realised it had been fifteen extraordinary years on the high seas since he had been there with Captain Cook in 1777, and less than four years since *Bounty* was anchored in the same bay. He also recalled it was here that the first real signs of dissension and confrontation in the *Bounty* crew had emerged. For any seafarer of this era to have once in a lifetime visited Adventure Bay, which was more than 10 000 nautical miles from Europe, would have been a remarkable achievement; for Captain William Bligh, this was an astonishing third time.

When looking from the deck of *Providence* and ashore, Bligh was once again captivated and intrigued by the natural beauty of this region. It was therefore understandable that he spent a considerable amount of time exploring and using his art brushes and exquisite watercolours to capture his observations of this unique, exotic and remote land. He also traversed much of what is now Storm Bay aboard a longboat, with young Flinders at his side, exploring many of the outstanding features of the land and all the time sketching and creating precise charts of Bligh's discoveries. Bligh also followed the lead of Captain Cook who, when he was there in 1777, carved a note into a tree trunk to confirm his presence. Bligh's inscription read: 'Near this tree Captain William Bligh planted seven fruit trees 1792: – Messrs S and W, botanists.'

During their excursions away from *Providence* to adjacent shores and waterways, Bligh and his men wrote glowing reports of the flora and fauna of the region. They were particularly amazed by the size and grandeur of the huge blue gum trees prevalent along the shoreline and into the hills, one of which measured 29 feet in circumference at its base. They also saw unusual animals: one 'a kind of sloth about the size of a roasting pig' which when roasted had 'a delicate flavour'. This was probably a wombat, while another, with a mouth like a duck bill and quills of a rusty brown colour, was an echidna. As was the case with Bligh's previous visits to Adventure Bay, his efforts to meet and try to communicate with the now vanished Aboriginals of Van Diemen's Land were near fruitless.

Two weeks after arriving in Van Diemen's Land, it was time to weigh anchor for *Providence* and *Assistant* and start another long haul, this time the 3500-nautical-mile final stage of the voyage to Tahiti. But before venturing on to the Tasman Sea and sailing towards New Zealand's southern cape, Bligh took time to survey and map interesting features surrounding Storm Bay, and to the north around what is now the Tasman Peninsula.

Fortunately, when they were established on the course to the south-east-by-east towards New Zealand, it was high summer in the southern hemisphere, a climatic influence that would wear well with the crews. It was the best possible time for them to be sailing deep into the Roaring Forties – the zone between 40 and 50 degrees south latitude renowned for howling westerly gales and mauling, mountainous breaking seas.

Unfortunately for Bligh, though, the longer this voyage progressed, the more unstable his health became. It would be easy to accept that his body was still trying to recover from the dire ravages of the launch voyage, little more than three years earlier. On many occasions, the severity of his crippling headaches required him to hand over the everyday operation of the ship to his senior officers. They could only watch helplessly during the month of March as their captain, often bedridden, endured pain so debilitating and excruciating that his face became distorted on one side due to the stress associated with twisted muscles.

There was no option but to press on and hope Bligh would pull through. As was usual when sailing to Tahiti from the west, the required course saw *Providence* and *Assistant* held well to the south of the latitude of the island, just so they could ride the south-east trade wind to the destination. It was a circuitous route, but the fastest, safest and easiest.

For Bligh, as ill as he was, there would be a wonderful bonus on this route – an explorer's equivalent of striking gold. He made yet another discovery, a beautiful low-profile atoll which is today known as Tematangi, but sometimes referred to as Bligh's Lagoon Island. Its location, at 21° 40' S; 140° 40' W, placed it about 500 nautical miles south-east of Tahiti, and ironically, much the same distance to the north-west of Pitcairn Island, where the *Bounty* mutineers were by then holed up in their secret world. It was 5 April, and Bligh elected not to stop at the atoll which, from their position about 3 miles off shore, appeared uninhabited, yet apparently it was.

Three days later the active volcanic peak of Mehetia came into view. It was important that sailors saw it because it was the signpost to Tahiti for square-rigged ships running down the trades on a course to the north-west. Apart from confirming *Providence* was on course, the sighting of Mehetia meant it was less than 48 hours before they would anchor in Matavai Bay. Bligh assembled his entire crew and addressed them on procedures, and what he expected of them, once there. He was most emphatic on three points: no one was to mention the death of Captain Cook, the loss of *Bounty*, or that they were there to collect breadfruit. Furthermore, he outlined strict regulations relating to ship's discipline and anyone associating with the islanders, adding that he promised 'disgrace and punishment to those who disobeyed' his orders.

After Tahiti loomed into view *Providence* made her way along the eastern side of the island before being guided around Point Venus and sailing into the sheltered waters of the bay. Obviously the islanders had no idea their latest visitors included their much-loved Bligh, but still the same enthusiastic welcome awaited both ships. The men watched with great interest as canoes full of eager islanders paddled towards the ship, then were surprised to see a whaleboat among them. Bligh soon learned the men aboard were some of the 21 survivors of the English whaler *Matilda*, which had been wrecked at night on a reef near Mururoa Atoll a few months earlier.

The 450-ton *Matilda* had transported convicts to Sydney before sailing to Peru then back into the Pacific in search of whales. Everyone survived the wreck, and once they struggled aboard the ship's four boats they sailed in company downwind for Tahiti. Soon after their arrival a small ship, *Jenny*, arrived in Tahiti and later took the captain, Matthew Weatherhead, and four crewmen to America, ostensibly to arrange a rescue mission. Three of the crew in Tahiti decided they couldn't wait and rigged one of the whaleboats with sails made from matting, then set out for Port Jackson. This boat was not dissimilar in design and dimensions to the launch Bligh and his exiles had sailed from Tofua to Timor, but sadly these men from *Matilda* were never seen again.

Hearing the tale from the remaining men was an all-too-bold reminder for Bligh and his crew of the life-threatening dangers all seafarers faced when sailing through the vast and uncharted waters that *Providence* and *Assistant* had just traversed, and would soon encounter between Tahiti and Torres Strait.

Bligh was eager to learn what he could of the mutineers and whether Captain Edwards had had any success in his hunt for them, and the islanders were equally keen to tell him all they knew – about *Bounty* returning twice to the island, of who stayed there and who left aboard the ship for an unknown destination. He learned there were several young girls and boys on the island who had been fathered by some of the renegades.

Within days of *Providence* arriving, word had reached Chief Tynah that Bligh had returned and he immediately made for Matavai Bay to renew the friendship he had enjoyed with the captain three years earlier. This reunion led to the mission securing the utmost support from the islanders for the collection of breadfruit plants, a task that would be considerably quicker than the *Bounty* experience, because at this time of year the seedlings quickly established themselves to a point where they could safely be potted and transported.

While the botanists did their work, Bligh made an observation that was causing him great concern. He believed a rot had set in within Tahitian society as a consequence of visits from foreign ships. The paradise of the Tahiti he had seen during the *Bounty* visit was being corrupted by European visitors, and it would never be the same. 'Our friends here have benefitted little from their intercourse with Europeans,' he lamented. 'Our countrymen have taught them such vile expression as are in the mouth of every Tahitian, and I declare that I would rather forfeit anything than to have been in the list of ships that have touched here since April, 1789.'

Bligh, a man who considered himself honourable in all things, continued to be alarmed at the changes in Tahitian customs and culture since his first visit. Local guests he invited aboard this time had changed their taste from wine to rum and, he noted bitterly, that owing to 'the quantity of old clothes left among these people ... they wear such rags as truly disgust us. It is rare to see a person dressed in a neat piece of cloth which formerly they had in abundance and wore with much elegance ... they are no longer clean Tahitians, but in appearance a set of ragamuffins with whom it is necessary to observe great caution.'

Bligh's health was again at a low ebb. The savage migraines that had struck him down during the voyage persisted and, making matters worse, the high humidity in Tahiti was sapping his energy. On many evenings he sought respite and solitude by going ashore and bathing in the cool waters of an island stream.

However, even when his health was at its nadir, the 37-year-old commander was still driven by a steely determination to prove his supporters, particularly Sir Joseph Banks, justified in their faith in him for this mission.

By 16 July 1792 the first of the three stages of this mission was nearly complete: *Providence* and *Assistant* were fully loaded and ready to depart for the return voyage to England via the West Indies. This would take them on a course to the west above the Tropic of Capricorn and south of the equator, one that would hopefully see them negotiate the dangers of Torres Strait before rounding the Cape of Good Hope and sailing north to the West Indies, where their cargo would be delivered.

Bligh must have been greatly relieved at this time. With the homeward journey about to begin, there had been no friction or confrontation of any significance with his men, and very few floggings. Better still, there was no evidence of unrest among the crew: none had shown any desire to desert despite the temptations of Tahiti that had led the *Bounty* mutineers astray three years earlier.

Just as *Bounty* had departed Tahiti a virtual floating nursery, so now did *Providence*. Bligh's count was 2126 breadfruit plants and 500 other plants, including various 'curiosity' plants, all meticulously catalogued by the gardeners for Sir Joseph Banks.

Bligh also had extra passengers: fifteen of the rescued survivors from *Matilda* took up his offer of a safe passage home, while five others had no desire to leave their newfound paradise. Seduced by the beauty of the island, they absconded without trace.

Also aboard *Providence* was a 22-year-old Tahitian, Mydidee, whom Tynah insisted Bligh take back to England to see and learn all he could before returning to Tahiti. Bligh conceded to this request, having refused Tynah's pleas that the chief be allowed to go himself. Three days after the two ships set sail, *Providence*'s crew increased by one more when a stowaway was found hiding below deck. 'I had not the heart to make him jump overboard,' Bligh wrote. 'I conceived he might be useful in Jamaica ... therefore directed he should be under the care of the botanists.'

CHAPTER FIFTEEN

Torres Strait, 1792

Success and slander

When the crews of *Providence* and *Assistant* saw the profiles of Tahiti's lush and towering volcanic peaks dissolve into the horizon behind their ships, Bligh had already set himself three immediate objectives: to search the myriad islands they would encounter en route to Torres Strait for any news of *Pandora* and even the *Bounty* mutineers themselves; to explore, as much as possible in the time available, the Fiji Islands; then to explore and survey Torres Strait in a bid to find a safe passage through it to the west.

Providence was running under full sail before a refreshing and steady south-easterly trade wind and making excellent progress during daylight hours, but when it came to night they probed their way through the darkness slowly under greatly reduced canvas, 'in an anxious lookout'. The responsibility placed on the seaman stationed high on the mainmast was enormous: these were still very dangerous, uncharted seas where in an instant an unseen coral reef or low-lying atoll could bring tragedy similar to that which had befallen *Matilda* and its crew.

As she was steered to the west, *Providence* weaved her way past numerous islands, including Bora Bora, and after sailing more than

600 nautical miles she arrived at Aitutaki, which arguably boasts the world's most beautiful island lagoon. It was a sweet reverie for Bligh as he had discovered this heavenly part of paradise aboard *Bounty* just seventeen days before the mutiny in April 1789. When he went ashore this time and communicated with the islanders in a fractured dialect and with hand gestures, the captain became convinced that *Pandora* had been there, but there was no evidence of *Bounty*.

Departing Aitutaki on 26 July 1792, within days Bligh was again back in all-too-familiar waters. He was in close proximity to the Friendly Isles, the region where, three years earlier, the famous, or infamous, mutiny occurred, and the incredible open-boat voyage to Timor began. Not far away was the island of Tofua, where he and his men went close to meeting a grisly death at the hands of islanders. However, there was little time for reflection and certainly no desire to stop this time.

For the leader of this expedition there was a far greater temptation to the north-west-by-north, one he could not resist: he had the opportunity to mount a more thorough investigation of one of his earlier discoveries, Fiji – or Bligh's Islands as the large patchwork of tropical peaks and atolls was then known. Also, he hoped that his track to Fiji would allow him to prove that other explorers had got it wrong, that the Friendly Isles and the southern part of what were called Maurelle's Islands were the same. This he did.

Dutch explorer and seafarer Abel Janszoon Tasman had been the first to sight some of the Fiji islands, in 1643. In fact he was almost wrecked there when his ship was swept alarmingly close to dangerous reefs that stood as a natural barrier around the atolls and islands making up the north-eastern part of the Fiji or Bligh Islands. Then, in 1774, Captain Cook recorded a sighting of the southernmost island in the group but ventured no further. Bligh is largely credited with making the most extensive discoveries among the 332 islands of the archipelago scattered across 200000 square miles of ocean: first during the launch voyage, when he sailed through the centre of the group, and now with *Providence*. However, as great as this exploratory passage would prove to be, the captain certainly didn't endear himself to historians, because of the very basic method he adopted to identify the islands.

Since there were so many islands in the group, Bligh decided, quite understandably, that it would be too difficult to give every one of them a name, so instead he used the letters of the alphabet.

Sailing with the utmost caution, the exploration continued through the reef-strewn region. All the time Bligh was recognising the magnitude of the demands placed on his navigational skills and the constant pressure the lookouts positioned high in the rig were experiencing. At no stage was there room for complacency or assumption; these treacherous waters were a maze of coral reefs and shoals, and every one of them held the potential to claim one or both of the ships.

Prudent seamanship was paramount in this situation. The security of the expedition was at stake, so Bligh gave orders for the sails to be taken in and progress slowed to little more than 1 knot. As an extra precaution, he added a warrant officer to each watch, and when the threat of navigational hazards was at its greatest he would send either *Assistant* or one of the ship's small boats ahead to sound the depth with the lead-line then report back.

When light faded after a long day's sailing and his instincts told him it was too dangerous to proceed, Bligh gave the order to anchor at night so that they didn't run aground. It was slow going.

During the launch voyage Bligh had done everything possible to avoid the Fijian natives in case they held murderous intentions like those he had encountered at Tofua. But this time it was different – he wanted to make contact – but the opportunity only presented itself once. 'A canoe, manned by four natives, approached the ship,' he wrote. 'Two came on board and looked about them with some surprise.' They were extremely hesitant and soon departed.

By 10 August, Bligh had gone through the entire alphabet for place names: the first island, named 'A', is today known as Mothe, located 170 nautical miles east-by-south of the Fijian capital, Suva. His island 'Z', we now know as Viti Levu. So, with 26 islands named, he switched to numbers, but as it turned out he needed to use only two numerals because Island Number 2 (today Kadavu) was where he realised there was no more land to be seen to the west. He correctly assumed it was the outer island of the group – in fact the southernmost island in Fiji.

He wistfully noted in his log that he would have liked more time for exploration because, with so many islands in the distance, there was obviously much more to be discovered. But more importantly the wily seafarer, whose knowledge of this region was second to none, was well aware that the 'contrary monsoon season' was approaching. It was a season that could bring havoc, even tragedy, to unwary mariners through heinous storms. He recorded that the pressure of time associated with his orders from the Admiralty called for 'my utmost exertions to avoid delay … in exploring my way between New Holland and New Guinea'.

Having sailed away from Fiji for the final time in his life, it was a further nine days of sailing across the warm blue seas of the tropics before land was sighted again. This time it was a group of islands positioned to the north of Vanuatu which he had previously seen and charted during his launch voyage in 1789, and Captain Cook had seen in 1774. But they remained unexplored, so Bligh took the time to do so. He named the group after Sir Joseph Banks – the Banks Islands.

As the two ships continued on towards Torres Strait through August, their progress remained uneventful until a surprising, almost disconcerting, observation was made by *Providence*'s sailing master. Portlock registered the incident:

> About this time the master reported to me that during the forenoon he had seen pass a stick that appeared very much like a white studding-sail boom. It was great neglect of his duty his not mentioning the matter to me. If I had known or had any idea that it really was a studding-sail boom or any other ship's spar, I most certainly would have hoist a boat out and picked it up, judging it must have belonged to a ship lost at sea hereabouts or cast on shore or some coast not far distant.

If this 'stick' had been recovered and identified as part of a ship's rig, it is almost certain Bligh would have insisted on a search for possible survivors. Had he done this and succeeded, he could well have solved one of the great maritime mysteries of the day: the disappearance of Jean-François de Galaup, Comte de La Pérouse and his ships *La Boussole* and *L'Astrolabe*. On 10 March 1788, La Pérouse, as leader of a grand French expedition to map the world on behalf of King Louis XVI, set sail with the two ships in company from Botany Bay, leaving with the British correspondence to be sent on to England via France. La Pérouse intended to reach France in December that year, his return voyage taking him via New Guinea, Tonga and New Caledonia, but unfortunately the two ships were mauled by a summer cyclone and vanished without trace. It was 40 years before the first clue as to the fate of these ships emerged: an Irish seafarer, Captain Peter Dillon, discovered one of the wrecks on a reef off the island of Vanikoro, just north of Vanuatu. It was not until the early 1960s, well over a century later, that divers found the wreck of the second vessel less than 1 mile from the first.

It was a tragic end to an ambitious voyage around the world that had begun in August three years earlier. The expedition had included 114 men – among them scientists, naturalists and illustrators, as well as an astronomer, a mathematician, a geologist and a botanist. Knowing La Pérouse was an admirer of Captain Cook, Banks had secured for him two inclining compasses Cook had used on his voyages.

It was Portugal's Luis Váez de Torres who had unknowingly discovered the strait in September 1606, when he sailed through it, but he did not name it. That came in 1769 when Scottish geographer Alexander Dalrymple was translating Spanish documents seized by the English: he found details of Torres' route and so named the stretch of water in his honour. Dalrymple was then hoping the Admiralty would commission him to go in search of this strait and explore some of the South Pacific, but instead they chose Captain Cook for the mission. This led to Cook discovering and charting the east coast of New Holland and eventually sailing through Torres Strait. This time, the Admiralty wanted finer detail of this stretch of water, and Bligh was the man for what would prove to be an extremely challenging, dangerous and near-disastrous mission. It is now known that there are 274 islands in Torres Strait, that it is stippled with a mass of reefs, shoals and shallows, and apart from exceptionally strong currents, the tidal range averages more than 16 feet. It is, to this day, an extremely hazardous stretch of water – a navigator's hell.

Bligh, whose health was now the best it had been for months, obviously had no idea of the magnitude of the navigational challenge he was about to encounter, nor did he realise his men would face an added human danger – armed and brutal warriors. This was a threat that Dutch explorer Willem Jansz had experienced first-hand when he was in the region with his ship *Duyfken*, just six months before Torres: nine of his crew were murdered by men he described as 'wild, cruel, black savages' when on the western coast of what is now Cape York Peninsula.

Even though Bligh had been through this region aboard the launch, he was facing far greater perils on this occasion because he really was entering unknown, shallow and undoubtedly treacherous waters. For this reason, he ordered that both ships make a slow and extremely cautious approach from the east, and once they entered the shallows they anchored so they could make observations and establish a plan for proceeding further to the west. It was a plan that became less complicated almost immediately after the anchor was set: the lookout stationed near the masthead reported he could see a relatively large island about 30 nautical miles to the west. Bligh would name this Darnley Island in honour of his kinsman, John Bligh, the 4th Earl of Darnley. Today we know it as Erub Island.

In the morning, the whaleboat and cutter led *Assistant* away to the west to start the search for a safe passage while *Providence* remained at anchor. Their quest was proceeding smoothly until four large canoes approached them under sail from Darnley Island and surrounded the cutter, commanded by Lieutenant Tobin. There was no doubt about the intention of these people: it was to attack and kill these unknown trespassers who had ventured into their part of the world. An ugly incident followed.

Soon after the islanders intercepted the cutter, those aboard *Providence* heard a round of musket fire, followed by the signal for assistance, which Bligh observed. Immediately he ordered well-armed men onto the pinnace to go to the aid of Tobin and his men. As they departed the ship, one of the canoes, with fifteen islanders on board, moved in to attack the cutter. 'Two of them now took a deliberate aim at the stern sheets of the boat, about 20 yards distant, while the rest were stringing and preparing their bows with great expedition,' Tobin recounted.

It was a desperate situation for the Englishmen. As their attackers took aim with arrows, the stricken men could see other canoes had also entered the hunt and were closing fast. Tobin's only option was to attack them before they were within a range of the cutter where they could be deadly accurate. It was an action, Tobin said later, that led to their survival. When the assailants heard the instant crack of musket shot and the invisible projectiles cut down some of their men, they took fright, diving into the bilge of their canoes so they were concealed below the gunwales.

With this attack put down, the crews of *Providence* and *Assistant* were on high alert for further attacks as they proceeded tentatively through the myriad submerged obstacles confronting them. Too much haste could destroy their mission in an instant. Ironically, over the following days they were only met by islanders who showed considerable friendship towards them, while all the time wanting items made from iron, which they referred to phonetically as *toore-toore*. Tobin noted that this reference sounded almost identical to the word used by the islanders throughout much of the South Pacific when talking of iron.

It was on 12 September 1792 that Bligh's life would take a turn for the worse in both England and the Torres Strait. It was the day when the courts martial commenced in Portsmouth for the ten *Bounty* mutineers who had survived the wreck of *Pandora*, and also the day when Bligh's already dangerous circumstances in the Torres Strait verged on the brink of tragedy. Both *Providence* and *Assistant* were off Warrior Island when as many as ten large canoes carrying at least 100 native men approached. Initially, it appeared they wanted to make friendly contact, but this was a ruse so they could move as close as possible to the ships to make an effective attack. Sensing great danger, Portlock called on some of his crew aboard *Assistant* to fire warning shots towards the men, and from this moment the trouble started.

Portlock was at the masthead, so he had the best vantage point for surveying the situation and directing those on deck. His greatest concern was for his men in the cutter rafted alongside his ship, being prepared to go on a sounding survey of the waters ahead. His call to fire was met with a salvo of arrows, wounding two men in the cutter and another on deck. Portlock then rushed down to the deck to better supervise the defence of his ship. His call for rounds of 'smart fire' aimed at the assailants in the canoes brought an immediate result: many took fright, jumping overboard to shelter behind their canoes.

The Englishmen continued their assault on the canoes and those islanders remaining aboard them. The islanders, quickly realising they had no way of countering an attack by weapons they could not even comprehend, retreated with their dead and wounded, and their battered canoes.

Of the three crewmen aboard *Assistant* wounded by arrows, one, the quartermaster, died two weeks later from gangrene. One other, who was wounded in the arm, never regained full use of the limb.

The two ships then continued on their slow, methodically planned passage to the west. Six days later when they were anchored near three small islands, Bligh sent two of his lieutenants, Guthrie and Tobin, ashore to one of them 'for the purpose of taking possession of all the islands seen in the Strait for His Britannic Majesty, George III'. Bligh ordered that it be named Possession Island; however, this was later changed to North Possession Islet to avoid confusion with the Possession Island off the northern tip of Cape York, which Captain Cook had named when he claimed New Holland. Bligh named the others Tobin's Islet and Portlock's Islet. This visit to the islet to complete Royal Navy formalities for the claiming of territory also presented the opportunity for the botanists to go ashore and collect previously unknown plants and specimens.

Bligh hoped that by now the most dangerous stages of this near three-week exploration lay in their wake, but that was not to be the case. The next phase proved to be an extremely dangerous, almost terminal, situation for both ships. With the whaleboat and cutter both searching for a channel that would take them between Mulgrave and Jervis islands, a current running at 4 knots suddenly took control of their progress despite every effort of both crews to escape its grasp. Their only option was to signal a warning to *Assistant*, which was trailing them.

But it was too late – both *Assistant* and *Providence* were about to fall into the same trap. Portlock, aboard *Assistant*, noted:

> Some sunken rocks appeared and almost forbid us a passage. At 8.55 in the morning the cutter fired some muskets as a signal for sudden shoal water, immediately signalled *Providence* and hauled towards and tacked and bore away to westward and ran in between two patches of broken water. The tide carried us through this dangerous passage at a great rate and was carrying us towards the reefs, therefore hauled under the shelter of the rocky lump ... and anchored. This tide was hurrying the *Providence* towards the reefs, and I signalled 'Good anchorage', but did not like to signal 'Follow without danger'.

Bligh, with meticulous skill, managed to guide his cumbersome, 107-foot ship through the turbulent water while at the mercy of the current, following Portlock's brave lead. 'I furled all sails and also came to anchor,' he logged. 'To my horror when the half cable came out it had the dog-stopper on, which although I cut it immediately and let go a second anchor, I only had it just in my power to save the ship from the rocks.' But Bligh kept a cool head: 'the men who had done this were no more faulty than the officer who was in command, so I did not punish them'.

Following their experience, Tobin would refer to this narrow passage as 'Hell Gates'. Torres Strait is littered with navigational threats such as this, so much so that since these two ships ventured into the strait, more than 350 vessels have been wrecked there. Unbeknown to Bligh, *Pandora*, with the captured mutineers on board, had already been wrecked on a reef just 150 nautical miles to the south-east of where *Providence* and *Assistant* almost met the same fate.

Had it not been for Bligh's request for *Assistant* to sail as tender to *Providence* in this expedition, there is every chance this particular incident would have seen *Providence* wrecked beyond repair. Without the smaller *Assistant* showing the way and immediately signalling the presence of danger, *Providence* would most likely have been driven uncontrollably onto the reef. Bligh's cautious approach to navigation and the teamwork he developed with Portlock also contributed to their safe transition through this particular part of the survey.

Relieved to have found their way through a narrow gap in the reefs and now in deeper water, both Bligh and Portlock knew they were still some time and distance from the point where Torres Strait would release them into safety. Late on the same day they were again entrapped by a raging current that threatened to bring their venture to an abrupt and disastrous end. With darkness on the march, they realised that if they were to have any chance of safety, they would have to drop anchor there and then in what was an extremely dangerous environment. Flinders wrote, 'the vessels were so closely surrounded with rocks and reefs, as scarcely to have swinging room', while Bligh declared that the circumstances were 'worse than before, rocks all around us and a dreadful tide running'. It was going to be a miracle if the two ships survived the night, but miracle it was.

The next day, with the small boats plumbing the depths of the waters ahead and searching for yet another gap in the reefs, success finally came and they made their escape to the western side of the strait. The channel they found was a mere 500 feet wide and, at its shallowest, just 4 fathoms. Appropriately, it would be named Bligh's Farewell. For the captain this nineteen-day probe through a challenging riddle of reefs confirmed yet again that this part of the world was the most dangerous he had confronted in his nautical career. Later, during his circumnavigation of Australia, Flinders would recall his earlier experience aboard *Providence* and recognise both Bligh and Portlock for their achievements. 'Perhaps no space,' he said, 'presents more dangers than Torres Strait; but with caution and perseverance the Captains Bligh and Portlock proved them to be surmountable.'

The threats of Torres Strait behind them, Bligh set a course for Coupang, but while the ships had survived their ordeal, the breadfruit plants in the nursery below deck were wilting and dying. Just ten degrees south of the equator, the tropical heat and stifling humidity were taking their toll. This loss would continue until they arrived in Jamaica. Part of the problem was caused by the ships encountering very little rain since leaving Tahiti, so the water supplies had not been replenished to any great degree. More importantly, with their water ration vastly reduced, the crew was also suffering from dehydration: some sailors resorted to licking the outside of the wooden buckets being used to water the plants simply to slake their thirst.

They finally reached Coupang during the first week of October, Bligh noting immediately it was 'a poorer place than when I last left it'. The priority was to have the ships re-provisioned and readied for sailing as soon as possible, and during this time the botanists went about their task of collecting more plants and specimens for Kew Gardens in London. This time they potted fruit trees, including mangoes and pomegranates, along with a number of native plants. After a brief stay, they left Timor and set a direct course around the Cape of Good Hope to St Helena in the middle of the South Atlantic.

Meanwhile the captured mutineers were back in Portsmouth, facing their courts martial. It was definitely a life-or-death experience for each one of them. The Admiralty had hoped to conduct the trials with Bligh present, but eventually decided that keeping the prisoners in dank confinement any longer would be inhumane, so proceedings commenced aboard HMS *Duke*. The adjudication panel comprised eleven captains who were presided over by Vice-Admiral Lord Hood. The charges were read: if found guilty of 'mutinously running away with the said armed vessel *Bounty* and deserting from His Majesty's Service', all ten men would hang.

When the time came to hand down the verdict, the court decreed the charges were proven against Heywood, Morrison, Ellison, Burkett, Millward and Muspratt. They were condemned to death. The charges against Norman, Coleman, McIntosh and Byrne (the near-blind fiddler) had not been proven, primarily thanks to Bligh's original evidence, so they were acquitted.

Fortunately for Heywood and Morrison, the court recommended mercy for them and both received full and unconditional pardons from the king. Heywood's family connections ensured his pardon and he went on to have a successful naval career. Morrison's account of the mutiny and his ordeal on *Pandora*, written while he was in prison, probably guaranteed his. This book was scheduled to be published after his execution, however, on seeing the manuscript the Admiralty most likely cut a deal with Morrison to suppress the book's publication and avoid a scandal in return for his pardon. Morrison went back to the navy but perished at sea off the coast of Madagascar in 1806. His book was published posthumously in 1870. Muspratt, too, was lucky to be pardoned. Conflicting testimony about his role in the mutiny meant he was acquitted and released. But there was no way out for Burkett, Ellison and Millward. All three were hanged from the foreyard aboard HMS *Brunswick* on the morning of 29 October 1792.

With the various plants in their pots and tubs having been aboard now for almost six months, Bligh sailed directly to St Helena, not stopping at Cape Town, to ensure that his precious cargo would reach Jamaica in a condition fit to be successfully transplanted. On 17 December, *Providence* sailed into the lee of St Helena and anchored close to shore, but still in the surge of wide open water. The tropical but near-barren island – famous for being Napoleon's place of exile – is the craggy peak of an undersea volcano and to this day it is considered to be one of the world's most isolated outposts. Bligh went ashore there and presented the governor with ten of the breadfruit plants, and in celebration of their safe arrival he had two of the Tahitians aboard the ship create a meal which included sago pudding made from the pith of some of the plants.

After celebrating Christmas on the island, Bligh elected to depart on 27 December and set a course to Kingstown Harbour, St Vincent, where they arrived one month later – on 22 January 1793. By now the weather and lack of fresh water had led to the loss of more than half the plants put aboard in Tahiti, but Bligh still managed to send ashore 544 healthy plants. At the same time the botanists, Wiles and Smith, continued their search for plants suitable for transfer to Kew Gardens and its patron, Sir Joseph Banks. They collected and potted 465 specimens. In the first week of February, *Providence* then moved on to its ultimate destination in the breadfruit mission, Jamaica's Port Royal, Kingston, where, with great fanfare and celebration – and great relief for Bligh – the balance of the breadfruit plants was delivered. Bligh was duly rewarded for his efforts; he received from the planters in St Vincent a special piece of plate valued at 100 guineas, while the Jamaican House of Assembly awarded him the remarkable sum of 1000 guineas. Captain Portlock received 500 guineas.

Over time the breadfruit plants were a successful crop on the islands of the West Indies, but as they grew, an ironic twist would emerge from what had been an obsession to establish the plant there. This mission was accomplished after two epic voyages to the South Pacific which led to mutiny, murder and men being hanged. It was all because of the need to provide a cheap food source for the slave labourers who worked on the vast sugar estates. Incredibly, after all this effort and drama, the slaves found breadfruit to be unpalatable.

With his South Pacific odyssey finally complete, Bligh's intention was to cross the Atlantic to England as soon as was practicable. As he prepared to depart, his plan was stymied by the arrival of the packet *Duke of Cumberland*. It brought news that England was back at war, and once again France was the enemy. This forced *Providence* and *Assistant* to remain in Jamaica until Bligh's ship was suitably prepared with arms for self-defence, and the circumstances on the high seas were deemed safe enough for them to cross the Atlantic and reach home. This meant a six-month wait until the middle of June.

After finally putting Jamaica in their wake, it was almost eight weeks' sailing for *Providence* and *Assistant* until they finally arrived in

England, anchoring at Deptford on 7 August 1793. Bligh and his two crews had been away almost two years to the day and in that time covered more than 35 000 nautical miles. Two days after their arrival Bligh made his last entry in his journal as captain of *Providence*. 'This voyage has terminated with success, without accident or a moment's separation of the two ships,' he wrote, with justifiable pride. 'It gives the first and only satisfactory accounts of the pass between New Guinea and New Holland, if I except some vague accounts of Torres in 1606; other interesting discoveries will be found in it.'

It was a superb achievement: Bligh had done it. He thanked his entire crew for being part of the mission, assuring them he would do everything in his power to help their advancement within naval ranks, and he kept his word. Unfortunately for Bligh, though, the success of this expedition was overshadowed by the fallout from the courts martial. In a matter of days he would discover that he was no longer the national hero of the Timor launch voyage and his version of what had happened on *Bounty* had been challenged, with disastrous consequences for his reputation, forever.

Bligh was now a much-maligned and controversial figure. The reasons for the mutiny had become the subject of gossip and speculation. With the court martial unfolding in his absence, the prosecution and family members of the mutineers on trial, including Edward Christian, Fletcher's older brother and an erudite barrister, had done their utmost to discredit Bligh. Morrison himself had begun writing his own somewhat biased account of the mutiny while he was in prison. It was critical of Bligh.

Public sympathy now lay with the mutineers; the campaign to besmirch Bligh's character was so effective that nearly a year after his own court martial, in which he was cleared of any wrongdoing, the new evidence portrayed him as tyrannical and abusive, a commander who had no hesitation in treating his crew with contempt and disrespect. It was a malicious and carefully orchestrated attack, designed to justify the reasons for the mutiny and save the mutineers from certain death. Speculation about Bligh spread across the country, and through English society. He became *persona non grata*, all because he had been away, as ordered, with *Providence* and therefore unable to defend his account and his honour in court. Even the Admiralty concurred with public opinion and shunned their one-time hero. The only captain in their favour from this mission was Portlock.

Understandably, being the proud man he was, Bligh struggled to contend with his fall from grace and the damage it wrought upon his reputation and his career. Still, there was work to be done: by the first week of September 1793, *Providence* and *Assistance* were formally paid off and he had a role to play.

On 6 September, *The Kentish Register* gave a glowing report of the event, saying that the high esteem the crew of both ships held for their captain was evident to all present. 'Every one of them cheered loudly as a mark of respect as he departed the ship and stepped ashore, then continued their rousing acclamation as he passed through the dock gates.' The report also noted how healthy and respectable the seamen appeared after such a long and perilous voyage.

Disconsolate as he may have felt at the time, there came a sign of great appreciation for his efforts little more than two months later when the Royal Society of the Arts bestowed upon him the honour of being the recipient of the society's prestigious Gold Medal. No doubt he would have been pleased to read the report of this award in *The World* newspaper on 3 December:

> On Wednesday evening last, the Society for the encouragement
> of Arts, Manufactures and Commerce, adjudged their gold
> medal to Captain William Bligh, of his Majesty's ship *Providence*,

being the premium offered to the person who should first
convey [breadfruit] from the Islands in the south-sea, to the
Islands in the West Indies.

As 1794 began to unfold, Bligh decided he had had enough: it was
time to stand up and publicly defend his honour and his reputation
against the opposing published accounts of the mutiny. Muspratt
had published his *Minutes of the Bounty Court-Martial* containing an
appendix by Edward Christian which was passionate in the defence
of his brother, Fletcher. This appendix did not directly condone
Fletcher's actions but it was a cleverly argued document and cited
a number of alleged incidents that presented Bligh's persona in an
unfavourable light. It asserted that Bligh treated his crew poorly
and that he had a mercurial side to his temperament, ignited by
trivial events. But as savage as this personal attack was, it only
strengthened Bligh's resolve to refute the accusations and save his
career. He wanted the Admiralty to appoint him once again to the
position of commander of a vessel, and this would allow him to put
all the unwarranted accusations behind him.

But Bligh's career as a naval officer was now all but dead. He
must have been wondering if it had been worthwhile undertaking
the breadfruit missions: the first voyage cost him his ship, and the
second cost him his reputation. The previous twelve months had
certainly been his *annus horribilis*, and making matters worse was the
fact that he was out of favour with the Admiralty; he had been stood
down and placed on half-pay. It would be another eighteen months
before he would again experience the pride of being posted as a
commander.

In the meantime, he had to contend with his family sharing the
weight of his suffering and the adverse notoriety that came with
his downfall. His only consolation during this period was that not

being at sea meant he could enjoy the otherwise rare pleasure of being a husband and father. By this time Harriet, his eldest child, was already twelve, and her father had been away at sea for much of her life. As happy as this period might have been, it too was a time of great sadness. Soon he and Betsy would learn that their sixth daughter, Anne, was epileptic. That distress was then countered by great joy: Betsy was pregnant again. Deep down Bligh hoped the birth would present him with a much longed-for son. That was to be the case. Much to his delight twin boys were delivered, but tragically this moment turned to crushing grief within twenty-four hours, when both boys died.

CHAPTER SIXTEEN

North Sea, 1795

Blockades, mutineers and battles

For almost eighteen months a heavy grey cloud of sadness, frustration and misfortune hung low over Bligh's life. He tried to stay focused, believing that one day soon there would be a glimmer of hope – a sign that better times were coming – but it wasn't to be. Instead, deep despair from the loss of the twin boys remained heavy in his heart; and despite England being at war with the French and the Dutch, the Admiralty saw no need to call on the services of a commander who, only a few years earlier, was a hero. Instead Bligh remained on half-pay and struggled to support his wife and six daughters.

With the cross-Channel naval hostilities escalating, the Admiralty finally decided to bring Bligh in from exile: as they put more ships into battle they were in need of qualified commanders, and Bligh was to be among them. Redemption came in April 1795 when he was appointed commander of the former East India Company ship *Warley*, which had been purchased by the government and renamed HMS *Calcutta*. His immediate role was to oversee the conversion of a merchant ship into a battleship during a refit at Blackwall. The new-look HMS *Calcutta* emerged as a 56-gunner destined to join Admiral Adam Duncan's North Sea Fleet based at the Nore, at the mouth of the Thames. This fleet's primary role was to harass the Dutch ships at anchor at the Texel with a blockade that gave them no option but to remain in port. If they tried to set sail, the British would do their best to blast the Dutch ships into splinters.

It was a defiant and bold Bligh who stood on the deck of the relaunched *Calcutta*, barking orders as she eased away from the dock at Blackwall and began heading down the Thames for the anchorage at the Nore, where she would join her squadron. As the ship rode the favourable tide and slipped past the low-profile buildings of London Town, he reflected on how this new posting was just a small part in the redemption of his naval career: the only way he could stand proud once more and reclaim his rightful place in the force, and society, was to prove himself on the high seas and in battle.

That first opportunity came on Thursday, 20 August, confirmed by *The London Sun* newspaper two days later. The news brief announced that Admiral Duncan had put to sea with a fleet of eight ships, including *Calcutta*, under the captaincy of William Bligh. 'The fleet is going in quest of the Dutch squadron said to be at sea,' the paper proclaimed.

During the last decade of the eighteenth century there was growing restlessness among the men of the lower decks in the Royal Navy, primarily because of poor wages and poor conditions and apparent mistreatment at the hands of some of the officers. The first real sign of what was to come surfaced in 1794 with a mutiny aboard HMS *Culloden*. It was quickly put down and the five instigators hanged – but this was not enough to deter others. One of the incidents following the mutiny involved Bligh, but it was through no fault of his own.

How strangely ironic it must have been for him when, as commander of *Calcutta,* he played a part in putting down a minor mutiny on another ship, the 74-gun third-rate HMS *Defiance.* After the actual incident, in October 1794, when Bligh was enjoying shore-time at home with his family in Lambeth, he wrote wryly to his still staunch supporter Banks, to tell him of the mutiny. Interestingly, in what was obviously an echo of the *Bounty* mutiny, he noted that one of the reasons behind the *Defiance* mutiny was that the captain, Sir George Horne, had no marines aboard to support him.

The rebels were demanding the replacement of Horne and a lieutenant they disliked; greater liberty to go ashore; and their grog less diluted. Bligh was called in by authorities to discuss how to subdue this uprising, and he suggested the most effectual course of action would be to have another ship carrying troops simply lie alongside *Defiance* and then take over the ship, fight or no fight. Eventually a similar plan evolved: 200 troops under Bligh's command and aboard smaller boats would force their way onto the decks of *Defiance* from all sides and take control. Bligh led the way in a boat containing 80 armed men, and, much to his pleasure, when the mutineers saw the troops approach, decided (not surprisingly) to recognise the error of their ways and surrender.

While Bligh was enjoying being back at the front line in the Royal Navy, he had to accept that his health was still not as good as it should be; the price he had to pay for the punishment his body endured during the 47-day open boat trek to Timor. These problems, including rheumatism, were exacerbated by the cold and the physical ordeals he faced when stationed on the North Sea during the early part of winter, 1795. Banks was aware of this, so on hearing of a vacancy within the senior management of Greenwich Hospital, he took it upon himself in early November to write to Lord George Spencer, the First Lord of the Admiralty, asking that Bligh be considered for the posting so he could enjoy better health. His letter said in part:

> The service he did by saving the part of the crew of the *Bounty*
> that did not mutiny was meritorious in the extreme, the
> rewards he met with an attack upon his character unfounded
> and illiberal which I trust he completely answered by the
> exhibitions of documents only, without the necessity of urging
> a single argument.
>
> His health has by the voyage from the *Bounty* to Timor
> been utterly ruined, his headaches in the hot climates nearly
> killed him in his second breadfruit voyage, and he now suffers
> as much from rheumatisms in the North Sea.
>
> Active and indefatigable in the service however he never
> either complains or solicits ... I have not heard from him for
> some weeks and nothing in his letter tended to express a wish
> for retirement. It is not by his desire that I solicit it – I take that
> liberty merely because I know that his constitution requires rest
> now or will soon require it.

Lord Spencer advised that while the position at the hospital had already been filled, Bligh would soon be rewarded with a posting to a larger ship. This news prompted an immediate response from Banks, saying that this promotion would 'assist greatly towards healing the wound his spirit had received by the illiberal and unjust treatment his character had met with from the relatives of the mutineers of the *Bounty*.'

By December Bligh had sailed *Calcutta* back into English waters to anchorage at Yarmouth Roads, on the Isle of Wight, at the western end of the Solent. Shortly afterwards he reported to Banks in a letter that it had been a most eventful voyage: *Calcutta* was continually lashed by alarmingly strong gales, and was also nearly trapped in an inferno when a ship laden with timber and anchored nearby caught fire. Bligh and his crew watched in horror when the ship 'in the most awful state of conflagration' broke free from its mooring and was driven rapidly and directly towards *Calcutta* by a fast flowing tide and a gale of wind. Knowing that if the blazing vessel struck his ship it, too, would be set ablaze, Bligh immediately shouted orders for all hands on deck and to set sail, then, with the inferno only feet away and no time to weigh anchor, he ordered for both anchor cables to be cut so *Calcutta* could sail away from the danger. They achieved this by the narrowest of margins and moored in safe waters nearby using their only remaining anchor.

On 7 January Bligh again wrote to Banks while aboard *Calcutta*, first to tell him some wonderful news – which Banks already knew in part. He had received an important new posting: captain of the considerably larger HMS *Director*, a 64-gun third-rate vessel of 1400 tons with a crew of almost 500 men, and his crew would be transferred with him. Apart from the importance the actual promotion brought to his now reinvigorated career – he was back in favour with the Admiralty – he suggested to Banks that the associated increase in salary was important for a man 'having a large family of young girls to bring forward in life'. He also thanked Banks for his consideration regarding the appointment at Greenwich Hospital.

D*irector* was readied for sea and in May 1796 Bligh was once more ordered to join the fleet patrolling the Channel and the North Sea.

Within days he became convinced that *Director*'s reputation for being one of the navy's superior fighting ships was well-founded. He confirmed this in a letter to Duncan Campbell, saying there was 'no faster vessel in the squadron'; however, he did hold some concern for her structural integrity as she was twelve years old and the hull had been fastened with iron, which had a limited life. 'I am not afraid, however, of her lasting my time,' he quipped. In that 'time' came experiences that would restore his reputation as an honourable and brave naval commander.

When *Director* crossed the English Channel and joined the Texel blockade, England was facing a maritime onslaught from the Dutch, French and Spanish navies. Once again, though, for the combined enemy, it brought with it defeat at the hands of the British, and a death toll that was almost beyond comprehension.

There was one huge loss during the summer that had little to do with a superior force. It came when the French deployed a large naval fleet out of Brest with the intention of attacking Ireland. This armada included seventeen sail-of-the-line ships, four frigates and an impressive array of other vessels, including six transports with 25 000 men aboard. As the ships approached the Irish coast a howling storm developed and decimated the fleet, leaving them no alternative but to run for home. Four ships sank with enormous loss of life, and thousands of soldiers drowned when some of the transports were lost. In another actual engagement that occurred a short time later, two English ships, the 44-gunner HMS *Indefatigable* and the 36-gunner HMS *Amazon*, engaged the 74-gun French ship *Droits de l'Homme* off Ouessant, an island at the southern entrance to the English Channel, leaving her a crippled and smouldering wreck on the coast of her homeland. Only 300 men in her complement of 1800 survived.

It was mid-May 1796 when Bligh retired to his spacious, heavily timbered captain's cabin at the stern of *Director*, which was at anchor at the Nore. He went to his desk near the many small-paned windows casting ample light into the interior and began penning one of numerous letters he would send to Banks over the next seven months, letters that provided a broader perspective of the life of a Royal Navy ship commander.

In that first letter Bligh's enthusiasm is evident after finally receiving his orders to put to sea with the squadron and cruise to Dogger Bank, where they were destined to engage the Dutch: '... our Order of Battle ... was given out yesterday ... I think we are equal to anything the Dutch will bring against us ... we shall return to port before the last of July or the first week in August.'

On 13 June 1796, when *Director* was part of the Texel blockade, Bligh wrote a letter which he sent via a ship from the squadron that was returning to England: 'Our cruise to this moment has not been attended with any event that should lead me to humble you with a recital, but to know that we are all as should be.'

It eventuated that the Dutch fleet laid low: there was little action to be seen, so *Director* and other ships in the squadron were ordered to return to home waters ahead of schedule. As soon as *Director* reached the anchorage at Yarmouth Roads on 26 June, Bligh again wrote to Banks: 'We arrived here on Friday evening, the squadron consisting of six sail of the line and one frigate. I had no expectation of the cruise being so short, I understand it is occasioned by a representation that no advantage will be derived from long cruises.' Bligh also voiced a strong desire to undertake a patrol before the end of summer with *Director* alone, not part of a flotilla. He was convinced that with his ship's speed under sail he would be able to pursue and engage the slower French naval vessels. The captain's desire for battle was again evident in a letter on 21 July when HMS *Glatton*, which would turn out to be his next command, arrived at the same anchorage after a successful fight with the enemy: '*Glatton* is much cut in the mast and rigging ... we have only to lament that the *Glatton* was alone.' Bligh also noted it was the effectiveness of the carronades *Glatton* carried that brought success against a larger enemy.

On 16 September Bligh's nemesis, Fletcher Christian, who was then living in hiding on Pitcairn Island, continued to haunt him. It was now eight years since the mutiny but Fletcher's brother, Edward, an English judge and law professor, was still doing his utmost to clear his family's name with publications biased towards the mutineers. These pamphlets would become one of the enduring sources of Bligh's bad reputation.

Bligh informed Banks: 'Mr Nichol has been so good as to send me down a pamphlet called Christian's Letters. Is it possible that wretch [Fletcher] ... has had intercourse [contact] with his brother, that sixpenny Professor, who has more law about him than honour? My dear sir, I can only say that I heartily despise the praise of any of the family of Christian and I hope thus yet that the mutineer will meet with his deserts.' This same letter also flagged Bligh's concern regarding his health: 'I continue to suffer much with headache and my eyelids are so constantly convulsed as to hurt my sight.'

During the next few months, Bligh, as ordered, kept *Director* fully provisioned and watered so that she could put to sea at a moment's notice if necessary. With Yarmouth Roads being only 2 nautical miles from the western entrance of the Solent, she could be sailing on the waters of the English Channel within an hour of weighing anchor.

In February 1797, when *Director* was back at anchor at Yarmouth, Bligh unexpectedly received orders to sail under the direction of Captain Parr, commanding HMS *Standard*, to proceed north to the port of Humber and lie there until further orders, 'to protect the peace'. He explained the reason for this voyage to the port, located halfway up the eastern coast of England and much closer to the Dutch coast than Yarmouth Roads: 'All accounts from the Texel state that the Dutch are laid up. Nevertheless the people here are very much alarmed from an apprehension that the French will pay them a visit.' Bligh had hoped he would also be able to survey much of the area close to the entrance of the Humber through to the town of Hull; however, he lamented to Banks that due to ill-health while there he did not have time to complete the survey, although he did take time to sketch 'a correct plan of the entrance, upon which you may rely'.

Two months later, in April, *Director* was again harassing the Dutch at Texel, and that same month saw a threatened uprising among Royal Navy sailors approach boiling point when men aboard sixteen ships from the Channel Fleet, at anchor at Spithead, mutinied. While refraining from any violent acts towards their superiors, the rebels refused to weigh anchor on any ship until their demands were granted and the ringleaders were guaranteed a pardon for their actions. The men won on all points, including a full pardon pledged by King George III on 23 April.

As alarming as it was, this mutiny at Spithead was just a short-lived and very small ember when compared with the insurrection that came only weeks later. It was the Mutiny at the Nore, an event that delivered Bligh one of his finest moments.

At the root of this rebellion was a core of men who could easily be classified as inferior samples of society: some former prisoners, some undesirables who had been press-ganged into service, others sordid scoundrels. However, there were also ordinary, well-meaning seamen who supported this action.

Having received word of the success achieved by their fellow 'jack tars' at Spithead, this group set about igniting their uprising while aboard a fleet of navy ships anchored at the Nore. The fleet included *Director* and HMS *Inflexible*, both 64-gunners. Bligh had sensed for some time a growing disquiet among his own crew, whom he had for so long considered to be a happy lot. When trouble surfaced he was forced to order floggings on eleven days during a two-week period to maintain control. By 1 May the message to captains of all ships was to strengthen their attitudes towards their crews, as signs of a pending mutiny continued to emerge. Captains were ordered to have their marines on high alert, weapons loaded, ready for action, and 'on the first appearance of mutiny, to use the most vigorous means to suppress it'.

On 6 May, as Bligh guided *Director* along the calm waters of the Thames to the Nore to undergo a refit, there were no indications of a mutiny in the making. Six days later, however, the mutiny came to life. That day, as part of the insurrection, Bligh received a deputation from his men demanding that the master and two of the ship's lieutenants be dismissed from duty for ill-treatment of the crew. Bligh established a compromise with the men by having the officers in question confined to their quarters.

The basis for this unrest across the fleet had its origins in London, where politicians, concerned by the nation's financial crisis, deferred a review of pay scales for the navy. The disappointment flowing from this decision was then overshadowed by a situation aboard HMS *Leviathan*, where the crew was owed two years' back pay. The crew of HMS *Nassau* faced similar circumstances: they had not been paid for nineteen months.

The rebellion proper erupted aboard the flagship, *Sandwich*, which was under the command of Vice-Admiral Charles Buckner. The rebels gathered on the fo'c's'le and trained their guns towards the quarterdeck and the captain's cabin, with the sole intention of shooting him or any officer who showed signs of opposing them. Simultaneously, to demonstrate that their intentions were as determined as they might be brutal, they tied nooses into yard ropes attached to the foreyards: they were ready to hang anyone else who stood in their way. Richard Parker, who had previously been discharged from two Royal Navy ships for immoral behaviour and was subsequently demoted, emerged as the leader of the mutiny.

The captain of *Sandwich* was immediately ordered into confinement in his cabin, while Parker and his committee of mutineers began to formulate their plan to spread their insurrection across the rest of the fleet at anchor at the Nore, which would eventually number 33 ships. The rebels' first action was to send ashore any captain or officer they considered to be insufferable. Interestingly, Bligh was not among them at that time; it would be a week before he was ordered to surrender his command and leave the ship. As he did, he realised for the first time that he had a nickname among the men of the lower deck: 'that *Bounty* bastard', a derogatory title stemming from when the *Bounty* mutineers defended themselves at their courts martial.

With all captains and officers who caused concern relieved of their postings, the mutineers followed the lead of their fellow seafarers who had achieved such success at Spithead: on 20 May they presented Vice-Admiral Buckner with a list of demands. This was immediately forwarded to the Admiralty, which had no hesitation in rejecting it, but promised a pardon for all mutineers. This decision was deemed totally unacceptable and with that, red flags of rebellion were hoisted aloft across the fleet of ships: the fight was on.

Soon the mutineers' log of claims expanded to the extent that it appears they believed their power was such that they were initiating a social revolution that would spread across all of England. They blockaded London by preventing merchant vessels from entering the port. Whenever possible, they also grabbed the opportunity to plunder the cargos of any ships docked close by.

Now on shore, Bligh communicated with the Admiralty, and was directed to involve himself in the negotiations aimed at ending the insurrection. However, despite his best efforts and those of other officers, there was no sign of a solution by 27 May, the day the Admiralty office suggested they consider resorting to the use of force. On 6 June, Parliament supported this move by declaring that the mutiny should be crushed at all costs. These decisions led to the establishment of batteries on shore and the guns they contained were trained on the rebels' ships. Additional batteries were also built at the entrance to the Thames in case offshore crews mutinied, took control of their ships and sailed to the aid of those at the Nore.

By 8 June, however, the mutiny was beginning to unravel: ships were seen to be replacing their red flags with the Union Jack and the Blue Ensign, then slipping their cables and trying to make good an escape from the anchorage. Suddenly the conflict had all the hallmarks of a civil war as crews fired on crews from ships of the same navy. For the mutineers the situation was becoming increasingly desperate, so the rebel leader, Parker, decided he had one last chance to save his pride, his men and his life. They would attempt to run the gauntlet of batteries and escape the Thames, then sail to safe sanctuary in France. It failed. *Sandwich* went nowhere.

On 14 June it was over: Parker was arrested and all ships had surrendered. Ironically, the last ship to raise the white flag was *Director*.

At eight o'clock on the morning of 27 June, a single cannon shot and the breaking out of a yellow flag from the masthead of HMS *L'Espion* signalled that everything was in readiness for an execution to take place. Small boats made their way from the shore to *Sandwich*, where a short time later, with hundreds of sailors looking on from the decks of adjacent ships and throngs of people watching from the shore, Richard Parker was hanged from the foreyard. In all, 29 sailors deemed to be leaders of the mutiny suffered the same fate, while others were flogged, imprisoned or transported to New South Wales; however, the majority of men aligned to this uprising were not subjected to any form of punishment.

Bligh's contribution towards bringing this uprising to an end, having successfully negotiated with many of the rebels, was noted by King George. He was rewarded with new orders to resume command of *Director*, and was lauded by his crew for the fair and effective manner in which he went about recognising those among them who had supported the mutiny from the outset and those given no option but to stay with the ship and be seen to back the rebel cause. The twelve offenders he culled from his crew were delivered to shore, arrested, and dealt the appropriate punishment, while those remaining aboard *Director* were pardoned.

The captain then set about organising his ship, until a few days later when, very much to his surprise and disappointment, Vice-Admiral Skeffington Lutwidge wrote to him suggesting that there was in fact a total of 31 men among *Director's* crew who were considered to be insubordinates. Bligh would have no part in this. He was determined to stand by his men. He immediately fired off a letter to the Admiralty in which he made an emphatic case in support of those who had previously been pardoned, and that only the twelve whom he had identified as mutineers would be sent to trial. It worked: Lutwidge backed down. He directed the captain to muster the ship's company and advise that pardons would be delivered to all of them as soon as possible.

Bligh now stood in favour with not only the Admiralty but also with his crew aboard *Director*. This single act yet again confirmed that the much-maligned great seafarer was in fact a fair-minded man, and now, after he had championed their cause, they would soon be supporting him in battle.

During much of 1797 the Dutch fleet remained holed-up at Texel, due to the supposed presence of the British North Sea Fleet on their doorstep. What they didn't know was that for an extended period in the middle of the year there were only two British ships out there. It was simply a clever act by Admiral Duncan, who had signals sent on a regular basis to make it appear that the entire fleet was just over the horizon, thus causing the Dutch to stay at home.

By mid August the British had decided it was time to confront the Dutch: surrender or battle were the two choices they offered. Four weeks later, there was still no indication of what might occur – partly because the British wanted their fleet to be at full strength – and Bligh wrote: 'We continue cruising without any advantage except what results from blocking up the Dutch fleet which I hope is of great consequence during the present negotiation.'

By October the time had arrived: the British had 21 ships off Texel, including *Director*. The first rumblings of what would become known as the Battle of Camperdown, or in Dutch, *Zeeslag bij Kamperduin*, began to surface. There would be no surrender; the Dutch had had enough of being bogged down in their own waters: it was time to take on their adversaries from across the Channel.

Until the mid-seventeenth century major sea battles had primarily been conflicts involving pursuit: the pursuing ship fired cannons from the bow, and the pursued fired cannons from the stern. However, in 1653, during the First Anglo–Dutch War, the British applied a new form of sea warfare, the line-of-battle, during the Battle of the Gabbard. As the lighter Dutch ships came alongside their enemy with the aim of putting men aboard and fighting to the death, the side cannons mounted on the British ships blasted away and inflicted severe damage on the Dutch, forcing them to retreat with the loss of two ships. Despite this obvious success, the line-of-battle wasn't refined until the second half of the seventeenth century, following the development of heavy cannons. It was then agreed that the most effective way to decide a sea battle was to have the ships of the opposing sides either anchor in a line opposite each other – and within cannon-shot range – or sail from opposing ends past each other at a similar distance. Once the battle commenced, it was either the last ships floating or the side that hadn't lowered its colours and surrendered, who became victorious. Only the most heavily armed and heavily built ships – the ships-of-the-line – took part in these brutal conflicts.

On the morning of 11 October the British watched as the Dutch fleet sailed out of Texel and towards them, determined to fight for Dutch honour. By the afternoon the opposing sides were under sail and in their respective lines, ready to do battle. The moment the signal to engage went aloft and cannons thundered into action, Bligh had his ship attack two of the opposition, *Alkmaar* (56) and *Haarlem* (64). Then, while the battle raged, Bligh took himself to a position on deck where he could observe developments and plan his next attack. He quickly became confident there were enough ships in the rear section of the British line to beat the Dutch into submission. Then, peering through the thick smoke the cannons were pumping into the sky, he could see the Dutch admiral's ship, *Vrijheid*, up ahead and in the perfect position to be attacked: 'There was no time to be lost as night was approaching,' he later explained. 'I made sail ... engaging some of the centre ships, for I considered now the capture of the Dutch Commander-in-Chief's ship as likely to produce the capture of those ahead of him [in the forward, or van division].'

Bligh ordered his ship's sails be trimmed for speed: he was determined to have *Director* alongside *Vrijheid* as soon as possible and engage the admiral in a showdown.

We began the action with him, lying on his larboard quarter within 20 yards, by degrees we advanced alongside, firing tremendously at him, and then across his bows almost touching, when we carried away his foremast, topmast, topgallant mast and soon after, his mainmast ... together with his mizzenmast, and left him nothing standing.

The wreck lying all over his starboard side, most of his guns were of no use, I therefore hauled up along his starboard side and there we finished him, for at 3.55 o'clock he struck and the action was ended.

Once the action ceased, Bligh was an elated man: 'My officers came to congratulate me, and to say there was not a man killed [aboard *Director*] ... it passed belief – we had only seven men wounded.'

With the Dutch admiral having struck his colours and surrendered, nine of his fighting ships followed his lead while the remainder changed course and 'ran off'.

Admiral Duncan's ship was then only a short distance away, so Bligh bore up with *Director* to speak with him. Duncan hailed him to take possession of the Dutch admiral's ship. This he did, sending his first lieutenant aboard to complete formalities amid horrendous carnage – 58 dead, 98 wounded and nothing left standing. The total Dutch loss was 540 killed, 620 wounded and some 4000 taken prisoner, the British lost 203 men and had 622 wounded.

It was soon time to head back across the Channel to home. On 17 October, *Director* sailed triumphantly into Yarmouth Roads and the following day Bligh proudly informed the Admiralty of his ship's success. 'Sir, My Commander-in-Chief not being here,' he wrote, 'I have the honour to inform you for the information of My Lords Commissioners of the Admiralty that I anchored here last night with His Majesty's Ship *Director* and *Egalité*, 64, a prize to the Fleet'. What Bligh didn't say in this note was that there were some 200 Dutch prisoners aboard the ship he had brought home as a 'prize'. Later, this and all other Dutch ships captured in the battle and taken back to England would prove to be anything but 'prizes'. They had been so severely damaged that they were of no use to the Royal Navy.

L ess than two months after the fleet returned victorious from Camperdown, Bligh returned to Sheerness, on the Thames estuary, this time to give evidence at the court martial of an old colleague. Held aboard HMS *Circe*, it was an event that would for Bligh put to an end something that had haunted him for eighteen years: the circumstances surrounding Captain Cook's death.

John Williamson, the captain of the 64-gun HMS *Agincourt* during the Battle of Camperdown, faced a charge that, through cowardice, negligence and disaffection he had held *Agincourt* away from the fight and not done his utmost to bring the enemy ships to battle. This was the same Williamson whom Bligh believed was in many ways responsible for Cook's death at the hands of the islanders on a beach in the Sandwich Islands. Williamson, captain of the cutter that had been conveyed to shore, was seen to do nothing to defend or assist his captain, or the four marines who died with him. Instead, he moved the boat further away from shore, apparently for his own safety. Bligh was equally aggrieved that Williamson returned to *Resolution* on that dreadful day having made no effort to recover Cook's body from the islanders.

After an intensive inquest during which Bligh was one of many to give evidence, Williamson was found guilty of the second charge of cowardice. The sentence effectively ended his naval career. His name was placed at the bottom of the captain's list; he would never serve on a naval ship again.

In January 1798, during the miserable cold of a bleak English winter, Bligh's health was being tested. He did his best to remain on duty, but the rheumatism and migraine-like headaches that had plagued him for years were pushing him to the limit of despair. He decided then to request a leave of absence from *Director* in the hope that he could find some relief. His concern was such that he advised Banks in one of their still regular exchanges of letters: 'I want much to have advice on account of an alarming numbness which has seized my left arm from a rheumatic affliction.'

The absence from a shipboard life must have brought a reprieve because he was back aboard *Director* during March. His letter to Banks from Yarmouth Roads on 3 April confirmed that. He said he had just returned from a cruise to Texel after word had come back 'suggesting the enemy were preparing to sail'. But his real battle was with his health. In May, having again sailed to the Dutch coast, he sent Banks what he believed to be an important document: 'I send you my dear sir a sketch of the Texel which I believe will give you a more perfect knowledge of the passage for ships ... I am sorry to say I have such an extreme weakness in my eyes that at times I can scarce see. I am always suffering much pain.'

Bligh spent the remainder of the year serving as commander of *Director*, all the time wondering what would come next in his career, especially if the ship was paid off because it had served its useful life. A clue came in October, in an unsolicited communication from Admiral Lord Duncan: 'I have mentioned to the Admiralty that if your ship is paid off I hope they will immediately give you another, as I have always observed her conducted like a man of war ...' It was high praise, something that surprised the modest captain. He told Banks of it, adding, 'this compliment has not been fished for as I have never written to him but on service according to order ...'

By now Bligh's 44-year-old body was beginning to feel like it was a battle-weary ship-of-the-line. Even so, there was no stopping him: there were more battles to be fought and won – on and off the high seas.

CHAPTER SEVENTEEN

Baltic Sea, 1801

Nelson and the Battle of Copenhagen

It was during 1798, while Bligh continued his command of *Director* as a front-line patrol ship on the English Channel, that news came of a spectacular victory for the Royal Navy. Admiral Horatio Nelson had crushed the French fleet in the Battle of the Nile at Aboukir Bay near Alexandria, on the coast of Egypt. The French had been there with the intention of invading Egypt to limit archenemy Britain's trade routes and challenge British authority over India. It was a component of Napoleon Bonaparte's long-term strategy to stretch British military resources and subsequently defeat the Royal Navy on the English Channel, a victory that would make England vulnerable to invasion.

Britain rejoiced with the news of Nelson's achievement. Bligh was certainly impressed, too: he made special mention of it in a communication with Banks. Little did he realise then that a few years later he would be fighting as a commander alongside Nelson in what would be another similarly meritorious British victory.

Bligh commanded *Director* in his trademark commendable manner through to the turn of the century, acquitting himself with distinction no matter what the order from Admiralty. What pleased him most, however, was that he was nearly back to full health. On a few occasions he again patrolled with the North Sea Fleet, and at the end of 1799 he was given the order to sail his ship to St Helena, where a wide range of plants were to be collected and delivered to Kew Gardens in London. It was an expedition he welcomed: a stimulating break from five years of sailing with squadrons on the often boisterous, cold and unwelcoming North Sea and English Channel. Bligh took considerable time during this sometimes rough passage to enjoy the then rare pleasure of creating charts. He took care to detail the ship's entire track and presented it to Banks for inclusion in maritime records to help future navigators 'eliminate the difficulties attending travelling by sea'. The map was subsequently published.

That reference came in another letter to Banks in what was then the new century, the eighteenth century. That same note, written in June 1800, made mention that Bligh expected *Director* to be laid-up, saying 'the ship is reported to require four months repair'.

It is likely that *Director* did go for repair because in the latter part of 1800 the Admiralty called on Bligh's exceptional surveying and hydrographical skills for a number of projects. He had already completed an extensive survey of the entrance to the Humber in 1797, although it was not as accurate as he had hoped because he was called away from there 'at short notice.' Where he did excel and display the full extent of his remarkable talent was in Dublin. His arrival in the town was noted in the *Lloyd's Evening Post* on 17 September 1800:

> At the desire of the Lord Lieutenant, the Lords of the Admiralty
> have recommended a skilful naval Officer, which is arrived in
> this city, for the purposes of making surveys of the harbour

and adjacent coasts ... providing means for the safety and accommodation of shipping. The officer who has come over for this purpose is Captain William Bligh, a gentleman distinguished in the navy for his professional skill, experience and enterprise.

The need for a safer approach to the port was due to the loss of many ships because of the unpredictable movement of sandbanks at the entrance to the harbour. Bligh's expertise extended to an incisive understanding of tidal flows and currents, which would prove to be vital for this project. Eventually Bligh decided he could wait no longer for the weather to improve: winter was approaching, so he set out in a small open boat to survey Dublin Bay and its tidal flows over many weeks. His recommendation was for the construction of two converging seawalls which, he declared, would create a Venturi effect on each ebb tide and this would scour away the sandbanks. What became known as the Bull Wall was so effective that it remains to this day – still doing its designed job.

Bligh also showed inventive skills during this time. Back in England he presented the Admiralty with a model of an instrument that would allow for the rapid calculation of bearings of land or ships 'when sudden emergency will not allow of time to use a compass for that purpose'.

As far as his naval career was concerned, his tenure as commander of *Director* was coming to an end – but it wasn't the end of his life in the navy.

For decades the British were the single enemy of many of the countries of Europe, none more so than France. In 1799 Napoleon – wanting to free up forces so he could concentrate on his desire to control much of Europe – tentatively offered a peace deal to England, but it was promptly rejected. It was a response he wouldn't easily forget.

Napoleon was closely allied to the mentally unstable Tsar Paul of Russia, and in early 1801 the Tsar convinced Denmark and Sweden to blockade a British lifeline – its sea trade into the Baltic. One of the first acts in establishing this embargo came when the Danes seized Hamburg, Britain's most important link for trade with the German states.

The British response was immediate and strong: the Admiralty ordered a formidable fleet to be gathered under the command of Admiral Sir Hyde Parker – whose father of the same name led the British fleet at Dogger Bank – and sail to the Baltic. The squadron's second-in-command was the recent maritime hero, Vice Admiral Lord Horatio Nelson – and Bligh, who on 18 March 1801 stepped aboard as commander of the 56-gun ship HMS *Glatton* and was to be part of Nelson's attack force.

Glatton was a hefty ship-of-the-line displacing 1256 tons. Initially she was armed only with carronades, the powerful short-range weapons which, because of the damage they could inflict with their 68-pound cannonballs, put extreme fear into the hearts of the enemy. Their effectiveness had been all too evident to Bligh at Camperdown when HMS *Rainbow* needed to fire just one round from its 68-pounder to cause the captain of the French ship *Hebe* to haul down his colours and surrender.

Bligh was at home with his family when he was informed of his appointment as captain of *Glatton* and was urgently required aboard. On 12 March he wrote of the circumstances to Banks:

> I was doing my utmost in proceeding according to my
> appointment, and in consequence severe as it was … I left my
> family at a moment's warning. Instead of going into Yarmouth

Roads, as I expected, the fleet being under sail I have joined
them at sea ... I am attached to this fleet of Sir Hyde Parker.

Once aboard and heading north under sail, Bligh soon realised
he didn't consider *Glatton* to be anywhere near as good as other
ships he had commanded. He noted: 'I do not like my ship, as
she has nothing to recommend her as a man-of-war, but her great
shot.' Despite this reservation, *Glatton* would present Bligh with his
greatest moment in battle.

Much to the surprise of the British, when they began their move
towards the Baltic by entering the narrow sound between Denmark
and Sweden, there was no hostile fire from the Swedish coast,
possibly because the Swedish guns did not have the range. However,
since they could see the Danish fleet anchored in a defensive
formation in the inner channel (Royal Passage, off Copenhagen)
Nelson, aboard his flagship HMS *Elephant*, declared those ships to be
the immediate target.

On 30 March the British fleet was anchored in the middle
of the sound off the island of Hven, 14 nautical miles north of
Copenhagen, and once there the plans were made for a fleet attack
on the Danish ships. At the same time the Danes advised the British
that if they proceeded through the extremely narrow entrance to
the Strait of Copenhagen, they would come under fire.

Ignoring this threat, the British went about preparing for battle
in the strait, including having Captain Hardy, of the 94-gun ship
HMS *St George* board a pinnace and, in the dead of night, covertly
travel almost right up to the edge of the Danish line so the depth of
water could be checked.

The battle took place on 2 April: Nelson, with the twenty
ships making up his squadron – all of 74 guns or less and including
Glatton – looped around and approached slowly down-current from

the south so they remained in formation and anchored parallel to the Danish line, the two sides a cable-length apart. Unfortunately for Nelson, while his squadron was moving into position, three of his most valuable ships, HMS *Bellona*, HMS *Russell* and HMS *Agamemnon*, grounded on a shoal and could proceed no further. Hyde Parker's ships stood guard to the north.

The scene was set, as Bligh described:

The enemy's line was nearly N & S. They had seven line-of-battle ships south of the Crown Battery, five low ships like sloops of war, and six floating batteries; in all, 18. Northward of the Crown Battery were two line-of-battle ships and four brigs; and within the battery, two line-of-battle ships and a frigate rigged. Total 27 ships and vessels of war, besides gun-vessels alongshore and batteries, all of whom threw shot at us.

It was late morning when the first broadsides were let loose, the booming sound that came with each barrage echoing across the sound and the city itself. Each time the pungent smoke was cleared by a puff of wind the dreadful impact of the cannon balls, weighing from 24 pounds to more than 60 pounds, was evident. Masts were sent crashing to the deck, bulwarks and topsides were being smashed into splinters and decks split open. The human toll was horrible: men were being crushed, drowned and blown apart. The firing was relentless. Each time a cannon ball departed a muzzle crew rushed to reload, and young boys, the powder monkeys, kept running powder from the magazine to the gun positions.

Bligh was in the thick of the action as *Glatton* was anchored south of *Elephant*. After more than two hours of engagement Hyde Parker, watching from the north from his flagship, HMS *London*, was growing concerned: the Danes appeared to be getting the upper hand in the onslaught. He decided that Nelson and his squadron should break from the action, so had the 'Leave off Action' signal hoisted aloft on *London*. What followed was one of the most famous moments in British naval history. Nelson, who was blind in one eye, took his telescope and put it to that eye, saying 'I really do not see the signal'. Bligh also did not acknowledge seeing the signal.

Nelson's squadron continued fighting, and it would turn out to be a brave and rewarded call. By two o'clock in the afternoon it was all over. The Danish line had ceased firing, many of its ships adrift and some on fire. Other commanders had lowered their colours and surrendered.

Bligh's log revealed the action as he saw it:

At 7.45, signal prepare for battle and anchor by the stern, with springs on the cables.

At 9.45 prepare to weigh. At same time *Edgar*, *Ardent* and *Glatton* to weigh, and the other ships in succession ... we anchored precisely in our station abreast of the Danish Commodore.

At 10.26 the action began. At noon, the action continuing very hot, ourselves much cut up. Our opponent, the Danish Commodore, struck to us, but his seconds ahead and astern still keep up a strong fire.

At 11.24, our fore top-mast was shot away, seven of our upper deck guns disabled by the enemy.

Soon after the British had secured victory there came an extremely important moment for Bligh: 'Lord Nelson in the *Elephant*, our second ahead, did me the honour to hail me to come on board, and thank me for the conduct of the *Glatton*.'

While this meeting took place both men could see the Danish commanding officer's ship, *Dannebrog*, in flames nearby. The fire had started as a result of the attack by *Glatton*.

At three o'clock Bligh decided it was time to move away. *Glatton*, with 'seven upper deck guns and two lower disabled by the enemy's shot', slipped her cable and sailed out, her mast was 'dangerously wounded' and the rigging and sails 'shot to pieces'. Bligh called for a course back to a safe anchorage where the Commander-in-Chief, Sir Hyde Parker, and his squadron were anchored.

As they anchored at around four o'clock there was a massive explosion. Bligh looked back towards Copenhagen and saw it was *Dannebrog* – the fire had obviously reached the ship's magazine. More than 250 men were killed in the explosion. Fifty-two survivors from the ship would later be put aboard *Glatton* as prisoners.

The morning after the battle it was time for a sober review for all captains in the squadron. While Nelson went ashore to Copenhagen to negotiate an armistice – which would give the British access to Copenhagen and the Baltic – Bligh, like the others, took stock of the situation aboard their ships. The dead had to be readied for burial, the wounded treated and the ship had to be repaired and readied for the passage back to England. Bligh had 60 seamen and 11 carpenters from HMS *Raisonnable* – a ship in Admiral Parker's squadron – come aboard to repair the damage, which was extensive. 'If there had been a fresh breeze', Bligh reflected, 'we must have been a mere wreck. Our lower masts must be double fished and mast heads secured by reefing the top masts. Lower yards also require fishes. We are in these respects the most cut up of any ship.'

The battle had delivered a heavy toll – the British had 253 killed and 988 wounded while the Danes had 790 killed,

900 wounded, nineteen ships lost and 2000 men taken as prisoners. Among the British losses was Captain Edward Riou of *Amazon*. He was literally cut in half when hit by a chain shot from the enemy.

Two weeks after the Battle of Copenhagen the British learned that Tsar Paul, a man considered by the majority of Russians to be insane, had been murdered and replaced by a new tsar who was not only intent on bringing peace to the region, but was also vehemently opposed to Bonaparte. Had this news reached the British as they prepared for the Battle of Copenhagen it probably would not have taken place.

Bligh's contribution to the victory at Copenhagen was not lost on the Admiralty. Immediately after the battle he was advised that he was being transferred to the command of the considerably larger HMS *Monarch*, a 74-gunner whose captain, Captain James Mosse, had been killed in the Battle of Copenhagen, along with 56 of his men. This was, however, a brief posting: less than a month. No sooner had Bligh sailed *Monarch* to anchor at the Nore he was promoted to the command of an even more important vessel, HMS *Irresistible*, Nelson's own flagship from his successful campaign against the Spanish at the Battle of Cape St Vincent in 1797.

Bligh's confidence and self-belief was now fully restored, so much so that he boldly asked Lord Nelson if he would write to John Jervis, the Earl of St Vincent and First Lord of the Admiralty, with a favourable appraisal of his role in the Battle of Copenhagen. Nelson had no hesitation in doing so. On 14 April 1801 he wrote:

> Captain Bligh (of the *Glatton*, who had commanded the *Director*
> at Camperdown) has desired my testimony to his good conduct,
> which, although perfectly unnecessary, I cannot refuse; his
> behaviour on this occasion can reap no additional credit from

my testimony. He was my second, and the moment the action
ceased, I sent for him on board the *Elephant*, to thank him for
his support.

In late May, while still at sea, Bligh was honoured to learn that
he had been elected a Fellow of the Royal Society, which had
then been in existence for 141 years and is today the world's oldest
scientific academy in continuous existence. It was a huge mark of
respect; one awarded 'in consideration of his distinguished services
in navigation, botany, and science'. Banks was then president of this
exalted organisation and Bligh could have wanted nothing more
than to receive the award from his great friend, but unfortunately
his ship, *Irresistible*, had become the flagship for Vice-Admiral
Parker, and Bligh 'dared not quit my ship'.

The next twelve months saw Bligh remain in command of
Irresistible either at anchor at Yarmouth Roads or with his squadron
cruising off the coast of Holland. Peace was now beginning to
settle across Europe – the warring factions, particularly Britain and
France, were starting to rest easy. Since 1793 these two sides had
constantly been engaged in confrontations, thanks in no small part
to Napoleon's belligerence and determination to see his country
control much of Europe, and eventually overwhelm England. But
the realisation was that this was not going to happen. At this time
England had a population of 11 million, while France boasted
27 million. However, this imbalance weighed in England's favour
through the country's far greater wealth and superiority at sea. The
Royal Navy had more than 100 ships-of-the-line at its disposal
while France had a mere 23.

It was now time for a tired 47-year-old William Bligh to
consider his options: 'I have so fully given up all my time and
exertions to the service that I feel worn out and want a little relief,'

he told Banks while aboard *Irresistible* at Yarmouth. 'Under these circumstances I have written to Lord St Vincent requesting he would take my long services into his consideration and as it was now peace I hoped he would allow me to be superseded.'

Lord St Vincent's answer was a very direct 'no'.

CHAPTER EIGHTEEN

England, 1802

Guardian and governor

Lord St Vincent rejected Bligh's request to be 'superseded' for the same reason he had for all Royal Navy captains at the end of 1801: no treaty had been signed by the French, and in short, the British would not trust them until it was. That meant everyone remained on a war footing even though the threat was at a low level.

Trans-Channel negotiations were underway: the Marquess Cornwallis had been sent to France to negotiate the truce. It eventuated, and on 25 March 1802 the Treaty of Amiens was signed in the French city of Amiens by Cornwallis and Joseph Bonaparte, Napoleon's older brother. It was said to be a 'Definitive Treaty of Peace' – but that peace would last only one year.

Regardless, this treaty was good news for Bligh: *Irresistible* was laid-up and he was able to go ashore and head home, but only on half-pay.

He enjoyed considerable time relaxing with his family in Lambeth, on the edge of the Thames, but in early 1803 the Admiralty once again called on his surveying skills, this time for waters around the heavily indented coast of Flushing in the southwest of England, and at Dungeness, in the southeast. There was good reason for the Admiralty having a man of Bligh's ability undertaking these surveys: they needed to be completed as soon as possible because, on the opposite side of the Channel, Napoleon was beginning to show a disregard for the treaty signed the previous year – another war between the two sides was becoming increasingly likely. The Admiralty had to be prepared for this eventuality: it needed to consider new anchorages for its fleets along the coast, and each proposed site had to be surveyed so accurate navigation charts could be created for the ships they intended to anchor there, lying in wait. So, Bligh again was the preferred man for the task. A Dover revenue cutter was requisitioned and put at his disposal for these investigations.

In May 1803, when this survey work was far from finished, the British Parliament decided Napoleon's provocative acts had gone too far, so yet again war was declared on France,

Bligh wasn't called up for active service until May 1804, when he was commissioned as commander of one of the navy's most prominent ships, HMS *Warrior*, a third-rate ship-of-the-line which had been under repair in Plymouth docks the previous year. She was launched at Portsmouth in 1781 and had seen action at the Battle of Copenhagen.

Napoleon's sabre rattling reached a point where rumours – probably of his own making – reached England that he was planning an invasion of gigantic proportions: a fleet of up to 2000 vessels and an army of 160 000 men. Again, Bligh's surveying and mapping skills came to the fore. This time he was sent on a secret mission to Holland where he was to survey the entrance to the River Scheldt, and report back on what he considered to be the most suitable positioning for a British blockade. The Admiralty believed that if Napoleon's threat was real then many of the ships that would join his invasion force would be built at the Scheldt.

Obviously, if that did occur, the British wanted to make sure they didn't get to leave port. Bligh agreed with this theory, telling his wife in a letter in June 1804: 'I think that if the French fleet were to come out, they would be full of men, and could take our inshore Squadron to pieces.'

Bligh's more localised concern was that he, like many other captains, was struggling to find a full complement of men for his ship, and because of this he had to accept men he would not otherwise choose. When *Warrior* was at sea she was either patrolling the Channel or providing provisions, hay and livestock to squadrons that remained offshore. Unfortunately for the captain, the good relationships he had enjoyed with his crew during recent postings weren't to be found aboard *Warrior*: it was a bad mix of men and it would prove to be one of his most frustrating appointments. His worst offender was an officer, second lieutenant John Frazier, whom Bligh had earlier had arrested and sent to a court martial for insulting language and disrespect towards the commander.

Frazier was acquitted at the court martial, principally because the word of the ship's surgeon contradicted that of Bligh. Frazier was then reinstated to the crew of *Warrior* and from that moment set himself on a course of revenge against his commander. An attempt came in November, 1804. He wrote to the Admiralty claiming Bligh had, among other things, grossly insulted and ill-treated him by calling him a rascal, scoundrel and shaking his fist in his face. He demanded that Bligh be court martialled.

Naval protocol had to be followed so Bligh was ordered to attend the court martial scheduled immediately after *Warrior* returned to Torbay, east of Plymouth, on 23 February 1805. The hearing lasted for two days, and on 1 March *The Times* newspaper in London reported the verdict: 'Captain Bligh was reprimanded with an admonition from the President, and restored to his command.' Bligh then returned to *Warrior* while Frazier was never again heard of in naval ranks.

This incident seemingly did nothing to harm Bligh's standing in the navy; he remained highly respected by the Admiralty, by the government and even more so by Sir Joseph Banks. This esteem was apparent when, that same month, Banks suggested to the government that Bligh be given the plum role of governor of New South Wales – an appointment following in the wake of governors Phillip, Hunter and King. All three governors were seen as being too lenient when it came to holding authority over the colony, and accordingly control was being lost to the militia and powerful individuals in the society. Banks, who could lay claim to being the father of the penal colony as it was established on his suggestion, wanted an unimpeachable man of firm discipline and integrity for the role of fourth governor, and Bligh was that man.

On 15 March 1805, Banks advised Bligh that he wanted him as governor:

> My dear Sir,
> An opportunity has occurred this day which seems to me to lay open an opportunity of being of service to you; and as I hope I never omit any chance of being useful to a friend whom I esteem, as I do you, I lose not a minute in apprising you of it.
>
> I have always, since the first institution of the new colony at New South Wales, taken a deep interest in its success, and have been constantly consulted by His Majesty's Minister, through all the changes there have been in the department which directs it, relative to the more important concerns of the colonists.
>
> At present, King, the Governor, is tired of his station; and well he may be so. He has carried into effect a reform of great extent, which militated much with the interest of the soldiers

and settlers there. He is, consequently, disliked and much opposed, and has asked leave to return ...

The words 'disliked and much opposed' carried far more relevance in this offer than Bligh appreciated at the time. Had he realised what was meant he could well have rejected the offer there and then.

As it was he was torn by the offer, and he shared his concerns with Sir Joseph:

Warrior at sea 21 March 1805

Thursday

You will I have no doubt kindly made every allowance for my not giving you a decisive answer in the generous and friendly offer you have made me respecting my occupying so advantageous as well as respectable situation as a Governor of NSW and I am sure you will feel for me [as I must have] family consultation with my wife and six daughters by letter on such a serious consideration between us, and which could have been settled in a day or two had we been together ...

At my time of life ... what a serious thing it is you will allow, to take leave forever of a wife who has united her lot with mine for 30 years, which I think would be the case if I should go without her; and her undertaking the voyage I fear could be her death owing to her extreme horror of the sea.

The moment I hear from Mrs Bligh I will write to you.

Bligh, sitting at his desk aboard *Warrior*, wrote a letter to his Betsy, telling her of the offer and assuring her that she would be the one making the final decision. He then sealed the letter and arranged for it to be delivered ashore. It would then be carried to the family home in London. He waited anxiously to hear her response.

It was a significant offer, with significant repercussions for Bligh's family and his career.

Betsy subsequently wrote to Banks:

> 6 April 1805
> Durham Place
> I have received a letter from Captain Bligh which makes me think he is inclined to accept of the offer your generous friendship has made him of the governor of New South Wales. His affection for his family made him wish we could have accompanied him ...
>
> He seems determined to undertake this voyage as he did all his others and I believe all sailors ever will do with the hope of return.
>
> He is anxious to know many things ...

As a result of this letter Banks advised Bligh he would receive as much as 2000 pounds a year, twice as much as Governor King was receiving, and King, Banks wrote, was living 'like a prince'. He also suggested that Bligh might take his daughters, saying: 'Your daughters will have a better chance of marrying suitably there than they can have here; for as the colony grows richer ... I can have no doubt but that in a few years there will be men there very capable of supporting wives in a creditable manner, and very desirous of taking them from a respectable and good family.' He apparently made sure Betsy was well aware of this information, and at the same time tried to allay any fears she might have about the proposed posting.

Regardless, this was an extremely difficult decision for her to make. Betsy had spent her entire married life raising six daughters, all the time waiting and wondering about the fate of her seafaring husband. Would she ever see him again? Had his ship been wrecked on an uncharted reef in a remote part of the Pacific? Had he been lost at sea or killed in battle? And how would she cope with six daughters if he didn't return home? Now, at a time in his career when he could soon retire ashore and establish a more normal family life with his wife and children, Bligh was considering spending up to four years on the opposite side of the world – without his wife and children. It was already accepted that Betsy could not, and would not, travel to the colony: the decision on accepting or rejecting the posting could only be based on what benefit the position of governor might bring to the family. Both parents were committed to providing for their daughters the best they could – and this was what influenced their final decision: the governorship would allow them 'to procure a little affluence' and further assist the girls. William Bligh was going to be the fourth governor of New South Wales.

Almost five weeks after being made the offer, during which time Bligh would have spent most, if not all that time aboard his ship, he confirmed to Banks in a letter written while on *Warrior*, at anchor in Cawsand Bay, at the edge of Plymouth Sound, that he would accept the appointment:

23 April 1805

I have just time to inform you we anchored this morning and received orders to refit with the utmost dispatch and victual for 6 months to be ready to push after the French in case they put to sea indeed I have just heard that all sail of the line, several frigates and many troops on board, have escaped from Toulon. I hope my dear sir you have received my letter of the 18th accepting of your kind and generous offer to me, and I have this moment heard from Mrs Bligh that you had sent her word of my appointment was fixed ...

Two days later he thought it best to advise Banks that he might be ordered to sail at short notice – to go in pursuit of the French:

> *Warrior* in Cawsand Bay
> 25 April 1805
> By the time you will receive this my former letter will
> have reached you with acknowledgement of my thanks and
> my acceptance of the appointment to the Colony of New
> South Wales, also of my arrival at this port very unexpectedly
> on Tuesday last. Yesterday the wind came so strong the
> eastward I could not get on shore but in the evening it
> moderated, and by the guard boat your letter of the 21st was
> sent out to me. I am much obliged to you my dear sir for
> the trouble and pains you have taken to explain to me what I
> may expect.
>   I think in a week's time I shall have the *Warrior* very nearly
> ready for sea and circumstances may require my suddenly being
> ordered to sail.

On 14 May 1805 – a year after he had taken command of *Warrior* – it was announced that Bligh would be the next governor of New South Wales. He took leave of the ship and returned to London to put his affairs in order and begin preparations for the journey to Sydney. *Warrior* would be the last ship of any significance he would command for the Royal Navy.

While he was making the final arrangements for his departure to what was then the most remote outpost in the British Empire, Bligh held one gnawing concern: the matter of his naval career. He had been advised that a governorship no longer went hand-in-hand with naval service, so his continued rise towards the rank of Admiral might be adversely affected. On 14 July he wrote from home in Durham Place, Lambeth, telling Banks of this: 'What I am anxious to obtain from the Admiralty is, that the Commission I am to have may be such as to prevent losing my rank for the time being according to the seniority I hold in the list of captains ...' Banks allayed those concerns, saying that he would not have encouraged him to take on the role of governor 'which may, I fear, on a future occasion be interpreted by the Admiralty into a dereliction of your chance of a Flag'. Time would reveal Banks was correct. Bligh kept his rank.

In February 1806, the soon-to-be Governor Bligh departed England for his term in the fledgling, yet foundering colony. It was a highly emotional farewell: besides leaving his beloved Betsy at home, five of his six daughters had decided to remain with their mother, which disappointed him immensely. It was only his married daughter, Mary, and her husband, John Putland, a naval lieutenant, who would join him in Sydney Town. They sailed aboard the ship *Lady Madeleine Sinclair* as part of a five-ship convict transport convoy being led by HMS *Porpoise*, commanded by Captain Joseph Short.

While the seven-month, 12 000-nautical-mile passage to Sydney was relatively straightforward, it proved to be extremely tough going for Bligh and Short on a personal basis. The two clashed regularly in violent quarrels over who was actually in charge of the convoy. The orders issued by the Admiralty were ambiguous. Short's interpretation was that he had been directed to take command over all ships, but to place himself under Bligh's command, as soon as they reached their destination. This, he believed, meant he was commander of the convoy in every sense, apart from Bligh making the call on the course to be followed and the ports they would visit en route. However, Bligh's understanding of the orders had him firm in the belief that he, by being superior in rank to Short, was in charge of the convoy, even though he was not aboard the lead ship, *Porpoise*. Short was also travelling with his wife and seven children, intending to settle in New South Wales.

This confrontation became increasingly heated as the ships made miles, and at one stage reached a point where it could have ended in tragedy. Bligh ordered his ship, *Lady Madeleine Sinclair*, to hold course after Short signalled from *Porpoise* to do otherwise. Short erupted when he realised Bligh was ignoring his directive, and decided in an instant to exert his perceived authority over the situation.

He ordered his men to fire a cannon shot across the bow of *Lady Madeleine Sinclair*, and when that drew no response from Bligh, he called for another to be fired across the stern. With Bligh still holding course, Short then ordered the cannon to be aimed for a direct hit amidships! Incredibly, to add an even greater display of authority over the moment, Short had Lieutenant Putland, who had earlier been transferred to *Porpoise*, direct the cannons to fire. Fortunately, common sense eventually prevailed and the third shot wasn't called for. All that this showdown achieved was an even greater level of animosity between Bligh and Short, as neither would retreat from their position.

'Putland can scarcely speak from agitation upon the subject of the shots which were fired at us, the day before yesterday,' wrote Mary to her mother. 'Captain Short had the brutality to make him fire them; [that is, he was officer of the watch] and told him to prepare a third, for if we did not bear down immediately, he was to fire right into us. I think such an inhuman thing as making a man fire at his father [in law] and wife was never done before.'

Bligh's pen vented his anger with Short: 'A wicked and most violent man ... the most irritating and insulting person.' Bligh and Short never reconciled. Bligh later ordered him back to England in 1807 to face court martial. He was acquitted but ruined.

After stopping in Cape Town for a brief period, *Porpoise*, *Lady Madeleine Sinclair* and the other ships in the convoy endured a rugged but safe 51-day downwind passage across the wild and wintery waters of the Southern Ocean and through the Roaring Forties until they reached the southern tip of Van Diemen's Land. Here they turned north and adopted a course that would see them sail up the coast of New South Wales.

On 6 August 1806, the impressively bold and vertical sandstone headlands that stand as protectors to the entrance to Port Jackson hailed into view on the port bow. Soon after, the ships changed course to the west and entered the magnificent deepwater harbour which had been noted and named by Captain Cook when he sailed north from Botany Bay in 1770. Once inside the harbour the wind was against them for the course they needed to sail to the south to reach the settlement in Sydney Cove, so the call was to anchor in sheltered water. Forty-eight hours later *Lady Madeleine Sinclair* had worked her way on the wind and tide up harbour and anchored off Sydney Town.

From the deck of the ship Bligh and his daughter could only have looked at their new home town with an element of disbelief: dusty, makeshift and somewhat uninviting. Banks, however, knew that Bligh, a man of distinction, conviction and great inner strength, was up to the challenge.

Bligh, a master mariner then aged 52, had achieved and experienced more than most of his contemporaries in the Royal Navy. He knew it was a great honour to have been chosen from naval ranks to be governor of New South Wales. What he didn't know was that this small colony would present him with a challenge as big as any he had ever faced on the high seas.

Sydney, 1806

Governor, rum and rebellion

When Sir Joseph Banks had offered Bligh the position of governor of New South Wales, informing him that King George III's current representative in the colony, Philip Gidley King, was 'disliked and much opposed', Bligh could not have imagined what was actually meant. Trouble was brewing. Corruption and dissent were rife and King, a naval officer like Bligh, could do nothing to stop it. What attempts he did make were treated with total contempt. Inevitably word reached England that King was all but powerless and the colony was collapsing. Something had to be done, and that 'something' was to appoint Bligh as governor.

King's greatest concern was that the root of the rot lay at the feet of one man, John Macarthur, a charismatic individual who had arrived in Sydney Town in June 1790 as a member of the New South Wales Corps. The Corps had been assembled in England the previous year as a replacement for the Marines, the original convict guard Governor Phillip had landed with when the convict settlement was established in 1788. The Corps was under the command of Major Francis Grose, and when the initial complement arrived with the Second Fleet in June 1790 their number represented ten per cent of the European population in the settlement. Macarthur, who was heavily in debt when he left England, was among them.

As soon as he set foot on land it seemed Macarthur's intent went far beyond being a military man: he was out to take every opportunity available to him and build his personal wealth, no matter what. As the years passed this grew increasingly apparent: he was ruthless in his pursuit of a personal fortune and had become a law unto himself: Governor King knew it, former Governor John Hunter knew it, and Sir Joseph Banks and the British Government knew it.

In 1801, however, Macarthur's plans were interrupted. He was sent to London by Governor King to face trial after seriously wounding another member of the New South Wales Corps, Colonel William Paterson, in a duel. The dispatch relating to the incident, which the governor sent to London on the same ship, mysteriously disappeared during the voyage. Macarthur returned to Sydney in 1805 without being tried.

Within ten years of his arrival in the colony the avaricious Macarthur had amassed a fortune amounting to £20 000, 'mostly at the public expense' through 'sewing discord and strife'. Governor King had scathingly quipped while Macarthur was in England: 'If Captain Macarthur returns here in any official character, it should be that of governor, as one-half the colony already belongs to him, and it will not be long before he gets the other half.' Knowing that a great number of the problems crippling the colony started and finished with Macarthur, King declared he should be investigated and dealt with. He made his views well known to London:

Experience has convinced every man in this colony that there are no resources which art, cunning, impudence and a pair of

basilisk eyes can afford that he does not put in practice to obtain
any point he undertakes ... persecution and opposition became
Captain Macarthur's system. If the records of this colony,
now in your office, are examined, you will find his name
very conspicuous. Many and many instances of his diabolical
spirit has shown itself before Governor Phillip left this colony,
and since, although in many instances he has been the master
worker of the puppets he has set in motion.

At the time the ailing Governor King was denouncing Macarthur,
a coup of sorts had already taken place. The New South Wales
Corps, to which Macarthur was still closely aligned, essentially had
free rein in the town. Wherever significant profits were to be made,
the Corps were in control. On the waterfront they ran unchecked,
purchasing all cargo of any worth that arrived from England, and
with rum being the local currency, it was their prime target. Under
the influence of Macarthur and Captain George Johnston Corps
members bartered brutally with the struggling settlers for stock,
produce and even their property. It was a system that ensured
maximum profits for the Corps members, and Macarthur, and
endless hardship for the colonists.

The British government could no longer ignore these problems.
They needed someone strong willed and tenacious if they were
to have any hope of breaking Macarthur's stranglehold on the
community. A decision had been made. Surely, the incorruptible
and indomitable navy man, William Bligh, was the one man who
could stand firm and hobble the unprincipled profiteer and his
supporters in the Corps? Bligh, having accepted the challenge, had
set sail with express orders to regain control of the colony from
Macarthur and his covetous cohorts and put this British outpost on
a solid path towards prosperity.

From that moment Bligh and Macarthur were on a collision course.

A crowd started to build as word spread that the new governor was arriving from England. William Bligh stepped ashore from a longboat to an audience wondering what this new man would bring to their troubled settlement. Welcomed by a worn-down Governor King, Bligh was then escorted to Government House, which stood on the corner of what is now Bridge and Phillip streets, where he was no doubt further briefed on the all-consuming troubles.

The colony was then under significant added pressure following a devastating flood five months earlier, in March. Floodwaters had surged down the Hawkesbury River to the northwest of the settlement and caused considerable havoc with the colony's food crops. This meant that Bligh was also going to have to deal with the resulting food shortages and skyrocketing prices.

Within days of him moving into Government House, Governor King made three land grants to Bligh: 240 acres on the southern fringe of the settlement, 105 acres near Parramatta and 1000 acres near Rouse Hill. Bligh named two in honour of his battles, Camperdown and Copenhagen, and the third Mount Betham, after his wife.

Bligh formally took office as the fourth governor of New South Wales on 13 August 1806. He was officially welcomed to New South Wales by three men, apparently self-declared, to be representatives of the community – George Johnston for the military, Richard Atkins for the civilian officers and John Macarthur for the free settlers. Bligh was by then well aware that the aspiring sheep grazier Macarthur was the man causing Sir Joseph Banks most concern, and that Governor King had dubbed him the 'Botany Bay perturbator [agitator]'. This knowledge left Bligh in no doubt it wasn't going to be an easy governorship, but at that time he had no idea how hard it would prove to be.

His concerns were reinforced when anti-Macarthur sentiment emerged as soon as the swearing-in ceremony had been completed: 135 free settlers sought an audience with him and declared that Macarthur in no way represented them in an official capacity – and further accused him of blatant and corrupt profiteering through the controlled supply of mutton to the community. Settlers from the Hawkesbury River region also accused Macarthur of infringing their rights and privileges by acting on their behalf when not authorised to do so.

Bligh commenced work quickly after his induction. Always a man of action, he immediately set out to tour the devastated Hawkesbury region and arranged relief for those struggling to find food. He made it clear he intended to assess the administrative processes to reform the colony and its dysfunctional economy. He did not tread lightly and within weeks the gloves were completely off.

Mindful of the shortage of available agricultural land, he wanted to slow down the pace of land grants. Of particular concern was the matter of an extraordinary grant to Macarthur when he arrived back in town from England: 5000 acres of prime agricultural land on the banks of the beautiful Nepean River. Macarthur was furious that his personal empire-building was suddenly under threat, but Bligh remained unyielding. The two men quarrelled famously and heatedly at Government House; Macarthur later reported that Bligh had said in one of these verbal stoushes: 'What have I to do with your sheep, sir? What have I to do with your cattle? Are you to have such flocks of sheep and such herds of cattle as no man ever heard of before? No, sir! ... I have heard of your concerns, sir, you have got 5000 acres of land in the finest situation in the country; but by God, you shan't keep it!'

By October 1806, in his ongoing efforts to curtail the crooked activities of Macarthur and the Corps, Bligh ordered new port regulations and was acting swiftly to enact laws to reduce the colony's reliance on rum as currency. Throughout the period of November 1806 to February 1807 he issued orders outlawing barter in goods and spirits and banned the importation of private stills for alcohol production.

The new governor continued to clash constantly with Macarthur over the next few months. Bligh introduced a system in which free farmers and settlers were no longer obliged to purchase exclusively from the monopolists the articles they required. Instead, they could now make purchases from the government's stores at a fair price. This move brought Bligh great respect and loyalty from the populace, but it was a direct attack on the powerbase of the corrupt Rum Corps, as the NSW Corps was now commonly known.

On 10 October 1807 Bligh's daughter, well aware of the difficulties her father was facing, wrote to her mother:

Papa is quite well but dreadfully harassed by business and the troublesome set of people he has to deal with. In general he gives great satisfaction, but there are a few that we suspect wish to oppose him; as yet they have done nothing openly; though it is known their 'tools' have been at work some time; that is, they are trying to find something in Papa's conduct to write home about; but which, I am sure, from his great circumspection, they will not be able to do with honour to themselves. Mr Macarthur is one of the party, the others are the military officers, but they are all invited to the house and treated with the same politeness as usual.

By the end of 1807 Bligh continued his march against Macarthur and the Corps, taking measures to up the ante. Earlier that year a sailing schooner, *Parramatta*, co-owned by Macarthur, sailed from Sydney to Tahiti with one of the colony's least desirable and most notorious convicts, John Hoare, as an apparent stowaway. When *Parramatta* returned to her home port, the government bond that had been lodged to ensure the ship complied with all regulations on departure – which included a search for stowaways – was forfeited because the ship was the means of Hoare's escape. Macarthur, arrogantly placing himself above the law, ignored an order to appear in court when the matter relating to this incident was heard. He was duly arrested on 16 August 1807, charged and ordered to face court on 25 January 1808. The accused was not concerned: he was then convinced he had the perfect arena for the ultimate showdown with the governor.

When the day of reckoning arrived, the court comprised the Judge-Advocate, Richard Atkins, and six officers of the New South Wales Corps. Macarthur immediately challenged the authority of Atkins to sit in judgement, using 'a great torrent of threats and abusive language' in disclosing that Atkins had been financially indebted to him for fifteen years. The bench of officers immediately adjourned to consult with the governor, only to be told that the court could not be constituted without the colony's Judge-Advocate. The officers immediately sided with Macarthur, their former superior in the NSW Corps. Atkins countered, demanding that the six officers be charged with treasonable offences. Bligh supported the decision. The die was cast.

For Bligh there was never greater evidence of Macarthur manipulating and controlling the colony for personal gain. He declared the action by the six officers to be mutinous behaviour and demanded in writing that Johnston, now ranked a major, meet with him so the matter could be dealt with accordingly. Johnston, who was at nearby Annandale, replied that he had been injured in an accident involving his gig and was unable to travel. From that moment Bligh was on his own.

On the morning of 26 January, twenty years to the day after the founding of the colony, Bligh ordered that Macarthur again be arrested and detained. Only hours later Johnston arrived at the jail and presented an order of his own that released the prisoner.

From that moment, Macarthur's 'mutiny' was underway. His earlier attempts to influence Bligh's recall to London had failed, so now he was taking matters into his own hands: the governor had to be overthrown by any means.

Macarthur returned to the Corps' barracks in the heart of the settlement – at what is now Wynyard Square on the western side of George Street – and together with Johnston he wrote and co-signed a petition with eight others, none of whom were members of the Corps. It stated, in part:

> The present alarming state of this colony, in which every man's property, liberty, and life is endangered, induces us most earnestly to implore you instantly to place Governor Bligh under an arrest and to assume the command of the colony. We pledge ourselves, at the moment of less agitation, to come forward to support the measure with our fortunes and our lives.

Johnston, who claimed he was acting on behalf of all his officers and the colony's 'respectable inhabitants', ordered his Corps to take up arms, and sent three officers to Government House with an order for Governor Bligh to resign. These officers were also to assure Bligh that there was no intention to harm him. The 400-strong regiment was assembled under arms and with bayonets fixed, then with flags flying and the band playing, they marched on the nearby Government House.

It was half past six in the evening of 26 January 1808, and still daylight when Bligh, dining with friends, received word of the uprising against him. His daughter, the now widowed Mary, took it upon herself to stride boldly to the gates of Government House and do her best to deter the entry of the Corps. 'You traitors, you rebels, you have just walked over my husband's grave and now come to murder my father,' she protested until she was forcibly dragged away.

On arrival, the Corps waited in the grounds of Government House while officers began a determined search of the building in a bid to find their man.

Bligh was eventually located: he was sorting through personal papers and confidential documents in a rear bedroom when the officers burst in and arrested him. The popular image of him hiding under a bed and being dragged out from underneath it was staunchly disputed by Bligh. He was indignant in his rebuttal, but in the days that followed it clearly suited the forces behind the rebellion to promote the idea of the deposed governor's cowardice.

With the insurrection complete and Bligh under house arrest, Johnston assumed the title of lieutenant-governor and declared martial law. Johnston promptly acquitted Macarthur of the charges brought against him by Bligh and he was appointed the inaugural 'Colonial Secretary'.

Seventeen months after being sworn in, Bligh's governorship was over. For the next six months Mary and her father remained under house arrest while a solution to their predicament could be found. Being so far from England and any hope of rescue, they were effectively political prisoners. Finally a deal was struck: HMS *Porpoise*, a twelve-gunner with a crew of 65 men, was put at Bligh's disposal on the condition that he would sail back to England. He boarded the ship with Mary but on clearing Sydney Heads Bligh turned to starboard, setting a course for Hobart Town. He was determined not to give up without a fight.

Sailing up the Derwent River and anchoring off the remote settlement in August 1808, Bligh hoped he would be able to muster the support of Lieutenant-Governor David Collins, to overthrow those who had usurped him. But it was not to be. Collins sent a communiqué to Sydney stating that Bligh had not sailed to England, instead he and his daughter were there. Collins had shown his hand: he had sided with the insurrectionists. Bligh had another enemy in his midst.

From that moment there was a remarkable stand-off between the pair. Collins tried to force Bligh to leave Hobart by cutting off all opportunities for the provisioning of *Porpoise*. Bligh was now completely isolated but he stood firm, hoping to receive word that support was coming from England. 'I remained on board my vessel getting some trivial supplies from the captains of ships,' he wrote. 'A few poor unfortunate settlers, who endeavoured to get off a few fowls and some mutton to my daughter, some were seized and flogged and one poor man received, I believe, 400 or 500 lashes and was imprisoned for the relief ...'

Bligh remained resolutely stubborn and the stand-off continued for more than a year. Finally, in January 1810, he received a letter advising him that Governor Lachlan Macquarie had taken office in Sydney and had declared the 1808 rebellion illegal. Also, the British Colonial Office had condemned his overthrow as mutiny. 'I shall be most happy to pay you every respect and attention in my power to bestow while you find it necessary to remain in the Settlement,' wrote Macquarie. It was the news Bligh had been waiting for. He sailed back to Sydney and arrived in Port Jackson little more than two weeks after the new governor had taken office.

On the day of Bligh's return, Macquarie arranged for the commander of his own 73rd Regiment, Lieutenant-Colonel Maurice O'Connell, to lead a guard of honour at Government Wharf in salute of Bligh, and to escort him and Mary to Government House for a reception.

Macarthur and Johnston were long gone. They had already fled Sydney and were in England by October 1808. Johnston was to face a court martial and Macarthur had escaped to England firm in the knowledge that if he remained in Sydney he would almost certainly be arrested and charged for his role in the events that led to Bligh's overthrow. The associated charge of sedition could have seen him face a lengthy jail term in Australia, but he knew he could remain in immunity in England, so he stayed there for the next eight years. Eventually, the British Government dropped the charges.

Back in Sydney Bligh made plans for himself and Mary to return home. Macquarie, too, was looking forward to the day when he saw the stern of HMS *Hindostan*, the ship that would carry Bligh back to England. He had had enough of Bligh being on his turf and was keen to see him leave. His departure would allow Macquarie to get on with the job of governing the colony without the division caused by the former governor's presence in the community.

A few days before Bligh and Mary were to leave he was astounded when Lieutenant-Colonel O'Connell proposed an offer of marriage to Mary. 'I gave him a flat denial because I could not believe it – I retired with her, when I found she had approved of his addresses and given her word to him,' he wrote to Betsy from *Hindostan* while sailing home. Conflicted and surprised, he had given his consent wishing his daughter every happiness. More than two years earlier Mary had endured the sad loss of her husband, John. He died as a result of consumption on 4 January 1808 – just 22 days before Bligh was deposed.

Bligh's planned departure celebrations evolved into wedding festivities for Mary and O'Connell, a man he summed up in his poignant letter to Betsy: 'Nothing can exceed the esteem and high character he has.'

On 12 May 1810, just shy of five years after he had first arrived, Bligh left Sydney. On October 25 that same year, *Hindostan*, along with the two naval ships that had sailed in convoy from the colony, HMS *Dromedary* and *Porpoise*, reached Spithead. Bligh went ashore as soon as he could and immediately set out for London to see Betsy and his much-loved daughters. His family had brought him emotional stability in an often turbulent life. He lived for them: their welfare and financial security were paramount as he worked his way towards the top in naval ranks.

In February 1811, nine months after he returned home, the then all but retired Bligh was elevated to Rear-Admiral of the Blue Squadron, backdated twelve months. Sadly, though, the time he spent with his wife was short: his happiness was shattered when Betsy passed away on 15 April 1812, aged 59. She was buried in the nearby churchyard at St Mary's Church in Lambeth.

The heavy silence in the family home that came with Betsy's absence would prove too much for Bligh to bear. A year after her passing he officially retired on a naval pension and moved to a country residence, the Manor House, in Farningham, Kent, with his four unmarried daughters – Elizabeth, Jane, Frances and Anne. Over the next two years Bligh did his best to enjoy the relaxation that came with the lush countryside of Kent, a far cry from the tempestuous and often threatening ocean he had shared his life with for more than 40 years. Some consolation came in May 1814 when he was advised that he had been promoted to Vice-Admiral of the Blue, but without Betsy by his side, they were lonely years.

His daughters could not compensate for the fact that his great love, and steadfast supporter, was no longer there.

Bligh's life mellowed over the following years and compressed into the quiet comfort of the reading room at his home where he was surrounded by hundreds of heavily bound, dark-covered books and an intriguing array of curiosities, all symbolic of a life spent at sea. Many years later a local, Dr. Alfred Gatty, revealed how as a young boy he would visit Bligh at Farningham: the Admiral would have him sit on his knee while he told the young lad stories, some based around the memento Bligh wore around his neck – a blue ribbon with a pistol ball hanging from it. It was the ball he used as a weight when sharing out the rations of rotten bread and water during the voyage in the open boat, a quarter of a century earlier.

By 1817 Bligh was diagnosed as suffering from a serious illness, possibly cancer. In December that year, however, he was pleasantly distracted from his failing health when he had the pleasure of seeing his daughter Elizabeth marry a cousin, Richard Bligh.

Within days of Elizabeth's wedding, while visiting doctors in Bond Street, London, Bligh collapsed and died. He was laid to rest alongside his Betsy in the churchyard at St Mary's.

When he passed away Britain was still ten years from enjoying the peace that had been so desperately fought for since 1792. Ironically, it was a battle with the French as an ally, not an enemy, which achieved this: the defeat off Pylos, in Greece, of a Turkish force that was out to prevent Greece from gaining independence. This same battle brought to an end the era of great conflicts fought under sail; within twenty years naval fleets included two new elements – power and steam.

Bligh played no small part in this historic period where the Royal Navy ensured that Britannia ruled the waves in a decisive and spectacular fashion; so one can only wonder, if it had not been for the *Bounty* mutiny and the heavy penalty it placed on his career, might he have been another Lord Nelson – the Royal Navy's youngest ever captain and the man who led his country to impressive victories in some of the most notable sea battles of all time? We will never know; but I do believe Bligh was one of the most accomplished seafarers of all time.

His personality combined complexities with cleverness: he was a principled man of incredibly strong character. He did have his shortcomings but what was then seen as acceptable conduct in the eighteenth century navy is now, two centuries later, seen as being cruel, harsh and unacceptable.

So what sort of man does Bligh's story reveal? The man was tough – he had to be if he was to control a crew that included reprobates, rogues and ragamuffins sailing into the unknown and into battle. For the same reason his tongue would lash hard with coarse and demeaning words of the day, often ignited by incompetence and insolence: the captain's men had to realise that dereliction of duty, when it came to shipboard tasks, could imperil the ship and its crew. And yes, he made enemies, primarily because he stood apart, and he stood for what he believed in; so powerful men like Banks recognised, respected and continued to promote him.

Was Bligh the cruel tyrant he is so often made out to be? I don't think so. He preferred encouragement over punishment and health over hardship. And, whereas Nelson became one the world's greatest naval leaders through grand victories in battle, Bligh's legacy to maritime history is more subtle – an explorer in every sense; an exceptional marine surveyor, cartographer and navigator; a strong leader of men in battle, and above everything else, a bona fide master mariner.

Bligh was a complex modern hero and a sailor that anyone with more salt water than blood in their veins would trust with their life at the height of the most ferocious of storms. Yet, in the end, the headstone on his grave said little about the man. Alongside brief references to his triumphs it carried a moving memorial to the twin boys he and Betsy lost. His daughter Anne, to whom he and Betsy were devoted, was later buried alongside her parents.

Bligh's simple epitaph hardly does justice to the sweep of his extraordinary life – but it is what mattered to him. If however, there was one last thing that would have riled this man who was meticulous about everything he did, with an assiduous attention to detail, it was that the age chiselled into his tombstone is incorrect. He was actually 63 when he died.

Sacred

To the memory of

WILLIAM BLIGH, Esq., F.R.S.

Vice-Admiral of the Blue

THE CELEBRATED NAVIGATOR

WHO FIRST TRANSPLANTED THE BREAD-FRUIT TREE

FROM OTAHEITE TO THE WEST INDIES.

BRAVELY FOUGHT THE BATTLE OF HIS COUNTRY;

AND DIED BELOVED, RESPECTED AND LAMENTED,

ON THE 7TH DAY OF DECEMBER 1817

AGED 64

Postscript

On 7 May 1811 the court martial of Major George Johnston began in London. After a month of evidence, including Bligh's, he was found guilty of mutiny. His sentence was lenient – he was cashiered from the army. This prompted the prince regent to declare it was a sentence 'so inadequate to the enormity of the crime of which the prisoner had been found guilty'. Johnston subsequently returned to New South Wales.

The mystery surrounding the whereabouts of the remaining nine *Bounty* mutineers, led by Fletcher Christian, was uncovered when an American sealer, *Topaz*, under the command of Captain Mayhew Folger, stopped at Pitcairn Island in February 1808. Only John Adams (alias Alexander Smith) was still alive. The majority of the mutineers had been murdered by the islanders they took to the island with them, Christian included. He was shot and killed while tending his garden in 1793. He had two sons, Thursday October and Charles, with his Tahitian wife. A daughter, Mary Ann, was born after his death.

In 1817 John Macarthur returned to Sydney from London, having been banned from holding public office – a ban that didn't stick. He became a popular hero, recognised as the great pioneer of the wool industry for the nation, and went on to become a parliamentarian. He died, insane, at his property, Camden Park, on 11 April 1834.

Sir Joesph Banks remained a champion of British society for his entire life. The greatly respected president of the Royal Society was eventually crippled by gout, but even when confined to a wheelchair he insisted on carrying out his presidential duties in full court dress and wearing the Order of the Bath. He died at his home at Isleworth, to the west of London, on 19 June 1820.

In November 1977, the wreck of the *Pandora* was located – 186 years after its loss. Its rediscovery by Steve Domm, John Heyer and Ben Cropp was the result of a methodological search based on analysis of historical information compiled by John Heyer. A magnetometer carried by an RAAF maritime reconnaissance aircraft initially indicated the approximate location of the wreck within Pandora Entrance. The exact location – near the spot where a flare had been dropped by the RAAF Neptune – was discovered the next day by Ron Bell, one of the divers on Ben Cropp's expedition vessel. The Museum of Tropical Queensland has a permanent exhibition, The *Pandora* Gallery, with many unique artifacts recovered from the wreck. More information can be found at www.mtq.qm.qld.gov.au and the affiliated Queensland Museum website: www.qm.qld.gov.au.

Bligh's many descendants including the O'Connell, Oakes and Nutting families are today spread across the UK, Australia and

New Zealand. The family tree extending from the union of Bligh's daughter Elizabeth and cousin Richard Bligh includes a great-great-great-great-granddaughter, Anna Maria Bligh, who became the first elected female premier of Queensland in 2009. The Hawkesbury settlers of Ebenezer, Richmond and Windsor never forgot Bligh's support either. Two hundred years later the descendants of those original settlers including Andrew Johnston and John Turnbull have continued the generational tradition of naming their sons in honour of Bligh. The federal member of parliament Malcolm Bligh Turnbull and his son Alexander Bligh Turnbull, and Penrith auctioneer James Bligh Johnston continue this tradition today.

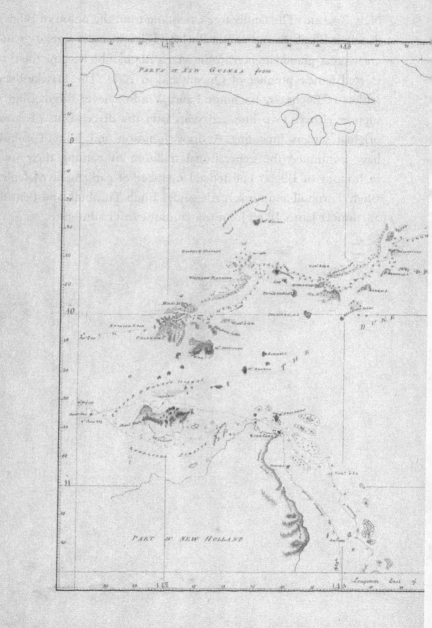

A CHART
OF
BLIGH'S STRAITS
in the
CLARENCE ARCHIPELAGO
Discovered & Explored
BY
Captain William Bligh
OF THE
ROYAL NAVY

SEPTEMBER 1792.

List of illustrations

Part openers

Adventure Bay, Van Diemen's Land, February 1792, map by William Bligh
– Charts, 1788–1805. Courtesy of the Dixson Library, State Library of
New South Wales, ref: Safe DL BLIGH/Chart 7.

William Bligh's *Bounty* Launch Notebook, 1789, ref: MS 5393, item 1, part
86. Courtesy of the National Library of Australia.

N.E. Coast of New Holland, c. 1792, map by William Bligh – Charts, 1788–
1805. Courtesy of the Dixson Library, State Library of New South
Wales, ref: Safe DL BLIGH/Chart 12a.

A Chart of Bligh's Straits in the Clarence Archipelago, by William Bligh,
manuscript map, ref: MS 6423. Courtesy of the National Library of
Australia.

Picture section

Portrait of Elizabeth Bligh by John Webber, © private collection.

Mary Putland (nee Bligh), ca. 1805, watercolour on ivory portrait miniature.
Courtesy of the Mitchell Library, State Library of New South Wales,
ref: MIN 399.

William Bligh, ca. 1814, watercolour on ivory portrait miniature. Courtesy of
the Mitchell Library, State Library of New South Wales, ref: MIN 53.

William Bligh's signet ring. Courtesy of the Dixson Library, State Library of
New South Wales, ref: DR 188.

The Death of Captain Cook by George Carter, 1781. Courtesy of the
National Library of Australia.

William Bligh's telescope, ca.1770–90. Courtesy of the Mitchell Library,
State Library of New South Wales, ref: LR 6.

In Adventure Bay Van Diemen's Land, 1792, watercolour by George Tobin.
Courtesy of the Mitchell Library, State Library of New South Wales,
ref: PXA 563/f.18.

Resolution and Discovery in the Arctic Sea, 1781, oil painting by Thomas Luny.
Courtesy of the Mitchell Library, State Library of New South Wales,
ref: ML 402.

*The Mutineers turning Lieut. Bligh and part of the officers and crew adrift from his
Majesty's Ship the Bounty*, 1790, hand-coloured aquatint by Robert
Dodd. Courtesy of the Dixson Library, State Library of New South
Wales, ref: DL PF 137.

Bligh's passage photographed by Rob Mundle.

List of mutineers, 1789, ref: MS 5393, item 2, part 1. Courtesy of the National Library of Australia.

Bligh's Notebook, 1789, ref: MS 5393, item 1, part 119. Courtesy of the National Library of Australia.

Bligh's Coconut shell, ref: F1345 © National Maritime Museum, Greenwich, London.

The attempt by Capt. Bligh of the Bounty who with 18 sailors had been set adrift in an open boat on April 28th, 1789, to land on Tofoa Island ... by Robert Cleveley, 1790. Courtesy of the National Library of Australia.

Lord Nelson's attack at Copenhagen, ref: PW4719 © National Maritime Museum, Greenwich, London.

Admiralty commission appointing William Bligh, Commander of HM Sloop *Falcon*, 3 Nov. 1790. Courtesy of the Mitchell Library, State Library of New South Wales, ref: Safe 1/35.

Action off Camperdown, 11 October 1797, by Thomas Sutherland. Courtesy of Photolibrary.

Sword, ca.1790–1811, steel and brass by S. Brunn, London. Courtesy of the Mitchell Library, State Library of New South Wales, ref: LR 5.

An animal shot at Adventure Bay, 1791–1793, watercolour drawing by William Bligh, Commander of His Majesty's Ship *Providence*. Courtesy of the Mitchell Library, State Library of New South Wales, ref: PXA 565/f.14.

Van Diemen's Land Heron, 1791–1793, watercolour drawing by William Bligh, Commander of His Majesty's Ship *Providence*. Courtesy of the Mitchell Library, State Library of New South Wales, ref: PXA 565/f.34.

Small Paroquet of Van Diemen's Land, 1791–1793, watercolour drawing by William Bligh, Commander of His Majesty's Ship *Providence*. Courtesy of the Mitchell Library, State Library of New South Wales, ref: PXA 565/f.26.

Glossary

abaft A direction indicating nearer the stern.

a making breeze A breeze increasing in strength.

beam ends The sides of a ship. 'On her beam ends' is used to describe the rolling effect of very rough seas on the ship; the ship is almost on her side and possibly about to capsize.

belay To secure a rope.

breadfruit A large and round fruit from the Pacific Islands.

boxed the compass When a wind changes direction through 360 degrees in a very short time.

bulwarks The planking along the sides of a ship above the upper deck which acts as a railing to prevent crew and passengers from going overboard.

bumpkin (boomkin) A small beam or spar usually made of oak or fir projecting outwards from each side of a ship's bow or the stern.

buntlines Ropes tied to the foot of a square sail that keeps it from opening or bellying when it is being hauled up for furling to the yard.

buttock lines Design lines showing the fore and aft hull shape of a vessel from bow to stern.

cable 1. A long, thick and heavy rope used to moor or keep a ship at anchor. 2. A naval unit of distance – 10 cables is one nautical mile.

caboose A small hut-like galley built on the deck.

calumny Defamation; false accusation.

capstan A large waist-high vertical winch turned by crew manning the capstan bars which lock into the head of the winch. The crew then walk in a circle to work the winch. Used to raise the anchor and other heavy objects.

Captains' List Each Royal Navy officer who reached Flag Rank came from the Captains' List. Their seniority determined which officer was next in line for promotion. See also Flag Rank.

carronades A short-barrelled limited-range gun, used for close-quarter action, which was enormously destructive to a ship's timbers.

carvel-planked A method of ship building where the planks are laid flush and edge to edge.

cathead A sturdy timber projection near the bow to hold the anchor.

cat-o'-nine-tails A lash used as a form of punishment aboard a naval ship.

caulking The material making the ship watertight, such as cotton fibres forced between the planks and covered with paint to stop leaks.

chain shot Two solid cannon balls linked by chain fired from a cannon to inflict major damage to a ship's rigging or masts.

clew The bottom corners of the square sail, or the lower back corner of a triangular sail.

clewed up To draw up a square sail to the yard by hauling on the clew lines.

colliers A cargo ship that hauled coal.

cutter A fast sailboat with one mast that carries several headsails.

dead-reckoning The method for estimating a vessel's current position based on its previously determined position then advanced by estimating speed and course over an elapsed time.

dog A hinged catch that fits into a notch of a ratchet.

Dogger Bank An extensive shoal in the North Sea, about 100 kilometres east off the coast of Northumberland, England. It is well known as a fishing ground. Over its most elevated parts there is a depth of only about six fathoms, but the depth is generally from ten to twenty fathoms.

Downs (The) An anchorage off the coast of England between Dover and Deal.

fathoms A unit of measurement for depth. One fathom is 1.83 metres or six feet.

fished/double fished Applying a large piece of wood. To 'fish the mast' means strengthening it with an extra piece of timber. Double fishing: reinforcing with two pieces of timber.

Flag Rank An admiral with the right to fly his flag at the masthead. Historically, the British Fleet was divided into three squadrons, and these were defined in order of rank by a colour – red, white and blue. Each of these divisions was then subdivided into three ranks, and the admirals commanding these fleets flew the ensign relating to their position. An officer achieving Flag Rank for the first time became a Rear-Admiral of the Blue Squadron. Each squadron's colour, and the Admiral's rank, also decided the formation each fleet would take when they lined up for battle with an enemy: the Red squadron, led by the Admiral of the Fleet, took up a position at the centre of the line; his Vice-Admiral's fleet would be at the front, and his Rear-Admiral's fleet would be positioned astern.

flagship The sailing warship carrying the admiral or fleet commander and his flag. Usually the best armed ship in the fleet.

fluke The pointed triangular end of an anchor arm, designed to embed the anchor in the sea floor.

fore castle [foc'sle] fo'c's'le The living quarters in the bow of the ship where crew is accommodated.

frap a rope To take up the slack on a rope.

frap a sail To make secure by lashing.

freeboard The distance from the water to the ship's gunwale.

frigate A three-masted sailing warship with two full decks, with only one gun deck. Usually armed with 30-44 guns, located on the gun deck.

grapnel A small anchor with four or five 'arms', used for anchoring a small craft and as a grappling hook.

gudgeon Part of a hinge: a socket for the pintle of a rudder.

gunwale/gunnel The top edge of the planking at the sides of the ship, named for the place where you rest your gun to take aim.

gybe Changing from one tack to the other away from the wind, turning the ship's stern through the wind. See also 'to wear ship'

HMS His/Her Majesty's Ship: prefix of Royal Navy ship names since 1789.

hove to Slowing a vessel's forward progress by fixing the helm and foresail so that the vessel does not need to be steered: a procedure usually applied in very rough weather.

Jack tar A sailor.

jolly boat An all-purpose boat on board the ship.

larboard The old name for port, the left hand side of the ship.

league A unit of distance in the eighteenth century equal to three nautical miles.

lee The sheltered side.

leeward The direction away from the wind; opposite of 'windward'.

logs Captains, masters and lieutenants all kept logs. The master's log was the critical log of the ship. It kept a record of a ship's movements and the weather for navigational purposes. From these the captain's logs (and the lieutenant's) were copied with the addition of whatever general information they chose to add (e.g. incidents, observations, shipboard routine, notes on stores). Private journals, particularly on the voyages of exploration were often kept in addition to the official logs.

luff The leading edge of a fore-and-aft sail. Or to change course into the wind.

lugsail A square sail that's bottom is wider than the top and is hung slanted to the mast.

lying-to/lying-a-hull Waiting out a storm by lowering all sails and letting the boat drift.

mal de mer Seasickness (Fr)

messed Dined

mizzenmast On a ship with three masts this is the mast nearer the stern.

packet ship A vessel that sailing a regular service between two ports, usually carrying mail.

pinnace A small sailing vessel with two fore-and-aft rigged masts.

pintle A pin forming the pivot of one of the hinges on which a rudder turns.

plantain A banana-like fruit.

poop deck The short deck towards the stern above the quarterdeck of a ship.

pooped To have a wave break over the stern of the ship and onto the deck.

Post-Captain An alternative form of the rank of captain. It distinguishes those who were captains by rank, from officers in command of a naval vessel who were recognised as captain regardless of rank, and commanders who received the title of captain regardless of them being in command or not.

press-ganged Forced recruitment into labour i.e. crew.

prow An alternative term for bow – the front end of the vessel.

quadrant A very simple instrument used to determine the altitude of a heavenly body.

quarterdeck The upper exposed deck at the stern of the ship from the mainmast to the back, usually the territory of the ship's officers.

ratlines Bands of ropes lashed across the shrouds like steps that allow crew to easily climb aloft.

reef/reefed To take in or reduce the area of a sail without furling it.

rigging All ropes, wires and chains used to support the masts and yards.

roads A sheltered place to anchor safely.

sextant A navigational instrument used to measure the angle of elevation of an object above the horizon.

shaddock A large pear-shaped fruit similar to a grapefruit.

Sheerness Docks An important naval dockyard at Sheerness, on the Isle of Sheppey, in the Thames estuary.

ship-of-the-line A sailing warship built to fight in the line of battle. In battle, each ship would form in a line, allowing them to fire broadsides at the enemy. First rate – a sailing ship-of-the-line warship with 100 or more guns on three decks. Second rate – a sailing ship-of-the-line warship with 84-98 guns on three or two gun decks. Third rate – a sailing ship-of-the-line warship with 64-80 guns on two gun decks. Fourth rate – a sailing ship-of-the-line warship with 50-60 guns on two decks. Fifth rate – a sailing warship with 32-44 guns.

slatted A sail flopping backwards and forwards in near windless conditions.

sloop A single masted sailing ship usually carrying a main sail and a single jib or headsail.

Spithead A stretch of water at the eastern end of the Solent located between Portsmouth and the Isle of Wight.

staving the boat To hole the boat.

stern sheets The stern area of an open boat.

taffrail A railing around the stern of the ship.

tenesmus Constipation over a long period of time.

thwart A seat across the boat, especially in a rowboat.

topgallant In a square-rigged ship, these are the spars and rigging at the very top of the masts above the topsails.

to wear ship A manoeuvre that comes when a square rigged ship changes course by turning the ship's stern through the wind so that the direction of the wind comes onto the opposite side of the ship. Today it is referred to as a gybe.

transom The surface that makes the structure of the stern from keel to deck.

warp To move or re-position a ship by hauling on a line or anchor line.

windage The exposed part of the hull and rig of a vessel causing wind resistance.

windlass A horizontal and cylindrical barrel used as a lifting device for a rope or anchor cable. It was turned by rods called handspikes.

Yarmouth Roads An anchorage in the Solent off Yarmouth on the Isle of Wight.

Venturi effect The decrease in pressure resulting from liquid flowing through a thinner section of pipe.

Bligh's ships

HMS *Monmouth*, 1761 • Ship's Boy and Captain's Servant

HMS *Hunter*, 1770 • Able Seaman

HMS *Hunter*, 1771 • Midshipman

HMS *Crescent*, 1771 • Midshipman

HMS *Ranger*, 1774 • Able Seaman

HMS *Ranger*, 1775 • Master's Mate

HMS *Resolution*, 1776 • Master

HMS *Belle Poule*, 1781 • Master

HMS *Berwick*, 1781 • Lieutenant

HMS *Princess Amelia*, 1782 • Lieutenant

HMS *Cambridge*, 1782 • Lieutenant

Merchant Vessel *Lynx*, 1785 • Commanding Lieutenant

Merchant Vessel *Britannia*, 1786 • Lieutenant

HMS *Bounty*, 1787 • Commanding Lieutenant

HMS *Falcon*, 1790 • Commander

HMS *Medea,* 1790 • Commander

HMS *Providence*, 1791 • Commander

HMS *Calcutta*, 1795 • Commander

HMS *Director*, 1796 • Captain

HMS *Glatton*, 1801 • Captain

HMS *Monarch*, 1801 • Captain

HMS *Irresistible*, 1801 • Captain

HMS *Warrior*, 1804 • Captain

HMS *Porpoise*, 1805 • Captain

HMS *Porpoise*, 1808 • Commodore

HMS *Hindostan*, 1810 • Commodore

A note on sources

More than 250 years have passed since William Bligh was born; and only a couple of decades less since the infamous mutiny happened aboard *Bounty*. Had it not been for that single event the man might simply have been recognised in history as one of the many great naval commanders of his day, especially in battle. The mutiny changed all that: it made him famous, even in his day, and forever controversial – a maritime hero to some, a tyrannical despot to others. Since then, stories about Bligh, particularly ones based around the mutiny, have escalated in drama and proportion with the passing of years and the help of four Hollywood movies. Recently, however, thanks to the internet, the cannon of literature either written by or inspired by Bligh is now at our fingertips, and there is an abundance of information to be found: some factual, some fanciful, some just plain wrong.

In researching *Bligh* I have cruised through many books, some dedicated to his life, others to events with which he has been involved. I have also trawled through countless websites – from the online collections of institutions such as the National Maritime Museum in the United Kingdom to those compiled by Bligh and *Bounty* enthusiasts, in search of facts, figures and fresh information. It's been a marathon.

Here now, to the best of my ability, I recognise as many as possible of those sources used in creating this book and that you too may choose to explore and read. My apologies to anyone I may have overlooked or omitted. The publisher would be pleased to correct any omissions or errors of fact in subsequent printings.

Prologue

We open with Bligh and his loyalists on the beach on the island of Tofua confronted by almost certain death. To set the scene I flew to Tofua via Google Earth (my airline of choice for many situations and locations dealt with in this book), and went to the many websites with images and information relating to Tofua to get a better appreciation of the island's form and what the castaways might have experienced. Much of the background and detail here was gleaned from *The Life of Vice-Admiral William Bligh RNFRS* (A&R, 1931), a masterwork written by prolific Australian academic and biographer of William Bligh, George Mackaness. This award-winning book is almost encyclopaedic in its presentation of information about Bligh. George Mackaness also published many additional papers and historical monographs on Bligh (and his correspondence) that can be found at the State Library of NSW. Kenneth S. Allen's excellent biography of Bligh, *That Bounty Bastard* (Robert Hale and Company, 1976), inspired much colour for this chapter and others. There was no better site for detail and accessing the primary sources of the mutiny and subsequent courts martial than www.fatefulvoyage.com which informed this chapter and many others across the book. Bligh's own two works on his *Bounty* adventure: his *Narrative of the Mutiny on Board HMS Bounty and the Subsequent Voyage of Part of the Crew in the Ship's Boat* and *A Voyage to the South Sea* were invaluable. The narrative written by *Bounty* mutineer, James Morrison, provided much colour, and an intriguing alternative view.

Chapters One and Two

The debate about Bligh's birthplace will go on forever, but here I am backing the detailed research done by Mackaness; I believe it was Plymouth, a belief I reinforced through contact with the Plymouth and West Devon Record Office in England. And while in England, the National Museum of the Royal Navy, UK, and the National Archives, UK, assisted with details of HMS *Monmouth* and HMS *Hunter*.

The Australian National University's website, www.adb.anu.edu.au, was a consistent source of excellent biographies and fact checking for me on Banks and the many significant personalities across the book.

Once Bligh reappeared in navy ranks and eventually went aboard HMS *Resolution* to sail as master under Captain Cook, Richard Hough's book, *Captain James Cook – A Biography* (Hodder & Stoughton, 1994), was of immeasurable help for detail, right through to Cook's death, the search for the Northwest Passage and *Resolution*'s long voyage home where Bligh was navigator. Hough's book also reveals that the Royal Navy's Surgeon-Admiral from 1972-74, Sir James Watt, considered Cook's reported symptoms when he was ill in Tahiti and suggested he was suffering from a parasitic infection of the lower intestine. Excerpts from Cook's journals, and the men who sailed with him (including Gilbert and Samwell) can be found at captaincooksociety.com and across the web. The originals for Royal Navy Captains and Masters logs of this period are held by The National Archives at Kew and a collection of Lieutenant's logs at the national maritime museum for more information refer to www.rmg.co.uk/discover/researchers/research-guides/research-guide-b7-royal-navy-ship-records.

Chapter Three

Just when it was that William Bligh met his wife-to-be, Elizabeth Betham, in Douglas on the Isle of Man is the subject of conjecture across many books and websites, and despite extensive efforts on my part, I'm no closer to an answer. Elizabeth Betham's uncle, Duncan Campbell, who became another mentor and lifelong associate of Bligh's, makes his first appearance in this chapter. Much of the background information on Campbell and his extensive business activities can be traced across the web and the fascinating work of 'The Blackheath Connection' at www.danbyrnes.com.au/blackheath/jamaica.htm.

This chapter is Bligh's first battle action – he smells the smoke of cannon fire at the Battle of Dogger Bank and is there for the Siege of Gibraltar. Mackaness, as a result of his exhaustive research, again provided fine detail, while cross-checking information from the numerous sites on the web provided the platform for these paragraphs.

It was difficult to find any information of much worth that could be applied to the era where Bligh was working in the merchant service, sailing across the Atlantic to the West Indies aboard ships owned by Duncan Campbell in the shadow of the notorious triangular trade. This was the first time he sailed with Fletcher Christian, the perpetrator of the mutiny. As to whether Bligh's service in the West Indies also saw him as the captain of any of the many slave ships of the Atlantic slave trade I could not ascertain, but I suspect there is a story to be found here. There was an intriguing reference in a Macakaness monograph – *Fresh light on Bligh: being some unpublished correspondence of Captain William Bligh, R.N., and Lieutenant Francis Godolphin Bond, R.N., with Lieutenant Bond's manuscript notes made on voyage of H.M.S. Providence, 1791–1795*, edited with an introduction, notes and commentary by George Mackaness – which could suggest that he may have. Thomas Bond makes a longish reference to William Bligh in a letter to a relative regarding Bligh's kindness to his son (also Thomas, and brother of Francis Godolphin Bond of *Providence*). The letter relates that William Bligh had told him he was tired of being a 'negro driver' and had long sacrificed his domestic comforts for the good of the service. Francis Godolphin Bond was a son of William Bligh's half-sister Catherine. It might well be that the displeasure Bligh experienced working in the shadow of the Atlantic slave trade, and possibly as master of a slave ship (as this curious reference might indicate) compelled him to jump ship and return to his naval career with the *Bounty* mission, even though it meant an enormous reduction in salary: from £500 to just £50 per annum (salary as noted in Dening's book).

Chapter Four

Lieutenant William Bligh is appointed captain of *Bounty* and commander of the breadfruit mission, but much to his disappointment he was not elevated in Royal Navy ranking to the actual title of captain. I found assistance for this section in David Divine's excellent read, *Six Great Sailors* (Hamish Hamilton, 1955), which gives a slightly different perspective on the life of Bligh. Snippets of other information from this publication surface elsewhere in this book. The website www.bountygenealogy.com/lamb.php provided some of the details of the men Bligh accepted as crew for *Bounty*, and www.findagrave.com is fascinating.

An interesting search came with the need for information on Larcum Kendall's No. 2 timepiece, which was aboard Bounty and used for navigation purposes. The website www.sullacrestadellonda.it/strumenti/strumenti_nautici_crono_en.htm gave the answers. Here also I must recognise another outstanding publication written by a man of considerable note in the world of seafaring: *Ship – 5,000 Years of Maritime Adventure*, by Brian Lavery, Curator Emeritus of Naval History at the National Maritime Museum, Greenwich. The words and images this book contains helped set many scenes in Bligh. It's a great read. My personal experience comes into play in this chapter as well: having raced yachts on the Solent and experienced its fickle winds and fearsome tides, I knew exactly the frustration Bligh was facing in trying to clear the Isle of Wight after weighing anchor and getting under sail from Spithead.

Chapters Five and Six

I am in my element here as Bligh exits the English Channel, enters the Atlantic and turns south. Having raced and cruised the English Channel, I could see *Bounty* leaving the coast in her wake and, like them, I have felt the frustration of Doldrum-like conditions on too many occasions. I know what it's like listening to the slatting of the sails while you desperately try to harness the slightest puff of wind and get moving. My writings about two Volvo round-the-world races, where competitors provided me with excellent detail relating to sailing south in the Atlantic to Cape Town, also helped, as did my own time in Cape Town and on the water there.

When it came to Cape Horn I turned my mind back to wonderfully relaxed conversations I had over glasses of red wine with my special, lifelong friend, Kay Cottee – the first woman to sail solo, non-stop and unassisted around the world. We talked at length about two heinous storms she confronted, one south of the Cape of Good Hope, and another that emerged as she neared the sailor's nemesis, Cape Horn. In both storms Kay was running with them; at Cape Horn, Bligh was trying to smash his way west against the storm in a ship that would not sail any closer than 70 degrees to the wind direction, and which made considerable leeway. My own touch came through my sailing in the Atlantic, especially when we had to endure a savage Force 10 storm while delivering a small yacht to Bermuda. That was memorable!

I could also see the weather and feel the loads on the ship when *Bounty* was deep in the Southern Ocean; and having enjoyed downwind rollercoaster rides on the south-east trade winds in the South Pacific, I knew exactly what Bligh and his crew were feeling as they approached Tahiti. George Mackaness, www.fatefulvoyage.com and Google Earth were all valuable in crafting these chapters, as was *Six Great Sailors*.

I would like to note the insightful paper of John F. Brock, *Cook-Bligh-Flinders-King: the quadrilogy of master mariners*, given at the Australian Museum, Australian Science History Club, Sydney, September 2005. It provided an insightful synthesis of the links between Cook, Bligh and Flinders in particular and their shared surveying legacy.

Chapters Seven and Eight

These two chapters deal with the incident that brought Bligh both fame and infamy – the mutiny and *Bounty*. The build-up to the revolt – from the moment *Bounty* sails from Matavai Bay until the plotters overrun the ship at dawn on 28 April 1789, is built around *Bounty*'s log, Mackaness' landmark research, and a cross section of websites too numerous to mention. Just type *Bounty* into Google and you will see what I mean. And, of course, Google Earth gave me a satellite's eye view of the scene as the ships circled and moved across the Pacific. Again, www.fatefulvoyage.com provides excellent detail and maps, especially through Bligh's narrative.

With the mutiny complete and Bligh and his eighteen supporters callously cast adrift, I could relate to the dilemmas they faced in such a small and overloaded boat. I started my sailing career as a bailer boy in small, undecked skiffs on Sydney Harbour, and they were extremely difficult to keep upright, even in moderate winds. But for Bligh and his men, rowing that heavy launch over great distances would be as demanding as sailing it in a breeze. As I wrote and researched this book, my old sailing mate, Don McIntyre, was reliving Bligh's nightmare by attempting to sail the same voyage under similar conditions: no charts, no toilet paper, not enough food or water, in a traditional eighteenth-century open-timber-whale-boat.

Chapters Nine and Ten

These chapters detail one of the greatest feats of open-ocean navigation, seamanship and survival in maritime history – eighteen men in a 23-foot open boat surviving a 3600 nautical mile passage over 47 days. I've sailed in these waters – from Sydney to Noumea, twice, through the northern waters of the Great Barrier Reef, in Fiji and the New Hebrides, Torres Strait and to the west – so I can relate to the undertaking. But, what brought home to me the enormity of this ultimate test of survival was to spend time appreciating the replica of the *Bounty* launch that is on display at the Australian National Maritime Museum in Sydney. I was in awe of how crowded it must have been for the men, how little freeboard the launch would have had, and how difficult it must have been to keep her afloat in a gale and big seas. Their survival was little short of a miracle. These two chapters were based on the log from *Bounty*, Bligh's narrative after the odyssey, the notes he kept during the launch voyage, and supported by visits to www.fatefulvoyage.com and many other related websites.

Chapters Twelve and Thirteen

Back with his family on home turf and facing a court martial (a Royal Navy procedure for any captain who loses his ship, even in a mutiny) we follow Bligh on the voyage and subsequent wreck of HMS *Pandora*, which was sent to search for *Bounty* and return the mutineers home to face justice. *Bounty* does come back onto the scene, but still in the hands of Fletcher Christian and a few of his faithful mutineers: they were on their way to find Pitcairn Island, and once there the ship was scuttled.

Having observed the Great Barrier Reef from air and sea, and having been through some of its narrow channels, it is easy to understand the dangers this coral bastion presented to vessels in Bligh's era when navigation was so basic and the actual whereabouts of the reef was known more by 'guestimation' than fact. For Bligh, who made a cautious and calculated approach, there was still an element of luck in finding what is now Bligh's Boat Entrance, but the wreck of *Pandora* is almost inexcusable.

The challenge of this book was always to keep the focus on Bligh, the mariner and Royal Navy man, so I regrettably had to make many decisions to not give extensive detail on some moments (such as the *Pandora* story) as they have all been well served by dedicated publications. Mackaness' book again provided much of the thread for these chapters, but it was the world wide web where the broadest information was found.

Chapters Fourteen and Fifteen

The voyage of HMS *Providence* fills these two chapters. Once again Bligh stopped at Adventure Bay, on Tasmania's Storm Bay, and this time he surveyed the region. Bligh was taken by the stunning natural beauty of this area, and I know why: you cross Storm Bay from Tasman Island to the entrance of the Derwent River when sailing to the finish of the Sydney to Hobart race, and I can say from my own experience in that race, Storm Bay is the highlight after departing Sydney. This part of the world remains almost untouched to this day, and the impressive stone columns, the 'organ pipes' at Cape Raoul, are now known the world over. Only the tall white lighthouse adorning the peak of Tasman Island is the obvious modern-day addition to the scene. After Bligh left Tahiti he sailed into one of my favourite parts of the world – the waters and islands of Fiji – which were somewhat appropriately recognised then as Bligh's Islands, because of the extent of his exploration there.

Then came Bligh's great challenge – finding and fighting his way through Torres Strait. Having sailed through the strait, and having stood on the summit of Thursday Island – from where you can see just a few of the hazards he faced – you recognise what a great navigator and explorer he was. It was the situation for me in relating to *Providence*'s arrival in Jamaica with her prized cargo of breadfruit plants. Having competed in the Miami to Montego Bay Race and sailed through the Bermuda Triangle from the Bahamas to Bermuda, one comes away with great respect for the masters and crews of the square-rigged ships that clawed their way through the myriad islands you find there.

The online edition of the Australian Dictionary of Biography was again valuable when it came to seeking accurate detail of individuals: this time it was Flinders. The usual sources again came to the fore, and an entertaining chat with Captain Welwyn Gamble, of Australian Reef Pilots, regarding the northern waters of Queensland and Torres Strait, was enlightening. Additional insight into the family background of the mutineers came through www.bountygenealogy.com.

Chapters Sixteen, Seventeen and Eighteen

Bligh was in the thick of the action at two great battles – Camperdown and Copenhagen, the latter being where he anchored his ship, *Glatton*, immediately astern of Nelson's flagship, *Elephant*, and blasted the powerful Danish fleet into submission in what was a monumental encounter. It was a similar story at Camperdown. In another ships-of-the-line confrontation, this time against the Dutch, the British either sank their opponent's ships, sent them running, or had them surrender. On each occasion Bligh returned home a proud man with his reputation restored, and rightly so. The offer of the role of Governor of New South Wales was to follow as a consequence. Both Mackaness and Lavery's books were of value in establishing the scenes for these chapters, and there was a plethora of websites to be scoured for information, including www.nmrn.org.uk and www.historyofwar.org, and to get the complete feeling of what these brave men and their crews were exposed to, you needed to go no further than Google images and the various online collections where many of the images for this book were sourced, of particular note is the National Maritime Museum at www.rmg.co.uk. Here, as in other chapters, www.ageofnelson.org helped when tracking down basic details of ships. The many letters between Bligh and Banks held by the State Library of New South Wales were of exceptional benefit in crafting these chapters.

Epilogue

Bligh's posting to New South Wales would be as tumultuous, testing and emotional as almost any other period in his life. It's a magnificent story in itself, but I have chosen not to cover this period in detail as it is a tangent in the life of a master mariner, and not the intention of my book. The State Library of NSW and its collection was a solid source of information. In particular, the book, *Politics and Power: Bligh's Sydney Rebellion 1808* by Paul Brunton, produced for the jointly curated State Library and the Museum of Sydney exhibition of this period, proved invaluable for background and detail of Bligh's impact on the colony. Anne-Marree Whitaker's chapter on Bligh in *The Governors of New South Wales: 1788–2010* edited by David Clune and Ken Turner (Federation Press) – was an insightful overview of Bligh's NSW stint and the earlier governors Bligh replaced. For the pen sketch biographies of John Macarthur and his cohorts I relied upon the www.adb.anu.edu.au for the necessary information. The wonderful quote of an enraged Bligh with Macarthur is from *Proceedings of a General court-martial . . . for the trial of . . . Geo Johnston* (Sherwood, Neely and Jones, London, 1811) and quoted from the State Library's *Politics and Power*.

The lovely story of old Admiral Bligh comes from Cornish Worthies, Walter, Hawken and Tregallas – www.bibliolife.com.

I have unashamedly taken Bligh's side in the complex Rum Rebellion in my brief summary of Bligh's NSW stint. The works of Michael Duffy, *Man of Honour: John Macarthur*, Sydney, Macmillan Australia, 2003; H.V. Evatt, *Rum Rebellion: A Study of the Overthrow of Governor Bligh*, 1943; and Ross Fitzgerald, and Mark Hearn, *Bligh, Macarthur and the Rum Rebellion*, 1988; as well as Paul Brunton's many lectures and papers on the topic, are the authoritative voices on this period and I would encourage you to discover their works.

A special note on the Bligh Collection held by the State Library of New South Wales

Any author writing and researching a work on Australian history relies greatly on the extraordinary collection of the Mitchell and Dixson Libraries at the State Library of New South Wales to create and research their story. I am no different, and the State Library's collection deserves particular recognition. It holds the most comprehensive collection of books, manuscripts, maps and pictures by and relating to William Bligh in the world. Bligh's personal papers, logbooks and journals, letters, commissions, maps, portrait, telescope and the personal papers of his wife, Elizabeth, were acquired throughout the twentieth century from a number of Bligh's descendants beginning in 1902 with a gift from his grandson, William Russell Bligh, which included the *Bounty* logbook and journal, 1787–1789. The Library acquires all published books, in any language, relating to William Bligh, the *Bounty* mutiny, and Bligh's governorship of New South Wales. It also collects associated manuscripts and pictures such as the journal of James Morrison, 1787–1792; the journal and sketchbook of George Tobin, 1791–1793 (whose original artwork provided the endpapers for this book); and pictorial works such as portraits of Mary Putland (née Bligh).

The Mitchell and Dixson collections at the Library also hold an extensive collection of the papers of Sir Joseph Banks. These amount to approximately 10000 manuscript pages and include correspondence – principally letters received – but also reports, invoices and accounts, journals, plus a small quantity of maps, charts and watercolours. Many of the letters quoted across the book are held in the Library's collection, and in the chapters relating to Bligh's years spent in the North Sea I relied on the online collection with Bligh's correspondence to Banks (series 58) mainly letters received by Banks from William Bligh while commander of HM Ships *Calcutta, Director, Glatton, Irresistible* and *Warrior.* Including a significant letter received by Banks from Elizabeth Bligh in 1805.

Much of the State Library's excellent collection is accessible online and I found their extensive provenance notes that accompany the collections a splendid source of additional detail on the stories behind Bligh's letters, work, images and personal objects. Detailed descriptions of this collection may be found at www.sl.nsw.gov.au. Members of the Library can also access online the astonishing 17th–18th Century Burney Collection Newspapers, which contains one million newspaper pages with titles from London, the British Isles and colonies. Included in the collection are newspapers, news-books, Acts of Parliament, addresses, broadsides, pamphlets and proclamations. I am grateful for the picture research of Linda Brainwood in sourcing the images from the State Library Collection and accessing the Burney Collection.

Further reading

The following additional books and articles were of particular assistance in researching and referencing various aspects of the Bligh story:

Alexander, Caroline. *The Bounty: The True Story of the Mutiny on the Bounty*, London, HarperCollins, 2003.

Brunton, Paul (Ed.). *Awake, Bold Bligh: William Bligh's Letters Describing the Mutiny on HMS Bounty*. Sydney, Allen and Unwin and the New South Wales State Public Library, 1989.

Dening, Greg. *Mr Bligh's Bad Language: Passion, Power and Theatre on the Bounty*. Melbourne, CUP, 1993.

Guttridge, Leonard F. *Mutiny: A History of Naval Insurrections*, Maryland, Naval Institute Press, 1992.

Kennedy, Gavin. *Bligh*. London, Duckworth, 1978.

Mackaness, George. *The Life of Vice-Admiral William Bligh, RN, FRS*. Two Vols. Sydney, Angus and Robertson, 1931.

McKinney, Sam. *Bligh!: The Whole Story of the Mutiny Aboard H.M.S. Bounty*, Horsdal & Schubart, 1999.

Nordhoff, Charles, and James Norman Hall. *The Bounty Trilogy*, Boston, Little, Brown and Company, 1951.

Rutter, Owen. *Turbulent Journey: A Life of William Bligh, Vice-Admiral of the Blue*. London, Ivor Nicholson and Watson, 1936.

Scott, Ernest. *The Life of Matthew Flinders*, Angus and Robertson, 2001.

Acknowledgements

Business was quite busy – writing and sailing – when an email arrived from Helen Littleton, non-fiction publisher at Hachette in Sydney. It presented an exciting opportunity – a wonderful idea for a book – a biography of Captain Bligh, the brilliant eighteenth-century seafarer, explorer and commander. Helen and a mutual friend, that old seadog and publishing legend, John Ferguson, had lamented how Bligh, 'the master mariner', had been overshadowed by his reputation. They thought I should right this wrong. I had a coffee with Malcolm Edwards, Fiona Hazard and Helen at Hachette and with that, life's course changed for me. I was honoured by this offer; so here now is my story of one of the great master mariners.

Producing the words for this book has been a far from solo effort. Had it not been for the contributions of many people *Bligh* would never have set sail. Firstly, I have to say that Helen Littleton is the most professional, encouraging, supportive and enthusiastic publisher I have worked with, as are the outstanding editorial team working with her at Hachette – Kate Stevens, Emma Whetham, Rachael Donovan, Jacquie Brown and proofreader Jon Gibbs. I am equally indebted to my dedicated assistant, Liz Christmas, whose contributions to the book were always generous and enthusiastic; and to Prue Stirling for her understanding and support when this project began to absorb a significant amount of my time. To Nigel Erskine, Curator, Exploration and European Settlement at the Australian National Maritime Museum in Sydney – and a 'Bligh fanatic' – I say thank you for your initial assistance in helping research the subject, and subsequent reading of the manuscript. Paul Brunton, Senior Curator of the Mitchell Library at the State Library of NSW, a man passionate about Bligh and an author of many works on Bligh and our colonial heritage, gave me guidance in the early stages on the extraordinary collection of Bligh material held by the library and provided invaluable assistance to my publisher in sourcing and crediting the images and charts that appear in the work. Also, I must recognise Captain Welwyn Gamble of Australian Reef Pilots and Troy Hamilton-Irvine of Antique Mapart Australia for their help.

Finally, I want to thank the booksellers in advance for their support of this book, and for what they achieved with my previous publications.

Index